S0-BNS-508

 Overview

The Daggett System for Effective Instruction

The Daggett System for Effective Instruction (DSEI) provides a coherent focus, across the entire educational organization, on the development and support of instructional effectiveness to improve student achievement. Whereas traditional teaching frameworks are teacher-focused and only consider what teachers should do to deliver instruction, the DSEI is student-focused and considers what the entire educational system should do to facilitate learning. This subtle but important difference is based on current research and a modern understanding of teaching and learning.

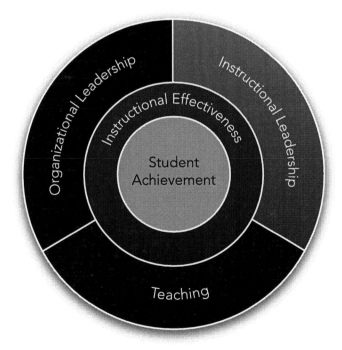

The three parts of DSEI are illustrated here. The following elements are the critical functions of each part of the system. Think about where you, as a professional educator, fit into this system.

Six Elements of Organizational Leadership

- Create a culture of high expectations.
- Create a shared vision.
- Build leadership capacity.
- Align organizational structures and systems to the vision.
- Align teacher/administrator selection, support, and evaluation.
- Support decision making with data systems.

Five Elements of Instructional Leadership

- Use research to establish urgency for higher expectations.
- Align curriculum to standards.
- Integrate literacy and math across all content areas.
- Facilitate data-driven decision making to inform instruction.
- Provide opportunities for focused professional collaboration and growth.

Six Elements of Teaching

- Embrace rigorous and relevant expectations for all students.
- Build strong relationships with students.
- Possess depth of content knowledge and make it relevant to students.
- Facilitate rigorous and relevant instruction based on how students learn.
- Demonstrate expertise in the use of instructional strategies, technology, and best practices.
- Use assessments to guide and differentiate instruction.

When all parts of the system are working together efficiently, teachers receive the support they need, and students are successfully prepared for college, careers, and citizenship.

DSEI and a Systemwide Approach to Embedded Literacy

The focus of this book is on using DSEI to create an environment of high expectations for student performance and to set in place the organizational and instructional leadership needed to implement an embedded literacy initiative. Embedded literacy is central to Common Core State Standards — the national educational standards that have been adopted by nearly every state. The goal of the standards is to prepare today's students to succeed in their future lives as workers, citizens, consumers, and parents. This book explains how to use DSEI as a framework for setting those aspirations in motion.

Chapter 1: Systemwide Support for Embedded Literacy

The first chapter defines terms and explains how and why embedded literacy is a critical feature of the Common Core State Standards.

Chapter 2: Research to Support a Focus on Systemwide Embedded Literacy

Chapter 2 presents some of the research supporting the emphasis on embedded literacy, including a look at how the CCSS Next Generation Assessments incorporate literacy skills across the curriculum.

Chapter 3: Organizational Leadership for Embedded Literacy

Chapter 3 examines the vital role that leadership can play in creating a culture of high expectations and in instituting a system for success. It outlines methods for building leadership, discusses the use of data, and offers suggestions for winning stakeholder support and participation.

Chapter 4: Instructional Leadership for Embedded Literacy

Chapter 4 looks at instructional leadership via the five DSEI elements, showing leaders how to use research to establish urgency, how to align the curriculum to CCSS and literacy expectations, how to approach the integration of literacy and numeracy, how to use data to inform instruction, and why it is vital to plan professional development to support literacy in the classroom.

Chapter 5: Teaching Embedded Literacy

Chapter 5 is also DSEI-based. Teachers see the importance of embracing higher expectations and building strong relationships with students. The chapter explores some CCSS shifts in instruction while offering a variety of strategies for teaching literacy in content-area classrooms.

Chapter 6: Successful Practices

Chapter 6 looks at methods used by successful embedded literacy programs. Some practices examined include team approaches, organizational approaches, the use of young adult literature; and a "literacy through happenstance" approach. The varied approaches incorporate a range of successful practices, including literacy coaches, a Freshman Academy, and an interventionist to support individual students.

Chapter 7: Actions for Implementation

In a step-by-step manner, this chapter directly outlines the issues to raise and the methods to employ when moving an embedded literacy initiative from planning to implementation. The chapter ends with a brief review entitled "Takeaways on Embedded Literacy."

 Chapter 1

Systemwide Support for Embedded Literacy

Embedded literacy is the incorporation of reading, writing, listening, speaking, and language across the curriculum. In other words, embedded literacy expands literacy strategies and instruction beyond the English language arts classroom. This approach to literacy not only makes good pedagogical sense, but also addresses the demands of the Common Core State Standards (CCSS), which require shared responsibility for student literacy across the disciplines and up the grades. This new focus on content-area literacy will require a shift in the culture of most schools. Systemwide support for embedded literacy can begin with adherence to the Daggett System for Effective Instruction (DSEI), which focuses on supporting instructional effectiveness with active, aware instructional and organizational leadership.

The Principle of Embedded Literacy

Most careers involve an element of literacy. There are few jobs, in fact, that do not require a worker to read a manual or guide or write a purchase order or memo. In the world of work, reading and writing are not isolated as English language arts tasks. They are skills that are seamlessly integrated with the general expectations for all workers. Recognizing that literacy skills are required for all adult tasks, proponents of embedded literacy strive to expand literacy instruction from its customary place in the ELA classroom into all areas of study.

The traditional pattern of instruction in schools separates literacy-driven instruction from content-driven instruction. In their book *(Re)-Imagining Content-Area Literacy Instruction,* Roni Jo Draper and her collaborators propose an alternative view, one that places all texts and the literacies required to interpret them at the core of all content-learning activities. A more authentic way to address literacy, they suggest, is to start from a content-rich text. Once you do that, you link the goals for ELA teachers to those of all other teachers in the school. Consequently, teachers across the curriculum will align themselves around the universal, shared goal of helping all students interpret and create content-rich texts. (Draper, et al., 2010)

Embedded literacy, then, entails literacy instruction that reaches across the disciplines and wraps around them, uniting all teachers in a single purpose — helping students to read, write, and discuss content-rich texts. The goal is not to convert content-area teachers into reading or literacy experts, but rather to have content-area teachers explore the literacy practices that fit their subject areas, encouraging students, for example, to read the way a scientist reads or to write as a historian writes.

For some students, the gap between learning to read and write versus reading and writing to learn is a chasm that they are afraid to leap across. But by showing students in every classroom and every course of study how they can read and write to learn, embedded literacy can make the leap achievable. By integrating reading, writing, listening, speaking, and language naturally into all courses of study, embedded literacy creates a more authentic path to literacy.

Embedded Literacy and the Common Core State Standards

The Common Core State Standards require instruction in reading, writing, speaking, listening, and language to be a shared responsibility within the school and across the district. The standards for reading, writing, speaking, listening, speaking, and language apply to a range of disciplines that include, but are not limited to, English language arts.

Accompanying the CCSS will be Next Generation Assessments (NGA) that will take testing well beyond the usual multiple-choice and short-answer questions. Instead, students will be required to apply their knowledge to real-world situations through performance tasks in interdisciplinary contexts.

The linking of goals across disciplines is reflected in how the Common Core State Standards fuse standards for English language arts with "Literacy in History/Social Studies, Science and Technical Subjects." These literacy standards do not apply directly to content knowledge; separate, specific content standards are being developed to assess knowledge in history/social studies, science, and technical subjects. Instead, the CCSS literacy standards provide content-area teachers with goals and expectations for how to incorporate literacy instruction into their classrooms.

CCSS Embedded Literacy at K–5

The grade K–5 standards, for instance, integrate content-area literacy with English language arts. Under grade-level-specific standards, you might find the following sample expectations:

Grade 1 Writing

7. Participate in shared research and writing projects (e.g., explore a number of "how-to" books on a given topic and use them to write a sequence of instructions).

Grade 2 Reading

3. Describe the connection between a series of historical events, a set of scientific ideas or concepts, or steps in technical procedures in a text.

Grade 4 Language

6. Acquire and use accurately grade-appropriate general academic and domain-specific words and phrases, including those that signal precise actions, emotions, or states of being (e.g., *quizzed, whined, stammered*) and that are basic to a particular topic (e.g., *wildlife, conservation,* and *endangered* when discussing animal preservation).

The 1st grade example refers to "how-to" books on a given topic, which might be books with a science or technical focus. The 2nd grade example specifically mentions "historical events," tying it directly to social studies instruction. The 4th grade example also suggests a connection to science. Throughout the K–5 standards, references like these abound, connecting reading, writing, listening, speaking, and language to the content areas.

In fact, all references to "texts" within the K–5 standards can be assumed to mean "texts in both ELA and the content areas," as is the case in this example:

Grade 5 Speaking and Listening

2. Summarize a written text read aloud or information presented in diverse media and formats, including visually, quantitatively, and orally.

Whereas state standards in reading, writing, listening, speaking, and language might have been limited to fiction and nonfiction texts in the ELA classroom, the new Common Core State Standards are broader in scope and might apply to written experiments in a science classroom, biographical information in a social studies classroom, and so on.

CCSS Embedded Literacy at 6–12: Reading

The standards for literacy in history/social studies, science, and technical subjects begin with the same anchor standards (college and career readiness standards) that apply to reading and writing in English language arts. It is within the grade-specific standards that they branch out to provide content-area specificity.

The content-area reading standards are subdivided into reading in history/social studies and reading in science and technical subjects. The examples below indicate how these differ.

Anchor Standard	History/Social Studies	Science & Technical Subjects
3. Analyze how and why individuals, events, or ideas develop and interact over the course of a text.	**Grades 6–8** 3. Identify key steps in a text's description of a process related to history/social studies (e.g., how a bill becomes law, how interest rates are raised or lowered).	**Grades 6–8** 3. Follow precisely a multistep procedure when carrying out experiments, taking measurements, or performing technical tasks.
6. Assess how point of view or purpose shapes the content and style of a text.	**Grades 9–10** 6. Compare the point of view of two or more authors for how they treat the same or similar topics, including which details they include and emphasize in their respective accounts.	**Grades 9–10** 6. Analyze the author's purpose in providing an explanation, describing a procedure, or discussing an experiment in a text, defining the question the author seeks to address.
9. Analyze how two or more texts address similar themes or topics in order to build knowledge or to compare the approaches the authors take.	**Grades 11–12** 9. Integrate information from diverse sources, both primary and secondary, into a coherent understanding of an idea or event, noting discrepancies among sources.	**Grades 11–12** 9. Synthesize information from a range of sources (e.g., texts, experiments, simulations) into a coherent understanding of a process, phenomenon, or concept, resolving conflicting information when possible.

Each broad anchor standard, then, is applied specifically to a particular content area. The development of steps (e.g., Reading Anchor Standard 3) might involve a historical process or a scientific experiment. Point of view (Reading Anchor Standard 6) might apply to a historical perspective or to a scientist's question. Comparison of themes (Reading Anchor Standard 9) might relate to primary and secondary sources in social studies or to a series of simulations in a technology course.

CCSS Embedded Literacy at 6–12: Writing

Unlike the reading standards, the content-area writing standards are combined for history/social studies as well as science and technical subjects. These standards focus on the writing of arguments that focus "on discipline-specific content" as well as informational/explanatory texts, "including the narration of historical events, scientific procedures/experiments, or technical processes." In all other ways, they parallel the writing standards for ELA. Content-area teachers at the middle school and high school level, in other words, will now need to approach student writing the way that ELA teachers do, with an eye toward having their students write routinely, construct strong arguments, draw evidence from multiple texts, and develop and organize their topics coherently.

Linking ELA to Content-Area Literacy

In the Common Core State Standards, ELA literacy and content-area literacy share strands and key ideas.

Key Points in ELA and Content-Area Literacy
(Media and Technology Blended Throughout)

Reading	Writing	Speaking and Listening	Language
• Build staircase for increasing text complexity. • Provide opportunities to read a wide range and quality of texts. • Progressively develop reading comprehension skills. • Teach some required texts (with most specifics left to states to determine).	• Focus on argument writing and research with substantive claims, sound reasoning, and relevant evidence. • Write routinely and include both short and sustained writing projects. • Use annotated student writing to establish expectations.	• Gain, evaluate, and present increasingly complex information, ideas, and evidence. • Guide informal discussions to answer questions, build understanding, and solve problems.	• Integrate vocabulary and conventions across reading, writing, speaking, and listening. • Build academic and domain-specific vocabulary through conversations, direct instruction, and reading. • Guide use of formal English in writing and speaking, and build knowledge of how to select appropriate language for expression.

These strands and ideas should no longer be confined to English language arts instruction. In all classes and at all levels, teachers must provide opportunities to read complex texts, guide informal discussions, or build academic vocabulary.

Examples of Embedded Literacy in Next Generation Assessments

To perform well on the Next Generation Assessments, students need to possess a foundational base of literacy as it applies across the curriculum. For embedded literacy to thrive in a school, systemwide support is critical. It is this systemwide support that will help students become literate in all content areas. When literacy is embedded throughout the curriculum, students are much more likely to succeed on the NGAs, and by extension, in college and their careers.

What follows are some sample NGA questions that address content-area literacy.

Grade 2 Next Generation Assessment

In this 2nd grade Next Generation Assessment activity, second graders are asked to perform a social studies activity that blends a variety of communication skills with a subject-relevant task. Literacy expectations include writing informative/explanatory text and demonstrating a command of the conventions of standard English.

> A new neighbor has moved into the house next to yours. There are two children. Their names are Megan and Jason. They are your age and you like them already. They don't know anything about the neighborhood. You decide to help.
>
> Write a description of a place in your neighborhood. Choose a place you like to go. Tell what is there. Tell why you like it.
>
> Draw a map showing how to get to this place from your house. Explain how to use the map in your description.
>
> When you finish, check and revise your work. Make sure you spell correctly. Be certain you use capitals and punctuation correctly.

Grade 10 Next Generation Assessment

The following 10th grade career and technology example asks 10th graders to use reading and interpreting skills, speaking and listening skills, as well as writing skills in an exercise on exchange rates that requires reading and writing to learn.

A United States dollar does not have the same value as a Canadian dollar, a European Euro, or a Japanese Yen. In other words, a U.S. dollar may be worth more or less than a unit of exchange in another form of currency. You can find out what a U.S. dollar is worth in another country by using a currency converter at a website such as http://www.xe.com/ucc/.

What's more, the exchange rate changes daily as economic conditions in each country shift relative to other countries. This can be vital information for a businessperson who conducts business with buyers and sellers in other countries. You can find the going exchange rate in any newspaper. The site above also reflects the current exchange rate between countries. Visit this site and see how much $1,000 will buy in Euros or Yen. Then discuss these questions with two or three classmates:

- What will be the effect for a U.S. businessperson if the U.S. dollar becomes more valuable in relation to a Euro?

- What will be the effect for a U.S. businessperson if the U.S. dollar loses value compared to a Euro?

- What can be the long-term effect of changes in the exchange rate on a U.S. businessperson who does business in another country?

- How can a businessperson take advantage of changes in the exchange rate to make more money?

Write a summary of the group's discussion of these questions.

To improve student achievement on the upcoming NGAs, all teachers must become proficient at designing informal assessments that incorporate literacy skills.

It Takes a System to Effect Change

Any school or district that takes on the challenge of implementing the new CCSS requirements will need an organizationwide commitment to the task. At the heart of the DSEI lies an understanding of the need for this kind of commitment. With this principle in mind, the DSEI provides a coherent focus across an entire education system: organizational leadership, instructional leadership, and teaching. Because teachers exert the most powerful influence on instruction, the entire system must focus on ensuring that teachers are effective.

The DSEI emphasizes *vertical alignment* — with organizational systems and structures as well as instructional leadership — but also *horizontal alignment* — with teaching colleagues and classroom resources — as keys to success.

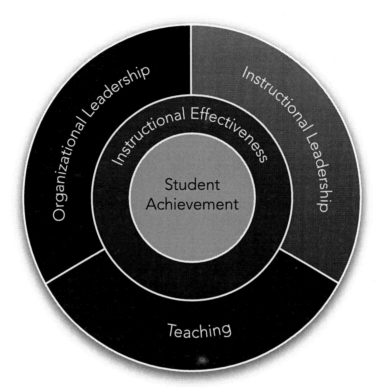

Throughout our discussion of embedded literacy, we will refer to the DSEI model frequently. It provides a sound basis for incorporating the kind of systemwide change that will be crucial if students are to succeed with the Common Core State Standards and Next Generation Assessments.

Summary

Embedded literacy refers to the incorporation of literacy instruction — instruction in reading, writing, listening, speaking, and language — across the curriculum. The Common Core State Standards both require and support embedded literacy in schools through their linking of standards for literacy in history/social studies, science, and technical subjects with standards for English language arts. Teachers in all disciplines and all grades must achieve a level of comfort as they take on aspects of literacy instruction. As teachers face this new challenge, the DSEI provides a model that can help districts to bring about the changes required to provide teachers, and ultimately students, with the support they will need.

Questions to Consider

- How successful has your school or district been with past systemwide changes?
- What types of interdepartmental or cross-curricular programs do you already have in place?
- How much training have the teachers in your district had on Common Core State Standards and Next Generation Assessments?

References

Common Core State Standards. Online: www.corestandards.org

Daggett System for Effective Instruction. Online: http://www.leadered.com/dsei.html

Draper, Roni Jo, et al., eds. *(Re)-Imagining Content-Area Instruction.* New York, NY: Teachers College Press, 2010.

 Chapter 2

Research to Support a Focus on Systemwide Embedded Literacy

The new focus on embedded literacy stems from a perfect storm of challenges. Research measuring the state of literacy nationwide indicates that the United States is underperforming when it comes to teaching the kinds of literacy required in the global workplace. Text complexity in school textbooks has declined, whereas expectations in the real world have increased. Technological advances require us to be literate in a number of platforms, not merely on paper. The Common Core State Standards seek to address our national underperformance by integrating literacy skills across the curriculum, making all teachers at all levels responsible for students' literacy.

A variety of recent research supports a focus on systemwide embedded literacy. From studies that compare student performance internationally to those that consider how best to support effective teachers, the research we will review here points in the direction of embedding literacy throughout the curriculum to improve student success.

Definition of a National Catastrophe

We have a rich supply of data measuring the state of literacy in our country. Adult literacy is assessed by the U.S. Department of Education approximately every ten years through the National Assessment of Adult Literacy. The 30 industrialized nations in the Organization for Economic Co-operation and Development (OECD) survey literacy. Colleges and community colleges also participate in literacy studies. The National Assessment of Educational Progress (NAEP) assesses school-age children, and state assessments are required under the *No Child Left Behind Act*. In numerous countries, the Programme for International Student Assessment (PISA) is given to 15-year-olds.

Still, despite all of the data available, we have been too slow to act. In the United States, we are data rich and action poor. Consistently, the data tell us that we are underperforming when it comes to helping students handle forms of embedded literacy that are essential to the global workplace. Among industrialized nations, we rank poorly, even when comparing similar groups such as high-achieving students or economically advantaged adults. But while most of the countries in the OECD have geared a national effort toward these forms of literacy, we in the United States have not. If we continue moving on this path, it will be difficult — to put it mildly — for the country to remain competitive in the world. (Lemke, et al., 2005)

National Evidence: 2003 National Assessment of Adult Literacy (NAAL) Results

The 2003 National Assessment of Adult Literacy found that 55 percent of all adults perform at a basic or below basic level of literacy when dealing with documents that contain numbers and numerical concepts, 34 percent also score poorly with simple documents, and 43 percent perform poorly with prose text (fiction and nonfiction).

It is difficult to remain a dominant world economic force when one-third or more of the population cannot perform the typical literacy tasks required in today's workplace. The situation is reaching catastrophic proportions.

Defining Below Basic Literacy

To underscore the scope of the problem, we should remind ourselves of what "below basic literacy" actually means. On the National Assessment of Adult Literacy (NAAL) assessment, for instance, below basic literacy includes adults who can read but cannot perform simple tasks with documents or enter information on a form. Consider the following alarming statistics from the NAAL (2003):

- 43 percent of adults at below basic levels of literacy were living in poverty, compared to 4 percent of those at proficient levels.
- Three out of four food stamp recipients performed at a basic or lower level on this assessment.
- Seven in ten prisoners performed in the lowest two literacy levels.
- Adults at the below basic level earned a median income of $240 per week compared to $681 for those at the highest levels of literacy.

Skills of Adults at Below Basic Level

Can Usually Perform	Cannot Usually Perform
Sign one's name Identify a country in a short article Locate one piece of information in a sports article Locate the expiration date information on a driver's license Total a bank deposit entry	Locate eligibility from a table of employee benefits Locate intersection on a student map Locate two pieces of information in a sports article Identify and enter background information on a Social Security card application Calculate total costs of purchase from an order form

(South Carolina Adult Education, 2006)

More negative signals came from a study by Murray, Owen, and McGraw (2005):

- Adults at below basic worked an average of 19 weeks per year compared to 44 weeks per year for those at the proficient levels.
- Minorities represented a disproportionate number of those scoring at the lowest two levels of literacy.

More National Evidence: National Survey of America's College Students

How do professionals and college graduates fare on literacy assessments? The National Survey of America's College Students (NSACS) assesses students in their final year at two- and four-year institutions. The survey measures the same characteristics as the NAAL scores do, in a similar way. (American Institutes for Research, 2006)

According to the NSACS results, 30 percent of students in two-year institutions and 20 percent in four-year institutions possess only basic level literacy skills in document and quantitative literacy. Yet most of them will enter a workforce in which nearly 80 percent of the literacy tasks will require acting upon documents of some kind. Prose and basic document literacy performances are higher for those students who take college level classes that require analytic thinking, such as evaluating the strength of arguments or applying theories to practical problems or new situations. (National Institute for Literacy [NIL], 2006)

The study also found that there are no significant literacy differences between students who attend public or private institutions of higher learning. Likewise, students do not differ substantially across majors with regard to literacy levels. Perhaps most surprisingly, four-year college and community college graduates fare no better than other adults in these critical areas of literacy. Given such findings, we should be asking whether our colleges, community colleges, and postsecondary technical training programs are truly preparing adults for the future.

International Evidence: Results of the 2003 International Adult Literacy and Life Skills Survey

How do we in the United States compare internationally in literacy? The highest literacy scores, according to the 1994–1995 international Adult Literacy and Life Skills Survey (ALLSS), were found in Switzerland, Norway, the Netherlands, and Germany. Canada also outscored the United States, when similar age groups and levels were compared. After the assessment was administered again in 2003, it was clear that the United States profited little from acquiring the earlier results. (Lemke, et al., 2005)

The 2003 version of the ALLSS also showed that Norway, Bermuda, and Switzerland all outscored the United States. Italy and Mexico, in fact, were the only countries in this recent study that were surpassed by the United States. The ALLSS scores become even more troubling when you learn about some correlations between low scores and future success. For instance, the survey concluded that younger workers were more likely to become employed if they scored at Levels 3 or 4 on the test. Scoring at the lowest levels also increased the probability of unemployment, especially over time.

Workers who were unemployed for 52 weeks or more were 30 percent more likely to get jobs if they scored at higher levels of literacy. This effect of literacy has been seen across all the countries tested. When poverty is coupled with literacy, the problem grows worse for workers in all countries and decreases the likelihood of employment even further.

The most interesting conclusion drawn by the survey was a direct and significant correlation between literacy level and computer usage. Across all countries tested, individuals who said they used computers on a regular basis had significantly higher scores than nonusers. This fact may have ramifications for U.S. secondary schools as we design comprehensive literacy programs that address 21st-century needs. We will address technological literacy later in the chapter.

International Comparison of Skill Levels

Summaries of international performance on the 2003 ALLSS are shown in the following charts. The charts compare countries and the percent of participants scoring at various levels of performance as defined on the assessment. Level 3 represents the essential minimum for competency in the workplace. While the United States performs better in prose than in other forms of literacy, we still lag behind most other countries in overall performance on this assessment.

2003 Adult Literacy and Life Skills Survey Results
for the First Phase of OECD Countries

Average Prose Literacy Scores of 16- to 65-Year-Olds in 2003	Scale Score	Average Document Literacy Scores of 16- to 65-Year-Olds in 2003	Scale Score
Norway	290.1	Norway	295.1
Bermuda	289.8	Canada	280.6
Canada	280.8	Bermuda	280.0
Switzerland	272.1	Switzerland	276.6
United States	268.6	United States	269.6
Italy	229.1	Nuevo Leon, Mexico	226.2
Nuevo Leon, Mexico	228.3	Italy	225.8
Average Numeracy (Quantitative) Literacy Scores of 16- to 65-Year-Olds in 2003	**Scale Score**	**Average Problem Solving Literacy Scores of 16- to 65-Year-Olds in 2003**	**Scale Score**
Norway	289.8	Norway	284.2
Switzerland	284.9	Switzerland	279.0
Canada	272.3`	Canada	273.8
Bermuda	269.7	Bermuda	272.8
United States	260.9	Italy	224.9
Italy	233.3	United States	Not taken in 2003
Nuevo Leon, Mexico	Not taken in 2003	Nuevo Leon, Mexico	Not taken in 2003

These tests are reported using a scale score system from 0 to 500. The average (mean) score is 250 points. (Murray, T., Owen, E., and McGraw, B., 2005)

Addressing a Growing Gap

The evidence is clear. We are not competitive enough when it comes to literacy, and if we do not act accordingly, this short-term deficiency threatens to turn into a long-term decline. As Western nations struggle to recover their economic equilibrium after the financial crisis of 2008, China and India are using their size and human capital to become global economic powerhouses. Emerging economies such as Vietnam, Argentina, Brazil, Indonesia, and Panama are increasingly capable of winning greater shares of international business. The ability to compete in the interconnected global economy is leveraged primarily through technical innovation and a highly-skilled workforce. To drive both levers, a more rigorous and relevant curriculum is needed.

One way to make the curriculum more relevant is to incorporate more nonfiction prose and more "reading to do." Research shows that middle-level skilled workers spend between 35 and 95 percent of their time in literacy-related tasks interacting with documents and other nonfiction prose forms of literacy. Even the average shipyard worker spends almost two hours a day reading and writing or performing entry data. Of the reading required at a typical shipyard job site, 60 percent involves "reading to do" or reading to carry out a specific purpose — 76 percent if we count the reading of symbols.

But while reading has become more common and more complex on the job, reading-level requirements for students have not kept pace with the increased complexity and diversity of texts that are now common in the modern workplace. Even entry-level job positions require the reading of texts that can be significantly more complex than those required for the average student. Lexile scores make this clear. Lexile measures are a measure of readability used by many textbook publishers and the Common Core State Standards. One analysis revealed that in 2006, entry-level job reading requirements ranged between approximately 1200L and 1500L, while the 75th percentile of 11th grade students were just over 1200L. Perhaps even more surprising, entry-level job reading requirements exceed the reading requirements of all but the most technical college coursework. (Daggett and Hasselbring, 2007)

While our schools are working hard at improving, the reality is that the rest of the world is changing faster, leaving a growing gap between what we hope to do and what they can, in fact, do. The requirements for success in college and careers grow ever more challenging, while research shows that the requirements for most secondary schools have not kept pace.

Lexile Measure	High School Students (Middle 50% at Midyear)	Classroom Materials (Middle 50%)	Personal Use Reading	Newspapers	Career Clusters Entry Level 75th Percentile
1700L					Law & Public Safety (1740)
1600L					
1500L					Ag./Natural Resources (1510)
1400L				Reuters (1440)	
1300L			Safety Manual for Spa (1390) Aetna Health Discount Form (1360)	New York Times (1380) Washington Post (1350) Wall Street Journal (1320) Chicago Tribune (1310) Associated Press (1310)	Education & Training (1370) Trans./Dist./Log. (1350) Arch./Construction (1340) Manufacturing (1310) Business and Admin. (1310) Health Science (1300)

Lexile Measure	High School Students (Middle 50% at Midyear)	Classroom Materials (Middle 50%)	Personal Use Reading	Newspapers	Career Clusters Entry Level 75th Percentile
1300L		Grades 11/12: 1100-1300	Medical Ins. Benefit Pkg. (1280)		Retail/Wholesale (1270)
1200L	Grades 11/12: 940-1210	Grade 10: 1100-1200	Application — Student Loan (1270)	USA Today (1200)	Hospitality & Tourism (1260)
1100L	Grade 10: 905-1195		Federal Tax Form W-4 (1260)		Scientific Res./ Engr. (1250)
1000L			G.M. Protection Plan (1150)		Human Services (1200)
900L					Arts/AV Tech/Comm. (1190)

By increments, the text complexity of K–12 textbooks has become less challenging over the last 50 years. The Common Core State Standards underscore this point, citing research that shows steep declines in the average sentence length and vocabulary level found in reading textbooks. During the same time period, the literacy demands of college and careers have remained consistent or even increased. College students are routinely expected to read complex texts with far greater independence than are high school seniors.

As a result, a significant gap yawns between students' reading abilities in school and the textual demands of their postsecondary pursuits. Research shows that this gap is equal to a Lexile difference between 4th grade and 8th grade texts on the National Assessment of Educational Progress (NAEP). (Daggett and Hasselbring, 2007)

Posing additional challenges to American educators is the large and growing percentage of students whose first language is not English. This population includes wide ranges of proficiency, including those who speak no English at all. In fact, students from many neighborhoods hear, speak, and read no English outside of school.

From 2000 to 2011, U.S. students made modest gains in reading achievement. The percent of America's 4th graders scoring at or above proficient in reading increased from 29 percent in 2000 to 34 percent in 2011, according to the National Assessment of Educational Progress (NAEP). Unfortunately, more than 65 percent of 4th graders continue to score below proficiency in reading, and half score below basic. Students who are behind in reading by 4th grade often never catch up. (Balfanz, et al., 2012)

Research shows that the academic achievement students attain by 8th grade has a greater impact on their college and career readiness by the time they graduate from high school than any other factor. (ACT, 2006) In fact, struggling in middle school can put students on a track to drop out in the future. Research shows, as well, that a student's decision to drop out may be rooted in loss of engagement and motivation in middle school, which in turn may stem from academic difficulties and resulting grade retention. (Balfanz, et al., 2012)

It may be significant that education spending in Finland, a nation among the highest performers on the international PIRLS assessments of reading and the PISA in math, is weighted toward the middle school years. Finland spends about the same as its OECD counterparts in grades 1–5, much less in grades 10–12, but substantially more in the middle years, grades 6–9. (Bassett, 2008)

To address the various academic gaps we have considered, the Common Core State Standards have been established. Developed in collaboration with content experts, states, teachers, school administrators, and parents, the Common Core State Standards establish clear and consistent nationwide goals that will prepare America's children for success in college and careers. These standards define the knowledge and skills that K–12 students should develop in order to graduate from high school and be prepared for college and careers.

The CCSS aim for standards that are fewer, higher, clearer, and deeper. This initiative follows analyses showing that top-achieving countries generally teach fewer topics more deeply, focus on applications of knowledge and reasoning skills, and employ well-crafted instruction and assessment based on developmental learning progressions, both within and across domains. (Darling-Hammond and Pecheone, 2010; Mullis, et al., 2007)

The Common Core State Standards hold all learners to the same expectations. To address the gap between real-life reading and school reading, the CCSS have extended the Lexile levels for reading materials, working from high school backwards down through the lower grades to prepare all students more effectively for the material they will read in college and career.

Text Complexity Grade Band in the Standards	Old Lexile Ranges	Lexile Ranges Aligned to CCR* Expectations
K–1	N/A	N/A
2–3	450–725	450–790
4–5	645–845	770–980
6–8	860–1010	955–1155
9–10	960–1115	1080–1305
11–CCR*	1070–1220	1215–1355

*College and Career Readiness

Anchored by Next Generation Assessments (NGA), the CCSS will raise the bar. They can help states ensure that every student is challenged to achieve and succeed on a path to college and career. Proficiency levels will also be set higher. Assessments will measure both what students know and what they can do with that knowledge. Consequently, the CCSS will have a major impact on learning and instruction. To achieve this goal, one major emphasis embedded throughout the CCSS is the development of process skills, not just knowledge.

The CCSS standards for English language arts, for instance, reflect a heightened awareness of the need for functional reading and writing. A major portion of the taxonomies, in fact, includes multifaceted informational texts; evidence-based content; speaking, listening, and literacy beyond the classroom; as well as the use of technology and digital media. (Daggett and Gendron, 2010)

Because careers and colleges require workers and students to read and write a substantial amount of informational texts, the Common Core State Standards call for a special emphasis on the reading and writing of informational texts in the content areas, adhering to the National Assessment of Educational Progress (NAEP) Framework developed over the past five years.

NAEP Distribution of Literary and Informational Passages by Grade

Grade	Literary	Information
4	50%	50%
8	45%	55%
12	30%	70%

(NAEP, 2009)

NAEP Distribution of Writing Purposes by Grade

Grade	To Persuade	To Explain	To Convey Experience
4	30%	35%	35%
8	35%	35%	30%
12	40%	40%	20%

(NAEP, 2007)

So why now? Why all the urgency to adopt the CCSS and to alter the way we teach? Quite simply, that answer is that what we have been doing and continue to do is no longer working. Digital technology, global competition, an evolving marketplace, and changing job requirements have accelerated our need to improve students' achievement. Today's global competition across many job categories requires a high degree of literacy and an unprecedented level of readiness for retraining in new jobs and technologies.

Preparing Students for Next Generation Assessments

> And last but not least, for the first time, the new assessments will better measure the higher-order thinking skills so vital to success in the global economy of the 21st century and the future of American prosperity. To be on track today for college and careers, students need to show that they can analyze and solve complex problems, communicate clearly, synthesize information, apply knowledge, and generalize learning to other settings.
>
> — *Arne Duncan, 2010*

The Basics of Next Generation Assessments

Correlated to CCSS and employing universal design principles, Next Generation Assessments will test higher order thinking and applications. Next Generation Assessments are designed to provide state-to-state comparability, with standards set against research-based benchmarks that will measure both current achievement and growth across time. Beyond providing a means for maintaining accountability, these assessments are meant to drive and improve instruction.

In order to show progress toward college and career readiness, assessment items will be constructed to include tasks that are required for success in college and careers. For example, both employers and postsecondary educators regard the ability to make effective oral arguments and conduct significant research projects as essential skills. These skills are difficult to assess, however, using a paper-and-pencil test. (Achieve, 2004) Therefore, the assessments will combine selected responses, short constructed responses, extended constructed responses, technology enhanced responses, and performance tasks. (Gendron, 2012)

Adaptations, including computer adaptations, will be available to serve learners with a variety of abilities and needs. Special attention will be given to the large numbers of English language learners in the nation's schools. An expert panel convened in 2007 and 2008 found, for instance, that the majority of accommodations used in state testing programs actually came from special education and do not address the linguistic needs of ELLs. (Rivera, 2008; Darling-Hammond and Pecheone, 2010)

A Move toward Assessment-Driven Learning

Since No Child Left Behind, assessment has dominated and driven teacher efforts. Too often, the focus on assessment as an accountability measure has resulted in teaching to the test, as well as a single-minded focus on tested disciplines.

Some pressure to teach to the test originates from influences outside the school system. For example, state test data dominate the media and may be all that the public learns about the performance of teachers and schools. Too often, the school system lacks control over the message.

Current high-stakes tests are often used as a punitive tool, not a growth tool. Students are retained and teachers evaluated, pressured, and sometimes fired based on test scores. By contrast, effective assessment-driven learning would provide continual, detailed feedback to guide students' learning and feed back into instructional and curriculum decisions. (Beatty and Gerace, 2009; Gendron, 2012) Unfortunately, most current teacher preparation programs fail to teach teachers how to use data to drive instruction (Grossman, 2008), so most teachers will need professional development in this area.

The result of this knowledge gap is that formative assessment is often underutilized or not used effectively to guide and differentiate instruction. Yet, according to a recent analysis, the effective use of formative assessment data can boost growth by almost two full years in a single year. (Hattie, 2009) The effective use of formative assessment to drive instruction can also help students in poverty or other high risk circumstances to catch up with their peers. (Gendron, 2012)

Formative assessment often incorporates literacy across the content areas, as students are asked to use speaking or writing to describe and explain what they have learned. For more about formative assessment, see the International Center's publication, *Formative Assessment for Increasing Rigor and Relevance* (2012).

A Move toward Interdisciplinary Content

Teaching individual disciplines in isolation has led to a concentration on these tested disciplines at the expense of others. The late 1970s through the late 1980s saw growth in the use of integrated curricula and interdisciplinary teaching practices. (Drake and Burns, 2004; Haney, et al., 2007; Palmer, 1998) Beginning in the early 1990s, however, the push toward standards-driven, discipline-based curricula posed challenges for interdisciplinary learning. (Drake and Burns, 2004; Haney, et al., 2007) Currently, some effort is being made to apply reading, language arts, and math to interdisciplinary content in classroom instruction. In particular, reading and language arts instruction is often organized around interdisciplinary themes. Authentic problem-based interdisciplinary teaching and assessment, however, remain rare.

The Common Core State Standards will require teachers to delve deeper into content. Cross-disciplinary lessons and project-based learning can help prepare students for the new assessments. The development of these types of lessons can be guided through the use of the Rigor/Relevance Framework described in the section that follows. High rigor/high relevance Gold Seal Lessons provide appropriate levels of rigor and relevance to prepare students for Next Generation Assessments. (Daggett and Gendron, 2010)

Because the Common Core State Standards that address reading, writing, listening, speaking, and language also cover History/Social Studies and Science and Technical Subjects as well as English language arts, content-area teachers must understand the fundamentals of literacy and be able to impart literacy strategies that their students can use to succeed on the Next Generation Assessments. In fact, the kinds of skills usually associated with language arts are now required even in mathematics. Just a glance at the CCSS for Mathematical Practices confirms that the new emphasis on reading, writing, and multiple steps will require math teachers to have some knowledge of literacy strategies as well as strong numeracy skills:

1. Make sense of problems and persevere in solving them.
2. Reason abstractly and quantitatively.
3. Construct viable arguments and critique the reasoning of others.
4. Model with mathematics.
5. Use appropriate tools strategically.

6. Attend to precision.

7. Look for and make use of structure.

8. Look for and express regularity in repeated reasoning.

Here are some examples of the kinds of performance tasks that students may be expected to perform on the Next Generation Assessments.

Performance Task A: Grade 2–3 Math

Task	What to Do	What to Submit
1	Count the students in our class.	Recorded number
2	Imagine that our class is at a picnic. Each picnic table can hold three students on a side. Draw our class at the picnic tables. How many tables would we need?	Drawing
3	Look at your drawing. Are there tables with too few students? How could you arrange the students so that the tables have nearly equal numbers of students? Draw or write your answer.	Drawing or one-paragraph written explanation
4	Explain why your second plan might be better than your first.	One-paragraph reflection

Performance Task B: Grade 11–12 ELA

Task	What to Do	What to Submit
1	Find 3–5 texts on the theme of moral courage. Take notes on those texts.	One page of notes per text, saved electronically
2	Synthesize what you have learned from the texts about moral courage into an essay on the topic. Cite specific examples.	1,000 word essay, saved electronically
3	Research a historical figure who exhibited moral courage, or write about a person you know who has that quality.	750- to 1,000-word essay, saved electronically
4	Write a brief reflection about what you learned from these tasks.	250- to 500-word reflection

Note that even the primary-level mathematics task requires competence in writing. The high school ELA task requires strong reading and writing capabilities. Both require high-level critical thinking.

Thinking about Learning Systemically

To move from teaching content in isolation to incorporating literacy across the curriculum requires a new mindset about learning. Thinking about learning as a continuum can help teachers move students toward success. Two models that are useful in organizing instruction and thinking about it logically are learning progressions and the Rigor/Relevance Framework.

Learning Progressions

Research indicates that educators need to pay more attention to building common conceptions of progress. (Hattie, 2009) As we mentioned earlier, high-achieving countries tend to have a curriculum that is based on developmental learning progressions. When well-defined, a set of learning progressions can form the basis for organizing the curriculum and assessments within a subject area. Learning progressions are empirically validated descriptions of how learning typically unfolds within a curricular domain or an area of knowledge and skill. These progressions are meant to help teachers determine where students are along a learning continuum in order to guide their instruction. (Gendron, 2012)

A learning progression is, in essence, a sequence of steps that students must take and master en route to a specific learning goal. To construct a learning progression, teachers or teams might follow these steps.

1. **Identify the learning goal.** This might be a local objective or a Common Core State Standard.
2. **Break it down.** Ask yourself: "What does a student need to know or do to meet this learning goal?"
3. **Create a progression.** Plan an instructional sequence that gives students a step-by-step learning progression toward the learning goal.

After each step in the instructional sequence, teachers may use formative assessment tools to check students' understanding and determine whether to move forward as planned or to fine-tune the progression by adding additional steps, altering an existing step, or even skipping one step entirely. The purpose is to move *all* students toward the end of the progression and mastery of the learning goal.

An understanding of learning progressions helps teachers scaffold instruction and identify gaps in students' understandings and skills. In addition, such progressions should guide formative and summative assessments in order to evaluate and support students as they attain college and career readiness. (Gendron, 2012)

Developing useful learning progressions has been challenging, in part due to the patchwork development of large-scale assessment systems over the last few decades. State and national assessments, originally intended to monitor large-scale trends, focused on grade level expectations for milestone grades, such as 4th, 8th, and 12th. Rather than assessing individual learning, they compared students at a particular point in time. In 2008, the Council of Chief State School Officers (CCSSO) included learning progressions as part of their "Five Attributes of Effective Formative Assessment." This same organization would later turn its attention to developing the Common Core State Standards.

Here is an example of a learning progression for a simple 4th grade ELA objective.

1. **What is the learning goal?** (CCSS Grade 4) Describe the overall structure (e.g., chronology, comparison, cause/effect, problem/solution) of events, ideas, concepts, or information in a text or part of a text.

2. **What does a student need to know or do to meet this learning goal?** Define and differentiate structural terms; recognize the structure of part of a text; recognize the structure of a whole text.

3. **What progression can I use?** (1) Vocabulary Lesson (teach terms); (2) Apply Vocabulary (show examples of each structure, have students match to terms); (3) Identify Structure of Text Part (give students a three-paragraph passage and have them name the structure and give reasons for their selection); (4) Identify Structure of Longer Text (let students select a longer passage and write a short essay describing and identifying its structure)

Thinking about learning in this way can help teachers to differentiate learning without having to design entirely separate tasks for certain students. It can also help them decide where to incorporate literacy strategies in the course of a lesson plan. Teachers may use formative assessment to determine where students are on the learning progression and adapt instruction accordingly.

The Rigor/Relevance Framework®

The Rigor/Relevance Framework® is a tool developed by the International Center for Leadership in Education (ICLE) to organize curriculum, instruction, and assessment. The International Center identifies rigor, relevance, and relationships as three key elements found in successful districts across the country. The Rigor/Relevance Framework is based on two dimensions — one of rigor and higher standards (based on Bloom's Knowledge Taxonomy) and the other of relevance and student application (how students apply learning to life). Both rigor and relevance thrive in the presence of strong, supportive, teacher-student relationships.

Relevance enables students to connect what they are learning to their experience. Rigorous content that is interdisciplinary and connected to the real world engages students in learning by providing a context and impetus for making meaning. Relevance can vary depending on the culture of a school and its students.

The Rigor/Relevance Framework has four quadrants. Each is labeled with a term that characterizes learning or student performance at that level.

Quadrant A: Acquisition

Students gather and store bits of knowledge and information. Students are primarily expected to remember or understand this acquired knowledge. Quadrant A represents simple recall and the basic understanding of knowledge for its own sake. Examples of Quadrant A knowledge are knowing that the world is round and that Shakespeare wrote *Hamlet*.

Quadrant B: Application

Students use acquired knowledge to solve problems, design solutions, and complete work. The highest level of application is to apply appropriate knowledge to new and unpredictable situations. Quadrant B applications would include knowing how to use math skills to make purchases and count change.

Quadrant C: Assimilation

Students extend and refine their acquired knowledge so they can use that knowledge automatically and routinely to analyze and solve problems and create unique solutions. Quadrant C represents knowledge for its own sake but embraces higher levels of knowledge, such as knowing how the U.S. political system works and analyzing the benefits and challenges of the cultural diversity of this nation versus other nations.

Quadrant D: Adaptation

Students have the competence to think in complex ways and also to apply the knowledge and skills they have acquired. Even when confronted with perplexing unknowns, students are able to use extensive knowledge and skill to create solutions and take actions that further develop their skills and knowledge. Types of Quadrant D knowledge include the ability to access information in wide-area network systems and the ability to gather and use knowledge from a variety of sources to solve a complex problem in the workplace.

The Rigor/Relevance Framework is based in part on Bloom's Knowledge Taxonomy, which was updated and revised in 2001 by Lorin Anderson, a student of Bloom's, and David Krathwohl, a colleague, to reflect the movement in education towards standards-based curricula and assessment. Nouns in Bloom's original model were changed to verb forms (for example, *knowledge* to *remembering* and *comprehension* to *understanding*) and slightly reordered. We believe that the original Bloom's Taxonomy, as can be seen in the Rigor/Relevance Framework, clearly describes expectations for Quadrants A, B, C, and D. The revised Bloom's, by comparison, elevates the importance of Quadrants B (Application) and D (Adaptation) and indicates how 21st-century lessons should be built. We regard both the original and revised taxonomies as necessary and important. Both taxonomies accurately describe the expectations established by the CCSS.

The following examples for technical reading and writing illustrate students working in the four quadrants.

- **Quadrant A:** Define vocabulary terms needed to understand content of a classroom simulation.

- **Quadrant B:** Complete a simulation following the directions given by the instructor.

- **Quadrant C:** Compare and contrast the information gained from two simulations with that gained from reading a text on the same topic.

- **Quadrant D:** Synthesize information from a range of sources (e.g., texts, media sources, and simulations), presenting solutions to conflicting information.

All four quadrants are of equal importance for student achievement. Embedding literacy into instruction can provide the scaffolds to shift instruction from one quadrant to the next. For example, a quick-write at the end of the class in which students reflect on their learning can increase the rigor and relevance of a particular lesson.

Neuroscience and Increased Rigor and Relevance

The use of Quadrants B and D (or the prefrontal cortex) is what will ultimately make an individual successful in the 21st century. Computers and technology are superb at Quadrant A and are becoming better at Quadrant C. But computers cannot think, as artificial intelligence is still some years away. Therefore, the individual who can use the prefrontal cortex in areas of creativity, design, innovation, and creative thinking will be the person who has the greatest probability of success in the 21st century.

— *Paul D. Nussbaum and Willard R. Daggett, 2008*

How can students wire their brains for future career success? Key findings from neuroscience and cognitive science, as well as our expanding knowledge of the mechanisms of human learning, help to underscore the importance of the Rigor/Relevance Framework. Here are just a few examples.

1. Learning can affect and change the physical structure of the brain. (National Research Council, 2000; Zadina, 2008) For example, learning can add synapses in the hippocampus, which is important to memory formation. (National Research Council, 2000; Zadina, 2008)

2. Learning can also change the functional organization of the brain, organizing and reorganizing it as it imposes structure on the information available from experience. (National Research Council, 2000; Shaywitz, et al., 2002; Simos, et al., 2002; Temple, et al., 2001; Zadina, 2008)

3. Enriched, novel, and complex environments may also grow brain cells in the hippocampus (Nussbaum and Daggett, 2008) and increase motivation and engagement (Zadina, 2008).

4. Different kinds of experience affect the brain in different ways. (National Research Council, 2000; Zadina, 2008) What we ask the brain to do builds its neural wiring and alters its structure. (Zadina, 2008)

5. Adolescent brains are still developing. The brain does not fully mature until around age 25, so it is important for teenagers to utilize all parts of their brains in their learning. (Zadina, 2008)

An area located in the parietal cortex, near the back of the brain, receives, pools, and integrates sensory information. (Nussbaum and Daggett, 2008) Pattern recognition also takes place in the back of the brain. As they work in Quadrants A and C of the Rigor/Relevance Framework, students are mostly using this part of the brain, plus the sensory networks themselves. (Nussbaum and Daggett, 2008)

The frontal cortex is responsible for executive function, such as planning and strategies, as well as application. (Nussbaum and Daggett, 2008; Shaywitz, et al., 2004; Sandak, et al., 2004) Students working in Quadrants B and D are using this part of the brain. (Nussbaum and Daggett, 2008)

Rigor and relevance are part of a holistic approach to learning that integrates disciplines rather than isolating them. Judicious use of the Rigor/Relevance Framework allows learners to use all parts of their brains to solve real-world, interdisciplinary problems. See Chapter 3 for more about the Rigor/Relevance Framework.

Supporting Quality Instruction

Effective teachers are widely recognized as the key to raising student achievement and bringing the nation's schools into the 21st century. Of the variables under school control, no single variable has more impact than the quality of instruction. (Daggett, 2011; Darling-Hammond, 2006; Hattie, 2009; Marzano, 2007; Nye, Konstantopoulos, and Hedges, 2004) In fact, the difference between the most effective and least effective teachers can be as much as year's difference in student growth. (Chait and Miller, 2009)

Every teacher needs a thorough understanding of pedagogy as well as a versatile and comprehensive repertoire of literacy strategies to draw from in planning and providing instruction so they can match teaching approaches with learning objectives, subject matter, and targeted learners. Teachers also need a clear understanding of today's students, who are "wired differently" from students in the past. The abundance of recent discoveries in neuropsychology and brain research can and should inform teachers' understanding of 21st-century learners. (Daggett, 2011)

Sadly, in hard-to-staff, struggling schools, variations in teacher effectiveness have a more profound effect on student achievement than in more affluent schools. (Grossman, et al., 2009) Students in these schools require teachers with strong remediation skills. They require teachers who are trained to handle the many academic and social challenges facing students. Despite their greater need, these students tend to be taught by less experienced teachers. (Grossman, 2008) In fact, both new teachers and new principals disproportionately work in struggling schools. (New Teacher Center, 2009). In hard-to-staff schools, turnover rates are nearly double what is found in other schools.

Administrative Responsibilities

The critical role of principals in overseeing a literacy initiative cannot be overemphasized. Rather than haphazard approaches to improving instruction, schools need to use an approach based on assessment data. It is the responsibility of principals to implement the latter approach. (National Association of Secondary School Principals, 2005) States, as well, need to address school leadership development in their strategies for recruiting and evaluating principals. Currently, no strategies or requirements exist to show how states should identify effective principals. (New Teacher Center, 2009) The National Association of Secondary School Principals recommends multiple measures to evaluate principals. These include state assessments, exams at the end of courses, self-assessments, supervisor site visits, climate surveys, teacher evaluations, and teacher retention and transfer rates. Principals themselves must also demonstrate the ability to manage resources and to recruit and retain high-performing teachers. (Grossman, et al., 2009)

Instructional leadership is linked to teacher effectiveness and student growth. Unfortunately, current principal preparation programs do not require prospective principals to lead school improvement efforts as part of their preparation. In order to develop the skills they need, principals may need models, and they also will need strong mentoring. (New Teacher Center, 2009) Principals can learn from observation in schools where a strong principal is already leading active efforts to improve student learning. States can also offer all incoming principals professional development, as North Carolina has, about strategies to improve teacher recruitment, retention, and working conditions. (Grossman, 2008)

Effective principal assessments of teaching are strongly related to better-than-predicted elementary student achievement in mathematics and reading. (Jacob and Lefgren, 2005) However, a recent evaluation revealed that principal preparation programs do not prepare principals to recognize effective instruction. This skill is necessary for improving schoolwide student achievement.

Support for Effective Teaching

How do we know whether teachers are successful at imparting literacy strategies and increasing student literacy across the curriculum? The entire system needs to be focused on making teachers effective because teachers are the most powerful influence on instruction. This includes teacher evaluation. School systems need to embed evaluation in a broader system of professional support and development for teachers. They need to make teacher evaluation one component in a comprehensive cycle of development, supervision, support, and evaluation.

Current methods of evaluation that focus on accountability tend to overemphasize their instructional focus on state standards and the scores their students receive on standards-driven bubble tests. These methods, however, do not assess teachers' rigor and relevance in the curriculum. Thus teachers are not encouraged to increase rigor and relevance, nor does professional development emphasize the need.

It is important to use multiple measures to determine a teacher's evaluation. (Gordon, Kane, and Staiger, 2006; MET, 2001) Future leadership will probably do so, because current proposed legislation requires districts to develop teacher-evaluation systems that use student achievement data as a "significant factor" accompanied by other multiple measures in determining a teacher's evaluation.

Classroom observations are associated with improved student growth. (MET, 2012) Observing teacher performance, however, requires the rigorous documentation of skills, knowledge, and behaviors associated with effective teaching. It requires repeated observations by trained principals, teacher leaders, and/or peer evaluators, usually with the aid of detailed rubrics tied to standards describing effective practices. (Chait and Miller, 2009)

The 2012 MET report recommends a series of observations, including some by trained outside evaluators. Such observations are more effective with observation rubrics. For such purposes, a number of observation rubrics and checklists are available. Creating a rubric must begin with discussions and assumptions about what effective instruction looks like. The International Center's Collaborative Instructional Review focuses on the ultimate goal of any school evaluation or improvement program: student outcomes.

Observations improve instruction only if useful feedback is provided to the teacher. Providing clear feedback to teachers following rubric-enabled observations has led to substantial improvements in student growth, even without a targeted professional development effort. (MET, 2012; Taylor and Tyler, 2011)

Incorporating Formative Assessment

Teachers should be equipped to assess students' initial literacy and other basic skills, to make regular formative and summative assessments of content mastery, and to use the data gained to drive appropriate instruction. A necessary element for effective teaching is the ongoing use of formative assessment to inform instruction. Hattie's 2009 meta-analysis deems the use of formative-assessment data to inform instruction as the number one factor driving instructional effectiveness.

The quality of classroom assessment practices can have a substantial impact on student achievement. (Black and Wiliam, 2006; Nitko and Brookhart, 2007; Gusky, 2007; Matsumura, et al., 2006; Torgesen, 2009) Formative assessments are only effective, though, when followed by appropriate types of feedback or instructional responses (Fuchs and Fuchs, 2002; Shute, 2007; Torgesen, 2009), and assessments should allow teachers to see and evaluate student learning in ways that can feed back into instructional and curriculum decisions (Gendron, 2012).

Teacher preparation programs should include the development of requisite assessment skills. Raw assessment data must be organized and combined with other data to produce usable information, and for most assessments this requires considerable training and experience. (Torgesen, 2009) Precise information must be provided for teachers to benchmark and eventually use as part of the summative process. (Gendron, 2012)

In addition, teachers should learn to evaluate commercial programs for the quality of their initial, formative, and summative assessments as well as their corrective feedback. Principals, too, should learn to evaluate the level of support programs provide to teachers with tasks such as assessment, the organizing of assessment data, record-keeping, and using the data to target instruction. It should be remembered that well-designed computer assessment programs can handle many of the nuts, bolts, and record-keeping required to assess and use the data to drive instruction.

The Case for Technological Literacy

The discrepancy between what students are asked to read in high school and what they read after high school is not new, but as globalization hastens the pace of change in the modern "information" economy, this difference is more troubling than ever before. Given our expanding technologies and resources, literacy is no longer simply about learning to read in a continuous text format. All forms of literacy, even those involving technology, are powerfully interconnected. Teachers can do much to provide students with powerful, nimble literacy skills — both for learning and doing — whether the medium consists of print, video, audio, or multimedia environments. Currently, however, we are not doing enough to access this variety of resources on behalf of students. Textbooks alone are insufficient for 21st century preparation. (Rafferty, 1999) Increasingly, programs such as Scholastic's *Expert 21* ELA program provide multimedia platforms, with texts plus web-based reading support, scaffolds, and learning tools.

Three major societal trends or developments favor the increased use of technology in education:

- widespread wireless connectivity, creating a hyper-connected world
- a boom of inexpensive devices in the form of tablets, smart phones, and laptops
- extensive developments in cloud-based learning applications

Teachers and administrators are increasingly becoming technology-enabled themselves, using emerging technologies such as mobile devices, online classes, and digital content to improve their own productivity. As a result, more educators are thinking creatively about how to use these same tools in the classroom. Digital textbooks, for example, are already in use. Most textbook publishers offer digital versions for all or part of the programs now in development.

The newest K–12 generation has grown up using digital technologies, which are now fully integrated into their lives. (Klopfer, Osterweil, Groff, and Haas, 2009) Educators should build on these preferences and capabilities by adopting similar digital technologies for educational use. (National Science Task Force, 2008)

In addition, students are demanding a different kind of learning experience, and that is forcing even the most reluctant teachers and administrators to re-evaluate their perspectives on the value of technology within learning. As noted in prior Speak Up national reports, students have a very clear vision for 21st-century learning. Their preference is for learning environments that are socially-based, untethered, and digitally rich. Parents are also supportive of this new learning paradigm. (Speak Up, 2010)

Since Speak Up 2007, three times as many high school students now have access to on-line learning, and twice as many middle school students are learning online. *Learning in the 21st Century: 2011 Trends Update* highlights the Speak Up 2010 survey data collected from 379,285 K–12 students, parents, and educators, and describes how online learning is changing instructional models within our nation's schools. (Speak Up, 2010)

Unfortunately, some teachers report that teacher education programs do not prepare them adequately to use technology effectively in instruction. (Darling-Hammond, 2006) In addition, administrators are uneasy about the ability of teachers to integrate these new technologies effectively into instruction. (Speak Up, 2011)

The advantages to digital materials are also revealed by research on the brain. This research explores three broad learning networks: recognition networks, strategic networks, and affective networks. These networks form the basis for the three principles of Universal Design for Learning that technology leverages to support the increased differentiation and individualization of instruction. (CAST, 2009; Meyer, Pisha, Murray, and Rose, 2001; Meyer and Rose, 2000; Rose and Meyer, 2002; Rose, et al., 2005)

An advantage to digital materials is that they may provide additional resources on demand, such as pronunciations, definitions, or background information. Multiple illustrations can appear simultaneously, concepts can be defined and explained, and links can lead to expanded or supportive information. Immediate, computer-assisted corrective feedback in digital texts has been found to be effective, especially with special needs students. (Epstein, Cook, and Dihoff, 2005)

English language learners also benefit from supports such as links to definitions and pronunciations of key vocabulary words in both English and their heritage languages. They benefit, too, from electronic translation tools or links to multilingual glossaries. (CAST, 2008) In addition, technology that gives students control of the screen gives them a sense of engagement and independence (Hasselbring, Lewis, and Bausch, 2005), and leads students to remain on task longer. (Distel, 2001; Hitchcock and Noonan, 2000)

Many of the existing technology tools can provide multiple contexts for facilitating the transfer of learning, and for situating learning in a setting similar to the real-world context for performance. (Bransford, et al., 2003) Moreover, digital-based graphics, animations, or video can be the best way to present information about the relationships among objects, actions, numbers, or events. (CAST, 2008)

Technology can also be used advantageously in the following ways (Bransford, et al., 2003):

- bringing real-world problems into classrooms through the use of videos, demonstrations, simulations, and internet connections to concrete data and working scientists

- providing "scaffolding" support, such as visualization and model-based learning, for complex cognitive participation that would be difficult or impossible without such technical support

- increasing opportunities for learners to receive feedback from software tutors, reflect on their learning processes, and improve their learning and reasoning through progressive revisions

- building local and global communities of interested learners

- expanding opportunities for teachers' learning

In some schools, teachers are using technology as a way to optimize learning despite dwindling budgets. Some teachers schedule virtual field trips, for example, when they lack funds for travel. These virtual field trips, many of them free, might involve an interactive museum exhibit or a spacewalk on the moon. Schools also access online tutorials for students who need extra help when appropriate staff are not available, and they offer online courses off campus when no funds are available to hire a specialized teacher. Schools across the country also are beginning to take advantage of "virtual desktops" as a low-cost way to bring computing into the classroom.

The Next Generation Assessments aligned to the Common Core State Standards will be entirely computerized. Just as media and technology are integrated in school and life in the 21st century, skills related to media use are integrated throughout the Common Core State Standards. Literacy in the 21st century is not just about paper and ink. Educational leaders must ensure that all formats and platforms of text are available to students and that students are gaining technological expertise along with reading, writing, listening, speaking, and language skills.

Recommended Literacy Models

A major goal of the CCSS is to set high achievement standards in literacy that will prepare students for their future in the workplace. That goal requires preparation in a range of cross-curricular materials. The National Institute for Literacy recommends the following literacy model (White and McCloskey, 2005):

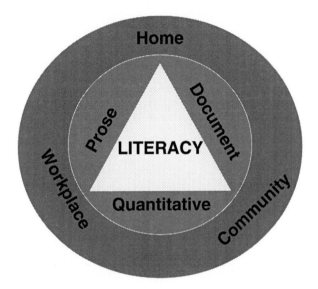

The forms and examples listed in this table more accurately reflect the demands of 21st-century literacy than the typical prose and textbook-based pieces currently used in U.S. schools.

Literacy Forms and Examples

Types of Literacy	Forms	Examples
Prose	• Fiction • Nonfiction	• Editorials • News stories • Brochures • Instructional materials
Document (includes technology-based sources)	• Array based • Form based • Visual displays • Media based or mimetic (forms of document literacy)	• Job applications • Payroll forms • Transportation schedules • Maps • Tables, charts, graphs • Drug or food labels • Ads • Web sites • Electronic media
Quantitative	• A form of document literacy requiring: • Mathematical action • Problem solving • Calculation	• Checkbook balancing • Tip calculation • Order form completion • Interest calculations • Benefit and nutrition comparison calculations • Advertisements comparing prices and other data

Compare the preceding chart to the range of text types recommended by the Common Core State Standards Initiative that follows.

CCSS Range of Text Types

Grade	Literature			Informational Text
	Stories	Dramas	Poetry	Literary Nonfiction and Historical, Scientific, and Technical Texts
K–5	adventure stories, folktales, legends, fables, fantasy, realistic fiction, myths	staged dialogue; brief, familiar scenes	nursery rhymes, narrative poems, limericks, free verse	biographies; autobiographies; books about history, social studies, science, and the arts; technical texts, including directions, forms, and information displayed in graphs, charts, or maps; digital sources
6–12	adventure stories, historical fiction, mysteries, myths, science fiction, realistic fiction, allegories, parodies, satire, graphic novels	one-act plays, multi-act plays, filmed plays	narrative poems, lyrical poems, free verse, sonnets, odes, ballads, epics	exposition, argument and functional text in the form of personal essays; speeches; opinion pieces; essays about art or literature; biographies; memoirs, journalism; historical, scientific, technical, or economic accounts written for a broad audience; digital sources

The National Assessment of Adult Literacy also recommends these areas of literacy in terms of key skill sets (NAAL, 2003):

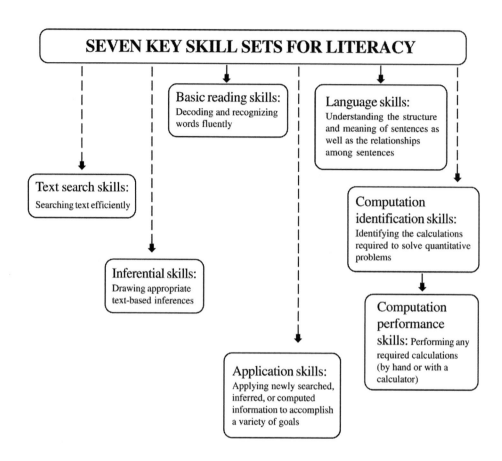

These models can help schools better plan a comprehensive literacy program that includes more than just intervention programs, fictional prose, and strategies for reading in the content areas. While all of these current aspects of literacy planning are needed, they are not sufficient. A comprehensive school literacy program will include "literacy to do," especially in relation to document, technological, and quantitative forms of literacy. When these aspects of literacy are added to a comprehensive school plan, student scores in math, science, and other assessments will improve.

The sheer number of items on Next Generation Assessments that include charts, graphs, maps, problems, and other document formats should convince educators to address these neglected areas of literacy. Embedding literacy throughout the curriculum is a natural and logical way to do so.

Summary

The 21st-century workforce is global and technologically savvy. Today's workers deal with complex documents, forms, technologies, and processes on a daily basis. Today, a skilled backhoe operator works with laser-guided grading and global positioning satellites in a computer based, high-tech environment. Despite our need to compete in a global marketplace, international statistics show that U.S. students are lagging behind some competitive nations in literacy skills. Meanwhile, our textbooks have decreased in complexity, and we are expecting less of students in school than we did a few decades ago.

The Common Core State Standards seek to address that discrepancy and to move students toward a goal of universal literacy. Schools must think systemically about how to integrate literacy across the curriculum to prepare students adequately for Next Generation Assessments. Support for effective instruction is part of a successful plan, and the integration of technology will be critical.

Questions to Consider

- How far along is your school with regard to implementing CCSS?
- How much does your school currently emphasize embedded literacy?
- Would you expect businesses in your community to support an embedded literacy initiative in the schools? How might you get them involved and interested?

References

Achieve Inc. "Do Graduation Tests Measure Up? A Closer Look at State High School Exit Exams." Washington, DC: Achieve, 2004. Online: http://www.achieve.org/files/TestGraduation-FinalReport.pdf

ACT. *Ready for College and Ready for Work: Same or Different?* Iowa City, IA: ACT, 2006.

American Institutes for Research. "New Study of the Literacy of College Students Finds Some Are Graduating with Only Basic Skills." Washington, DC: AIR, 2006.

Balfanz, R., Bridgeland, J.M., Bruce, M, and Fox, J.H. "Building a Grad Nation Report: Alliance for Excellent Education," *America's Promise Alliance*. Baltimore, MD: John Hopkins University, 2012.

Bassett, Patrick F. "The Finnish Model." *Independent School Magazine*. National Association of Independent Schools, Fall 2008. Online: http://www.nais.org/publications/ismagazinearticle.cfm?ItemNumber=151216

Beatty, I.D. and Gerace, W.J. "Technology-enhanced Formative Assessment: A Research-based Pedagogy for Teaching Science with Classroom Response Technology." *Journal of Science Education & Technology* 18: 146–162, 2009. Online: http://legacy.einstruction.com/support_downloads/assessment/pulse/CPSPulse-Research-Whitepaper.pdf

Black, P. and Wiliam, D. "Developing a Theory of Formative Assessment," in J. Gardner, Ed., *Assessment and Learning*. London: Sage, 2006.

Bransford, J., Brown, A., and Cocking, R. *How People Learn: Brain, Mind, Experience, and School*. Washington, DC: National Academy Press, 2003. Online: http://siona.udea.edu.co/~jfduitam/curriculo/doc/How%20people%20learn.pdf

CAST. "About Universal Design for Learning," 2008. Online: www.cast.org/udl/

Chait, R. and Miller, R. *Paying Teachers for Results: A Summary of Research to Inform the Design of Pay-for-Performance Programs for High-Poverty Schools*. Washington, DC: Center for American Progress, May 2009. Online: http://ww2.pwcs.edu/Admin/TIPA/EssentialElementsofaSuccessfulTeacherIncentive-research.pdf

Daggett, W.R. *The Daggett System for Effective Instruction — Where Research and Best Practices Meet*. Rexford, NY: International Center for Leadership in Education, 2011. Online: http://www.daggett.com/white_papers.html

Daggett, W.R. and Gendron, S. *Common Core Standards Initiative — Classroom Implications*. White paper. Rexford, NY: International Center for Leadership in Education, 2010.

Daggett, W.R. and Hasselbring, T.S. *What We Know about Adolescent Reading*. Rexford, NY: International Center for Leadership in Education, 2007. Online: http://www.leadered.com/pdf/Adolescent%20Reading%20Whitepaper.pdf

Darling-Hammond, L. "No Child Left Behind and High School Reform." *Harvard Educational Review* 76(4): 642–667, 2006.

Darling-Hammond, L. and Pecheone, R. "Developing an Internationally Comparable Balanced Assessment System That Supports High-Quality Learning." Princeton, NJ: Educational Testing Services, 2010. Online: http://www.k12center.org/publications.html

Distel, R.F. "Evaluation Series LS Class — netschools.net." South Bloomington, IN: PLATO Learning, 2001. Online: http://www.netschools.net/media/Evaluation%20 Studies/E/Eastern%20High%20School.pdf

Drake, Susan M. and Burns, Rebecca C. *Meeting Standards through Integrated Curriculum.* Alexandria, VA: Association for Supervision and Curriculum Development (ASCD), 2004.

Duncan, Arne. "Beyond the Bubble Tests: The Next Generation of Assessments." Secretary Arne Duncan's Remarks to State Leaders at Achieve's American Diploma Project Leadership Team Meeting. U.S. Department of Education, September, 2010. Online: http://www.ed.gov/news/speeches/beyond-bubble-tests-next-generation-assessments-secretary-arne-duncans-remarks-state-l

Epstein, G., Cook, J., and Dihoff, R.E. "Efficacy of Error for the Correction of Initially Incorrect Assumptions and of Feedback for the Affirmation of Correct Responding: Learning in the Classroom." *The Psychological Record* 55: 401–418, 2005.

Fuchs, Douglas, Fuchs, Lynn S., Mathes, Patricia G., and Martinez, Elizabeth A. "Preliminary Evidence on the Social Standing of Students with Learning Disabilities in PALS and No-PALS Classrooms." *Learning Disabilities Research & Practice* 17: 205–215, 2002.

Gendron, S., Mathematics Science Partnership — SMARTER: Balanced Assessment Consortium, June, 2012. Online: http://www.ed-msp.net/public_documents/ document/2012conferences/6_SMARTER%20Balance%20on%20Assessments%20by%20 Susan%20Gendron.pdf

Goldhaber, D. and Player, D. "What Different Benchmarks Suggest about How Financially Attractive It Is to Teach in Public Schools." *Journal of Education Finance* 30: 211–230, 2005.

Gordon, Robert, Kane, Thomas J., and Staiger, Douglas O. "Identifying Effective Teachers Using Performance on the Job." *Hamilton Project Discussion Paper*. Washington, DC: Brookings Institution, 2006.

Grossman, P. "Responding to our Critics: From Crisis to Opportunity in Research on Teacher Education." *Journal of Teacher Education* 59: 10-23, 2008.

Grossman, P., Compton, C., Igra, D., Ronfeldt, M., Shahan, E., and Williamson, P. "Teaching Practice: A Cross-Professional Perspective. *Teachers College Record* 111: 2055-2100, 2009.

Gusky, T.R. "Formative Classroom Assessment," in J.H. McMillan, Ed. *Formative Classroom Assessment: Theory into Practice*. New York: Teachers College Press, 2007.

Haney, J.J., Keil, C.P., and Zoffel, J. "From Problem Solving to Taking Action: A Problem-Based Learning Model for the Middle Grades." *Ohio Middle School Journal*, 2007.

Hasselbring, T.S., Lewis, P., and Bausch, M.E. "Assessing Students with Disabilities: Moving Assessment Forward through Universal Design." *InSight* 5: 1–15, 2005.

Hattie, John, C. *Visible Learning: A Synthesis of Over 800 Meta-Analyses Relating to Achievement*. London: Routledge, 2009.

Hitchcock, C.H. and Noonan, M.J. Computer-Assisted Instruction of Early Academic Skills. *Topics in Early Childhood Special Education* 20: 145–158, 2000.

Jacob, Brian A. and Lefgren, Lars. "Principals as Agents: Subjective Performance, Measurement in Education, NBER Working Paper Series." Working Paper 11463. Cambridge, MA: National Bureau of Economic Research, National Bureau of Economic Research Working Paper Series, 11463, 1–67, June 2005.

Klopfer, E., Osterweil, S., Groff, J., and Haas, J. "Using the Technology of Today in the Classroom Today: The Instructional Power of Digital Games, Social Networking, and Simulations and How Teachers Can Leverage Them." *The Education Arcade*. Cambridge, MA: MIT, 2009.

Lemke, M., Miller, D, Johnston, J., Krenzke, T., Alvarez-Rojas, L., Kastber, D., and Westate, L. "Highlights from the 2003 International Adult Literacy and Life Skills Survey (ALL)." Alexandria, VA: National Center for Education Statistics, May, 2005.

Marzano, Robert J. *The Art and Science of Teaching*. Alexandria, VA: Association for Supervision and Curriculum Development (ASCD), 2007.

Matsumura, L.C., et al. *Using the Instructional Quality Assessment Toolkit to Investigate the Quality of Reading Comprehension Assignments and Student Work. (CSE Technical Report #681).* Los Angeles, CA: University of California, National Center for Research on Evaluation, Standards, and Student Testing (CRESST), 2006.

Measures of Effective Teaching Project (MET). Online: http://www.metproject.org

Meyer, A. and Rose, D. "Universal Design for Individual Differences." *Educational Leadership* 58: 39–43, 2000.

Meyer, A., Pisha, B., Murray, E., and Rose, D. "More than Words: Learning to Write in the Digital World," in A. Bain, L. Baillet, and L. Moats, Eds., *Written Language Disorders: Theory into Practice,* 2nd ed. Austin, TX: PRO-ED, 2001.

Mullis, I.V.S., Martin, M.O., Kennedy, A.M., and Foy, P. *PIRLS 2006 International Report: IEA's Progress in International Reading Literacy Study in Primary Schools in Forty Countries.* Chestnut Hill, MA: Boston College, 2007.

Murray, T., Owen, E., and McGraw, B., Eds. *Learning a Living: First Results of the Adult Literacy and Life Skills Survey.* Paris, France: Organization for Economic Co-operation and Development and the Ministry of Industry, 2005.

National Assessment of Adult Literacy (NAAL). U.S. Department of Education, Washington, D.C.: National Center for Education Statistics, 2003. Online: http://nces.ed.gov/naal/. Follow links to "Key Findings."

National Association of Secondary School Principals. Online: www.nassp.org

National Institute for Literacy (NIL). "Facts and Statistics," 2006. Online: http://www.nifl.gov/. (follow links to "Facts and Statistics")

National Research Council. "How People Learn: Brain, Mind, Experience, and School. Committee on Developments in the Science of Learning." Commission on Behavioral and Social Sciences and Education, Washington, DC: National Research Council, 2000.

National Science Task Force. Online: http://www.nsf.gov/pubs/2008/nsf08204/nsf08204.pdf

New Teacher Center. Online: http://www.newteachercenter.org

Nitko, A.J. and Brookhart, S.M. *Educational Assessment of Students*. 5th ed. Upper Saddle River, NJ: Pearson Education, 2007.

Nussbaum, Paul D. and Daggett, Willard R. *What Brain Research Teaches about Rigor, Relevance and Relationships and What It Teaches about Keeping Your Own Brain Healthy*. Rexford, NY: International Center for Leadership in Education, Inc., 2008

Nye, B. Konstantopoulos, S. Hedges L. V. "How Large Are Teacher Effects?"*Educational Evaluation and Policy Analysis* 26: 237–257, 2004. Online: http://steinhardt.nyu.edu/scmsAdmin/uploads/002/834/127%20-%20Nye%20B%20%20Hedges%20L%20%20V%20%20%20Konstantopoulos%20S%20%20(2004).pdf

Palmer, Parker J. *The Courage to Teach*. San Francisco, CA: Jossey-Bass, 1998.

Pisha, B. and Coyne, P. "Smart from the Start: The Promise of Universal Design for Learning." *Remedial and Special Education* 22: 197–203, 2001.

Pisha, B. and Coyne, P. "Jumping off the Page: Content Area Curriculum for the Internet Age." *Reading Online* 5: 2001. Online: http://www.readingonline.org/articles/art_index.asp?HREF=/articles/pisha/index.html

Rafferty, Cathleen. "Literacy in the Information Age." *Educational Leadership* 57: 22–25, 1999.

Rivera, C. "ELLs: Developing an ELL-Responsive SEA Policy to Support Local Practice." Washington, DC: The George Washington University Center for Equity and Excellence in Education, 2008. Online: http://www.ctb-e.com/emails/images/pdfs/ELLAP_TestAccommodationsForELLsDevelopingELLResponsiveSEAPolicyToSupportLocalPractice_Rivera.pdf

Rose, D. and Meyer, A. *Teaching Every Student in the Digital Age: Universal Design for Learning*. Alexandria, VA: Association for Supervision and Curriculum Development (ASCD), 2002.

Rose, D., Hasselbring, T.S., Stahl, S., and Zabala, J. "Assistive Technology and Universal Design for Learning: Two Sides of the Same Coin," in D. Edyburn, K. Higgins, and R. Boone, Eds. *Handbook of Special Education Technology Research and Practice*. Whitefish Bay, WI: Knowledge by Design, 2005.

Sandak, R, Mencl, W.E., Frost, S.J., and Pugh, K.R. "The Neurobiological Basis of Skilled and Impaired Reading: Recent Findings and New Directions." *Scientific Studies of Reading* 8: 273–292, 2004. Online: http://www.brainmap.org/pubs/RichlanHBM09.pdf

Shaywitz B.A. and Shaywitz S.E., et al. "Development of Left Occipitotemporal Systems for Skilled Reading in children after a Phonologically-based Intervention." *Biological Psychiatry* 55: 926-33, 2004.

Shaywitz, B., Shaywitz, S., Pugh, K., Mencl, W., Fulbright, R., Skudlarski, P., et al. "Disruption of Posterior Brain Systems for Reading in Children with Developmental Dyslexia." *Biological Psychiatry* 52: 101–110, 2002.

Shute, V.J. "Focus on Formative Feedback." *ETS Research Report*, RR-07-11 (1-47). Princeton, NJ: Educational Testing Service, 2007.

Simos P.G., Breier J.I., Fletcher J.M., Foorman B.R., Castillo E.M., Papanicolaou, A.C. "Brain Mechanisms for Reading Words and Pseudowords: An Integrated Approach." *Cerebral Cortex* 12: 297–305, 2002.

South Carolina Adult Education, South Carolina Department of Education. *The State of Literacy in America: Estimates at the Local, State, and National Levels.* Columbia, SC: SCDE, 2006.

Speak Up. "Learning in the 21st Century: 2011 Trends Update." Released at ISTE, June 28th, 2011, Project Tomorrow and Blackboard K-12, Speak Up 2010 National Data, June 2011. Online: www.tomorrow.org/speakup/learning21Report_2011_Update.html

Taylor, E.S. and Tyler, J.H. "The Effect of Evaluation on Performance: Evidence from Longitudinal Student Achievement Data of Mid-career Teachers." NBER Working Paper No. 16877. Cambridge, MA: National Bureau of Economic Research, 2011.

Temple, V., Jozsvai, E., Konstantareas, M. M., et al. "Alzheimer Dementia in Down's Syndrome: The Relevance of Cognitive Ability." *Journal of Intellectual Disability Research* 45: 47–55, 2001. Online: http://apt.rcpsych.org/content/10/1/50.full.pdf

Torgesen, Joseph K. "Preventing Early Reading Failure and its Devastating Downward Spiral." New York, NY: The National Center for Learning Disabilities, 2009. Online: http://www.ncld.org/at-school/general-topics/early-learning-aamp-literacy/ preventing-early-reading-failure-and-its-devastating-downward-spiral

Torgesen, Joseph K. "The Response to Intervention Instructional Model: Some Outcomes from a Large-Scale Implementation in Reading First Schools." *Child Development Perspectives* 38–40, 2009.

White, S. and McCloskey, M. *Framework for the 2003 National Assessment of Adult Literacy* (NCES 2005-531). U.S. Department of Education. Washington, DC: National Center for Education Statistics, 2005.

Zadina, J. *Six Weeks to a Brain-Compatible Classroom: A Workbook for Educators.* January, 2008. Online: http://www.brainresearch.us/Zadina-Publications.html

 **Chapter 3**

Organizational Leadership for Embedded Literacy

In an era of global competition, school leaders need to recognize the significance of proficiency in embedded literacy and what it means to the future success of our students. This chapter will help school leaders make decisions about what is taught, how resources are allocated, and who is responsible for ensuring that students become proficient in embedded literacy.

The strategies traditionally used to promote reading comprehension need to be adjusted for embedded literacy materials because in many embedded documents readers are not dealing with long sections of prose text. Writing strategies also need to be adjusted to meet the demands of our era, with its electronic forms and workplace documents that require clear and accurate technical writing skills.

The CCSS have been developed to address these issues by providing logical and coherent standards for both teaching and measuring achievement in literacy with the goal of preparing today's students for college and the workplace. But while the standards define what literacy goals students should achieve, they do not identify what content students should master in literature, social studies, history, science, or technical subjects. Moreover, they do not present a method for reaching these goals. It remains in the hands of organizational leaders to put these last pieces in place.

The DSEI initiative provides invaluable support for leaders who implement these changes. Specifically, the DSEI helps leaders develop the following five key areas of leadership:

- High expectations and vision as a leader
- Instructional leadership
- Leadership through empowerment
- The personal, social, and emotional skills of a leader
- Leadership and community engagement

This chapter and the next one focus on organizational leadership and instructional leadership, respectively. These two segments move the system along a coherent pathway that enables teachers to see the district's focus and purpose in everything that drives the changes.

Organizational Leadership

No plan, however well-considered and practical, can succeed if the people it involves are not on board. Accordingly, leaders must work to create an environment in which those charged with implementing the plan and participating in it will willingly collaborate. Toward this end, organizational leadership must create six primary conditions:

- Creating a culture
- Establishing a shared vision
- Increasing leadership capacity
- Aligning organizational structures and systems to vision
- Aligning teachers and administrators to selection, support, and evaluation
- Using data systems to support decision making

Creating a Culture and Establishing a Shared Vision

The two elements of organizational leadership to focus on first are creating a culture and establishing a shared vision for your literacy initiative. The following rubrics have been developed by the International Center for Leadership in Education to assess the progress of organizational leadership and to guide the process toward the goal of "exceeding."

Organizational Leadership

Involves a Mentality, Structure, Focus, and Commitment to Create the Environment in Which Learning Is Optimized				
DSEI Element	**Beginning**	**Developing**	**Meeting**	**Exceeding**
Create a culture	• Expectations for students are low.	• Staff understand importance of holding high expectations for student success.	• Reference to high expectations for rigor, relevance, and relationships appears in vision and mission statements.	• All staff members, including bus drivers, cafeteria workers, custodians, and office personnel actively contribute to the mission of the school.
	• Staff are aware of state and local standards.	• Staff use state and local standards in their teaching.	• Teachers expect all students to meet state and local standards.	• Teachers and staff are committed to helping every student meet state and local standards.
	• State tests are seen as the finish line.	• State tests are seen as a part of student profile.	• Students are encouraged to meet or exceed expectations.	• Every student is expected to do his/her best work and is rewarded appropriately for the effort.
	• Few staff are actively involved in individual student success.	• Students perceive staff are concerned about them.	• Students have a caring and concerned adult advocate.	• Each student has an adult advocate and maintains a personal plan for progress.
	• There is little or no parent involvement.	• Parent involvement is encouraged.	• School conditions and personnel are welcoming to parents.	• Achievements of students and faculty are routinely celebrated by the district, parents, and community.

Organizational Leadership (Continued)

Involves a Mentality, Structure, Focus, and Commitment to Create the Environment in Which Learning Is Optimized			
DSEI Element	**Beginning**	**Developing**	**Meeting**	**Exceeding**
---	---	---	---	---
Establish a shared vision	• Few students or parents are aware of the district/school vision.	• Some students and parents can articulate the district/school vision.	• District/school vision is evident in conversations with students and parents.	• Students and parents understand the district/school vision and have a role in developing it.
	• Little or no evidence of commitment to providing a rigorous and relevant education is seen in district/school vision.	• Some attempt is made the district/school vision to share the importance of a rigorous and relevant education with faculty, staff, and students.	• Many opportunities exist for faculty, staff, students, and parents to share the philosophy behind, and importance of, a vision of rigor and relevance for students.	• Faculty, staff, students, and parents come together periodically to review and strengthen the district/school vision of a rigorous and relevant education for every student.
	• Little or no evidence of the importance of creating relationships between students, parents, and faculty/staff is seen in the district/school vision.	• The importance of creating relationships between students, parents, and faculty/staff is shared by some in the district/school community.	• Creating meaningful relationships between students and faculty/staff and between district/school personnel and parents is a vision shared by all.	• A foundational part of the district/school vision is the importance of establishing and nurturing strong relationships among all members of the school community to ensure student achievement.

Organizational Leadership (Continued)

Involves a Mentality, Structure, Focus, and Commitment to Create the Environment in Which Learning Is Optimized				
DSEI Element	**Beginning**	**Developing**	**Meeting**	**Exceeding**
Establish a shared vision	• Student achievement is measured solely by state test results.	• State test results are an important focus of faculty and student work.	• A few important priorities are the common focus throughout school. There's a focus on summative, benchmark, and formative assessment to describe student achievement.	• All staff, students, and parents focus on important priorities and play a role in identifying them. There's a balance between a focus on summative, benchmark, and formative assessment to describe student achievement.
	• Little or no evidence of students' future planning.	• Some students have a clear picture of their future plans.	• Students understand the importance of a clear plan for the future.	• All students have a clear and ambitious plan for future.
	• Very little evidence of emphasis on learning is displayed in the school.	• Some evidence of emphasis on learning in displays, posted materials, etc.	• Evidence of emphasis on learning is seen in displays, posted materials, and awards.	• There is a system in place to show emphasis on learning as an ongoing commitment.
	• Assessment data are available by request of faculty and staff.	• Assessment data are shared with faculty and staff.	• Assessment data are shared in ways understandable to parents and students.	• Assessment data are used by school community to support vision.

Increasing Leadership Capacity

Organizational leadership needs to support and develop existing leaders and identify and cultivate the skills of emerging, future leaders. Doing so broadens the leadership capacity of the organization immediately and paves the way for the continuous development and growth of new leaders.

Aligning Organizational Structures and Systems to Vision

Once a culture, mission, and empowered leadership are established, organizational leadership must:

- decide which external impediments to instructional effectiveness can be changed or compensated for and which ones are beyond the control of the educational organization
- ensure that enabling conditions and structures are in place to support instructional effectiveness
- identify which factors impacting effective instruction are most effective and efficient

The DSEI employs extensive data and research, provided by John Hattie and others, to accomplish these objectives. It allows decision-makers to consider the broader perspective of how to prioritize initiatives related to enhancing instructional effectiveness, and it does so according to what can reasonably be impacted. It then examines both effectiveness and efficiency.

Aligning Teachers and Administrators to Selection, Support, and Evaluation

Organizational leadership must develop systems for recruitment, retention, development, and evaluation that are understood, broad-based, focused on instructional effectiveness, and aligned both horizontally and vertically among all individuals who support instructional effectiveness and student achievement. These systems must reinforce the instructional vision of the organization.

Using Data Systems to Support Decision Making

Leaders must continually assess progress, which will never be constant or without setbacks. Data can be gathered through formative assessments, surveys, and summative assessments, among others. Analysis of the data will reveal deficiencies as well as successes, allowing for ongoing corrections and improvements. A data system is needed to provide information with which to measure instructional effectiveness. Additionally, stakeholders need to know how to use data and how to make decisions based on it. Leaders should create a regular schedule for analyzing data, building it into routine meetings with shareholders.

A sound data collection system and the knowledgeable use of the data can be applied to developing short- and long-term goals that will lead to ongoing progress toward more rigorous and relevant learning.

What Literacy Plans Are Already in Place?

As leaders develop instructional plans for achieving the high levels set by CCSS and for accomplishing an embedded literacy, an essential first step is to determine where the program currently stands. The following quiz can provide leaders with a glimpse of their current focus on literacy as a way to gauge the fidelity of implementation and to generate discussions about the culture of the school or district.

Focus on Literacy

Answer each question by checking the best answer. If you can answer "Yes" only to part of the question, check "Partially" as your response.	Yes	Partially	No
1. Can we walk through your building, program, or district and clearly see a focus on literacy?	☐	☐	☐
2. Does each and every teacher have a rich toolkit of research-based strategies for reading, writing, speaking, listening, production, and technology access?	☐	☐	☐
3. Does every staff member have a performance goal related to literacy and the achievement gains of students?	☐	☐	☐
4. Are your strategic plan goals, school/program goals, and resources clearly tied to literacy and numeracy?	☐	☐	☐
5. If we asked your staff members what is the single most important literacy achievement accomplishment that you hold them accountable for, would they know?	☐	☐	☐
6. Does your staff frequently share best-practice strategies around literacy?	☐	☐	☐
7. If we reviewed your meeting agendas, could we see a clear focus on literacy?	☐	☐	☐
8. Do parents know exactly what you are trying to accomplish in teaching literacy?	☐	☐	☐
9. Do students set their own goals in literacy achievement and have someone who helps them reflect on their progress?	☐	☐	☐
10. Is your professional development in literacy ongoing, with time for teacher dialogue and reflection on best practices, student work, and lessons or units?	☐	☐	☐
11. When your staff members talk about literacy for all students, do they mean it? Can they demonstrate that they mean it?	☐	☐	☐
12. Do you as a leader keep up with and articulate the best instructional practices for today's students in acquiring literacy?	☐	☐	☐

Focus on Literacy (Continued)

Answer each question by checking the best answer. If you can answer "Yes" only to part of the question, check "Partially" as your response.	Yes	Partially	No
13. Does your staff extensively use authentic and relevant documents and electronic resources to prepare students for the future?	☐	☐	☐
14. Do you have a plan for introducing and getting results with embedded literacy strategies aligned to the literacy standards set by CCSS?	☐	☐	☐
15. Is the dialogue in your school clearly focused on 21st-century literacy skills, including rigorous thinking and communication for 21st-century students?	☐	☐	☐

If you answered "yes" to at least 12 of the questions, this section will seem less revolutionary than if you have a smaller literacy focus in your school or district. Outstanding schools in this country and throughout the world have leaders with the courage to make achievement for every student a priority, and literacy is an imperative. The first step for leaders in the 21st century is to make certain the answers to all the above questions are "yes."

Learning from Best Practices

The International Center for Leadership in Education has devoted many years to studying the best practices of highly successful schools. For most of these schools, their improvement can be traced to a simple acknowledgement: "What we are now doing is not getting the results we want." In essence, the faculty and administration asked, "What plan for curriculum and instruction is necessary if our students are to graduate college and career ready?" Such a direct question produces a variety of responses and actions from teachers and administrators.

After responding to the previous questions to assess your school and its literacy development, several additional questions still remain:

- Who needs to be involved in this initiative?
- What resources are available or can be reassigned?
- What training is needed to accomplish our objectives?
- Are we prepared to devote the time necessary to reach our goals?

The following chart serves as a draft for a literacy initiative. Identify the key steps in the process, the action steps for your school, as well as people to involve and resources needed.

Key Action Steps for a Literacy Initiative

Action Steps	Person(s) Responsible	Dates	Resources
1.			
2.			
3.			
4.			
5.			
6.			
7.			
8.			
9.			
10.			

Implementing such an initiative is no small undertaking, and there are countless opportunities to take a wrong step or to overlook some crucial element of the foundation. So when poorly performing schools make this transition to becoming highly successful schools, it's worth examining what they achieved and how they brought it about. Some of the International Center's research has led to the following model for implementing a literacy initiative.

Four Stages in Literacy Initiative

Stage 1. Assess Needs

A. Establish a Shared Vision

- The administration uses faculty meetings to discuss the school's strengths and weaknesses, the vision of what is possible for students, and the school culture. The DSEI rubrics in the Organizational Leadership chart earlier in the chapter will be an invaluable resource for these meetings.

- Common observations and concerns are collected and communicated back to the faculty for revision and further discussion at department meetings.

- Key faculty and staff are asked to join a leadership or restructuring committee for regular meetings.

- The faculty reviews the mission as related to the program, activities, and student outcomes. Two questions structure their inquiry: What are our expectations for student performance and levels of achievement? Will these recommendations achieve these expectations?

B. Assess the School Culture

- A walkthrough and discussions by an administrative team determine the degree to which faculty accept the school's needs and the recommended changes.

- The restructuring committee gathers information from faculty about literacy issues in the instructional program and the possible need for more active engagement on this issue.

C. Assess Student Performance Data

- The faculty reviews data to determine answers to the following questions:
  - What are we doing well?
  - What is not working?
  - What needs to be addressed?

D. Incorporate School History

- The restructuring committee reviews past efforts to improve the school, what worked, what didn't, and what professional development and support was needed during the change process. The committee compiles comments from teachers for each meeting.

- The common factors typically identified by the faculty are low literacy skills, low student expectations, and the vision and culture within the school. Improved vision and culture within the school may be addressed using the DSEI rubrics.

E. Identify Challenges and Supporting Conditions

- The administration asks teachers:
  - What can we do to improve our students' success?
  - Where are we today with student success levels?
  - What is our vision for the future success of our students?
  - What needs to be addressed to get us to our goal?

- The restructuring committee meets to identify people, funding, and programs that can support the change initiative. The principal commits to reassigning available resources to support the initiative.

Stage 2. Plan for Change and Improvement

A. Share Leadership and Decision Making

- The restructuring committee meets regularly, and after all meetings have been held, a summary report of the discussion points, decisions, and plans is shared with the entire faculty. This report establishes a transparent leadership model to ensure that all individuals are "on the same page" and working toward the same goals. Opportunities for feedback are encouraged.

B. Build Trust

- The principal invites opinions and suggestions on school operational issues, student concerns, and community needs. The principal attends assemblies and school athletic events and visits classrooms and lunch cafeterias to interact with students, sharing ideas about changes and soliciting feedback.

- The administration demonstrates a commitment to the focus on literacy training by supporting it with school policies, structures, and resources.

C. Involve Stakeholders

- Communication with the faculty occurs after each meeting of the restructuring committee. At the end of the faculty meetings, teachers complete a set of reaction statements specific to the issues and decisions being discussed. The results of their responses are summarized and shared.

Stage 3. Implement Action Steps

A. Focus on Literacy Strategies

- The restructuring committee defines literacy in each of the four areas — reading, writing, speaking, and reasoning — and produces literacy charts with skill areas for all disciplines.

- The restructuring committee identifies areas of weakness in the existing literacy program, and strategies for resolving these issues are prepared. Strategies may include such elements as creating training scripts to introduce faculty to improved methods.

- Instructional resource specialists model revised classroom strategies and lessons, observe classroom management systems, and gather best practices in the building. Teachers who are most familiar with the best practices demonstrate them at faculty meetings.

- Applying best practices, teachers assess texts, model thinking aloud while reading, define the purposes for reading, and use strategies to assist in the retention of information.

- The principal distributes an implementation calendar that identifies specific dates for each department to incorporate the strategies of open response or active reading into their lesson plans and instruction. With this approach, students use the same strategies during the semester in a variety of subject areas.

- Department heads and administrators visit classrooms to observe strategies that were scheduled during the year. Teachers use rubric-graded open-response essays; department heads and administrators review the essays. Written comments are returned to each teacher based on these reviews.

B. Design Professional Development

- The restructuring committee develops scripts for workshops on open-response and active reading strategies. The workshops are used with inter-disciplinary faculty groups and content area teams — a train-the-trainers model is employed.

- Open-response training provides a set of writing steps, a scoring rubric, and model responses.

- Active reading strategies incorporate skills such as summarizing, Think-Pair-Share, and teaching the text backwards. The same process is followed for the speaking and reasoning aspects of literacy.

- Teachers list their annual professional goals for review by the administration and as part of an evaluation system. These plans reflect both personally selected areas of interest as well as schoolwide areas of literacy and improved student performance.

- Bi-monthly faculty and department meetings become vehicles for professional development.

- The administration adopts an implementation calendar, targets resources for the initiative, identifies ways that supervision activities will focus on literacy, and submits the initiative for review and comment as a written document.

- To monitor implementation, the administration collects lesson plans, uses formal and informal observations, and collects and reviews student work.

- Department offices serve as "bullpens" for professional discussions and for sharing reviews of material and instructional approaches.

- Training follows a sequence of general introduction (first meeting), application to subject area (second meeting), and then classroom "try outs," with time to react and refine strategies.

- Departments present examples to the entire faculty of target strategies that work well in their subject area. Department meetings incorporate discussions of Quadrant D, student work, and instructional techniques.

- The administration shares professional articles and publications, and encourages attendance at conferences and workshops.

- The overall focus is to share new ideas, best practices, and successes that will build a culture of collaboration that is tied to literacy.

C. Use the Leadership Team

- The members of the restructuring committee are selected by means of a formal applications process. The administration ensures representation from all departments and prioritizes new thinking, a willingness to assume leadership roles, and an ability to communicate a vision of what an effective literacy program looks like.

D. Organize Instructional Support

- During faculty meetings, teachers are introduced to the Rigor/Relevance Framework and other studies that suggest methods to improve the rigor of their lessons.

- The teacher evaluation system includes specific comments and suggestions for improvements based on administrative observations.

- Department chairs emphasize the literacy initiative skills during department meetings through critiques of student work, instructional designs, and model lessons.

E. Meet the Needs of All Students

- The literacy initiative addresses all students, including low performing, special education, and ELL students.

- "Safety net" programs — such as mentoring by teachers and senior students, after-school/summer tutoring, a Freshman Academy, and computer assisted instruction — support students who are struggling academically.

- The counseling staff organizes four-year career education plans for all students, provides an informational session each semester on study skills and time management, and maintains data on graduation and college application requirements.

- Freshmen academy students write education and career plans and attend counseling sessions on study skills and time management.

- Bilingual counselors and teachers place ELL students in immersion, transitional, and regular education programs. Bilingual teachers co-teach with content teachers as students participate in college preparation courses.

Stage 4. Sustaining Improved Performance

A. Assess Progress Toward Program Goals

- Departments engage in discussions about rigorous lessons, review student work samples, and apply best practices to their disciplines.

- Assessment results, graduation rates, college admissions, and college scholarship awards are used to judge progress toward goals.

B. Modify Goals, Action Plans, and Expectations

- The restructuring committee works with the administration to develop new action plans to ensure continuous improvement in literacy and in the school's operation.

Successful Literacy Plans

The four-stage literacy initiative provides a model strategy for implementing a literacy program, but the success of any initiative depends heavily upon each school's unique history in teaching literacy. Other considerations include the system's resources and its current literacy performance level. Every school is unique and organization leaders should begin with an honest appraisal of their system. These questions ought to be considered as a starting point.

Constructing a Literacy Initiative

Questions to Consider
• What data exist to support our direction?
• Who should be involved and consulted?
• What time frame would be appropriate for a literacy initiative?
• What policies, procedures, and school structures will need to be discussed?
• What new or existing resources will be needed for a literacy plan?
• How should staff training be designed and implemented?
• Is the school at a stage of development so that a full multi-year program can be designed or should the process ensue one step at a time (allowing "happenstance" to guide the implementation process)?

For more information about successful literacy initiatives, see the International Center's 2012 publication *Transforming Schools through Comprehensive Literacy Initiatives.*

Leading the Way to Student Achievement in Embedded Literacy

The Rigor/Relevance Framework

An essential parallel step in developing a literacy program is the need to build more rigor and relevance into the overall instructional program. Students need preparation for taking their skills and knowledge into college, the workplace, and beyond. As we have seen, the literacy demands of many workplaces exceed the reading levels attained by most high school and of many college graduates. Young people are, moreover, unprepared for the complexity of the embedded materials they must use and develop. As new literacy instruction is developed, our schools must make the instruction more relevant to real-world situations.

So how will the need for rigor and relevance be communicated in the context of growing job-market demands for students? Faculty members may have a general understanding and appreciation of the need for increasing the rigor of instruction as a result of past efforts to add AP and college-level courses. However, the Rigor/Relevance Framework provides a common vocabulary for describing any lesson design.

The Rigor/Relevance Framework is a tool developed by the International Center to examine curriculum, instruction, and assessment. The framework is based on the two dimensions of higher standards and student achievement.

First, the Knowledge Taxonomy represents a continuum based on the six levels of Bloom's Taxonomy, which describes the increasingly complex ways in which we think. The low end involves acquiring knowledge and being able to recall or locate that knowledge. The high end labels the more complex ways in which individuals use knowledge, such as taking several pieces of knowledge and combining them in both logical and creative ways.

The second continuum, known as the Application Model, is one of action. Its five levels describe putting knowledge to use. While the low end represents knowledge acquired for its own sake, the high end signifies the use of that knowledge to solve complex real-world problems and to create unique projects, designs, and other works for use in real-world situations.

The Rigor/Relevance Framework contains four quadrants. Each quadrant is labeled with a term that characterizes the learning or student performance achieved at that level.

As you review the framework, consider the following questions concerning the extent to which faculty understand and accept these concepts.

Rigor/Relevance Framework

Questions to Consider
• Do the faculty understand the need for more rigor/relevance in the instructional program?
• What evidence of the need exists in our school (e.g., test results, parent expectations)?
• Is training needed to develop a common understanding of, and language for, the Rigor/Relevance Framework?
• Do selected teachers possess the knowledge to present the framework to other teachers?
• Are successful examples of Quadrant D lessons being used in the building?
• How can an increased emphasis on content-area literacy help to increase both the rigor and relevance of instruction and assessment?

Think about your responses to these questions as you review the Rigor/Relevance Framework.

Rigor/Relevance Framework®

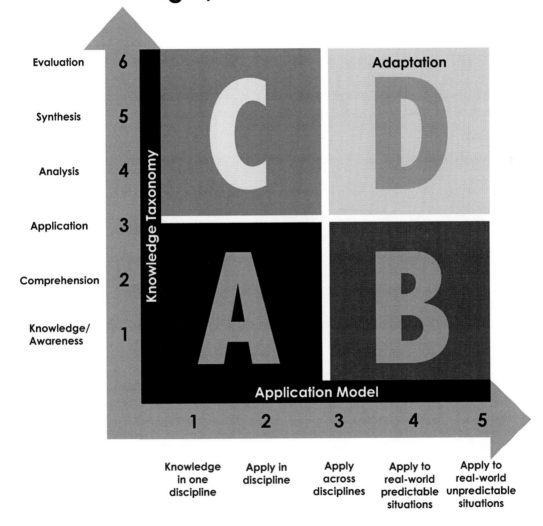

The Rigor/Relevance Framework is easy to understand. With its simple, straightforward structure, it can serve as a bridge between the school and the community. It offers a common language with which to express the notion of a more rigorous and relevant curriculum.

The Rigor/Relevance Framework is also versatile; it can be used to develop instruction and assessment. Teachers can use it to measure their progress in adding rigor and relevance to instruction. Finally, the Framework can help teachers select appropriate instructional strategies to meet the needs and higher achievement goals of their students.

Learning Criteria

The Learning Criteria tool was developed in partnership among the International Center for Leadership in Education, the Successful Practices Network, and the Council of Chief State School Officers (CCSSO) as part of a five-year initiative to identify and analyze both the nation's most successful high school practices and policies for achieving a rigorous and relevant curriculum for all students.

The Learning Criteria tool displays data in four dimensions to help schools set goals for improvement and to establish the need for change. Data, of course, are essential to any school's effort to measure and track its own progress. In short, any school instituting a literacy initiative must also be able to display data, set goals, and compare its own progress to that of other "benchmark schools."

Many schools are working diligently to improve. At the heart of these efforts lies a strong commitment to two important goals: meeting the needs of learners and raising scores on standardized tests in all academic areas. Ray McNulty, Senior Fellow of the International Center for Leadership in Education, explains how the very design of the Learning Criteria makes it a valuable tool for educators as they develop and implement plans for school improvement. McNulty notes (2009):

> School improvement initiatives are carefully constructed, appropriately viewed through the lens of a school's mission, driven by data, and accountable to multiple stakeholders. Other initiatives, however, are not so meticulously conceived. Rather than allowing data to drive goal setting and decision making, some schools are guided by little more than good intentions, faulty assumptions, hunches, and impressions. Often, such poorly supported plans inadvertently lose sight of learners' needs, even as they struggle to ensure compliance with state regulations.

In the hands of a thoughtful and broad-based school leadership team, the Learning Criteria helps a school clarify its mission, prioritize problems and interventions, and critically review school performance. Further, these analyses provide critical rationales for establishing goals and developing action plans.

The Learning Criteria is designed to provide a robust, comprehensive, and detailed portrait of school performance that clearly maps out a route for school improvement efforts.

Increasing expectations and testing demands have placed a heavy burden on schools. The Learning Criteria accounts for both expectations and demands and simultaneously breaks new ground in the territory of school improvement: the Learning Criteria redefines school success in terms that are unique to each school, in terms that meet standardized test measures of school success, and in terms that reveal the school environment in all of its complexity and depth. Learning Criteria empowers schools and school communities to craft meaningful, cogent, and comprehensive school improvement plans, to set powerful school change agendas, and to envision critical interventions that fortify the efforts of learners, teachers, and school administrators to achieve academic excellence.

Underlying The Learning Criteria are years of research on educational success stories. Of course, the specific indicators used will vary among schools based upon state requirements as well as the philosophy, focus, and curriculum of individual schools. To identify success and maximize its usefulness, data collected through the Learning Criteria should be examined from the following perspectives:

- **School Performance Data:** Expressed in objective terms
- **Sustained Data:** Trend data to show improvement or maintenance at high levels for 3–5 years
- **Disaggregated Data:** Comparisons of achievement among all subgroups
- **Benchmarked Data:** Compared to similar schools, schools in the state, schools in the nation, or to accepted norms from national/state surveys and/or reports

When schools are establishing their vision, the Learning Criteria can help guide this dialogue through measuring what matters. Often, emphasis on test performance alone is used to assess instructional effectiveness. Leadership teams that have established a vision including all dimensions of the Learning Criteria are providing a comprehensive view of student growth and achievement. The following data indicators are suggested for each dimension of the Learning Criteria. Leadership teams are welcome to establish their own set of data indicators per dimension — measuring what matters most to the culture if the main purpose is using the Learning Criteria as a lens through which to view achievement. Developing this mindset within a school involves a culture shift that requires organizational support and guidance.

Foundation Learning

Core Academic Learning in English Language Arts (Reading/Writing), Mathematics, and Science (Results of Required State Testing Plus a Minimum of Two Additional Data Indicators)				
Data Indicator	School Performance	Sustained	Disaggregated	Benchmarked

Sample Indicators

- Percentage of students meeting proficiency level on state tests (required)
- Percentage of students reading on grade level (i.e., Lexile level)
- Average scores on ACT/SAT/PSAT tests
- Achievement levels on standardized tests other than state exams
- Percentage of students requiring English/math remediation in college
- Follow-up surveys of academic achievements of graduates
- Percent of students graduating high school in four years
- Percent of students earning college degree within four years after high school
- Military ASVAB scores

Stretch Learning

Demonstration of Rigorous and Relevant Learning Beyond Minimum Requirements (Examples: Achievement/Participation in Higher Level Courses, Specialized Courses—Minimum of 3)				
Data Indicator	School Performance	Sustained	Disaggregated	Benchmarked

Sample Indicators

- Percentage of students improving beyond one year's reading level (Lexile growth)
- Number of credits required to graduate
- Average number of credits earned at graduation
- Interdisciplinary work and projects (e.g., senior exhibition)
- Participation/test scores in International Baccalaureate courses
- Average number of college credits earned by graduation (dual enrollment)
- Enrollment in advanced math or science courses
- Enrollment in AP courses/scores on AP exams/percentage scoring greater than 2
- Percent of students completing career majors or career/technical education programs
- Four or more credits in a career area
- Four or more credits in arts
- Three or more years of foreign language
- Value of scholarships earned at graduation
- Achievement of specialized certificates (e.g., Microsoft, Cisco Academy)

Learner Engagement

Extent to Which Students (1) Are Motivated and Committed to Learning, (2) Have a Sense of Belonging and Accomplishment, and (3) Have Relationships with Adults, Peers, and Parents that Support Learning (Minimum of 5)				
Data Indicator	School Performance	Sustained	Disaggregated	Benchmarked

Sample Indicators

- Student satisfaction surveys
- Student risk behaviors (asset survey)
- Dropout rate
- Attendance rate
- Graduation rate
- Discipline referrals
- Participation rate in extracurricular activities
- Follow-up survey on enrollment in higher education
- Percent of students taking ACT/SAT
- Tardiness rate
- Surveys on degree to which teachers know their students
- Surveys on positive peer relationships
- Percent of students going to two-year colleges
- Percent of students going to four-year colleges

Personal Skill Development

(1) Measures of Personal, Social, Service, and Leadership Skills, and (2) Demonstrations of Positive Behaviors and Attitudes (Minimum of 2)				
Data Indicator	School Performance	Sustained	Disaggregated	Benchmarked

Sample Indicators

- Participation or hours in service learning
- Students holding leadership positions in clubs or sports
- Assessment of personal skills: time management, ability to plan and organize work, leadership/followership, etc.
- Respect for diversity
- Work as a member of a team
- Trustworthiness, perseverance, other character traits
- Conflict resolution
- Reduction in number of student incidences of conflict
- Follow-up survey of graduates on development of personal skills

The Learning Criteria provides valuable information for schools, as should be evident when schools respond to the following questions:

Learning Criteria

Questions to Consider
• What data are currently available in each of the four dimensions?
• Do we need to collect additional data in some dimensions?
• What levels of growth should we target in each area?
• Which schools should be "benchmark schools" for us as we develop a literacy initiative?
• What timeline will we accept for growth targets in each area?
• How should we share this information across the school community?

Common Core State Standards Literacy Rubric

The International Center for Leadership in Education believes that the most empowering investment educators can make in middle and high schools is to implement a comprehensive literacy program that makes sure students are receiving literacy instruction across every content area. This has been reinforced with the advent of CCSS literacy standards for grades 6–12.

In the nation's most successful schools, literacy is the highest priority. If other schools wish to replicate the success of these schools, all teachers in all disciplines need to teach reading and writing skills that are both rigorous and relevant to the real world.

One key lesson learned from successful schools is that improving student achievement begins by creating a culture of literacy that engages teachers, students, administrators, parents, and the community alike in developing a vision of learning based on rigor, relevance, and relationships. This culture is sustained by translating beliefs about literacy into broad-based yet focused, measurable goals and actions.

To implement a comprehensive adolescent literacy program fully, the following essential components must be in place:

- well-developed data structures based on multiple measures of student learning and focused on the learning of students and teachers
- strong teacher and administrator leadership that implements a vision of high expectations and continuous improvement while also building capacity to sustain a culture of literacy

- research-based best practices and professional development designed both to improve classroom instruction and to integrate reading and writing strategies across all content areas
- comprehensive support systems that include targeted intervention

Building on these essential components, the International Center developed the CCSS Readiness Rubrics. The Literacy Rubric that follows is meant not only to examine a school's current level of literacy in its instructional program but also to determine how a literacy initiative based on the school's perceived needs should be designed. For schools wishing to use all CCSS rubrics, see *Shifting Instruction to Meet Fewer, Clearer, and Higher Expectations: Common Core State Standards*, published by the International Center for Leadership in Education.

Literacy Checklist	Exceeding	Meeting	Developing	Beginning	Absent
1. Literacy is an important priority throughout the school.					
2. There are clear, measurable goals for levels of student reading.					
3. A standard measure of reading, such as Lexile, is used to describe aspects of reading achievement.					
4. Literacy development is addressed in all disciplines.					
5. Student literacy levels are measured continuously, and the data are compared to literacy achievement goals of the school.					
6. Teachers have convenient access to data about student reading levels.					
7. Professional development opportunities are available to support an interdisciplinary approach to literacy.					
8. Teachers select rigorous and relevant instructional materials to challenge students appropriately.					

Literacy Checklist	Exceeding	Meeting	Developing	Beginning	Absent
9. Teachers use effective instructional strategies pertaining to vocabulary to improve reading in their content areas.					
10. Teachers know the reading level requirements for postsecondary opportunities, including college, employment, and personal use.					
11. Instructional coaches are available to help teachers improve strategies related to reading.					
12. Teachers personalize instruction to accommodate different levels of reading in the classroom.					
13. The school media center/library is aligned with reading-level information and is an integral part of the literacy program.					
14. Students are expected to engage in complex texts across all disciplines.					
15. State assessments in all subjects have been analyzed based on student reading levels.					
16. Teachers break tradition by emphasizing informational texts and literary non-fiction.					
17. Teachers emphasize analytical writing, quarterly research, and the expectation that students will analyze texts, cite textual evidence, and be able to cite sources.					
18. Teachers provide opportunities for students to develop comprehension and collaboration through speaking and listening.					
19. Teachers require students to present to a variety of audiences utilizing digital media, as well as visual and quantitative data.					
20. Students are expected to be able to answer a range of text-dependent questions based only on the text presented.					

Leadership in successful schools does not reside in a single position but reflects the attributes, skills, and attitudes of many staff members. Not surprisingly, then, schools developing high levels of literacy employ teachers who take action rather than defending the status quo. In the case of literacy promotion, it is deliberate, sustained action that ensures success. Highly successful literacy programs recognize the need to monitor student progress on a regular basis using formative assessments in an organized, deliberate, and ongoing fashion. Furthermore, schools use these data immediately to adjust instructional practices and intervene to meet student needs.

There are multiple approaches to thinking about how the rubric might provide useful information to schools. Key questions and possible responses follow.

How Does the Literacy Rubric Apply to Us?

- Members of the leadership team review the items in each section to select those that are appropriate.
- Administrative and leadership teams discuss how it might be used, when best to complete the rubric, who should complete the form, and how the results could be incorporated into their planning.
- As the literacy activities of the school increase, the rubric could be re-administered to evaluate change and to refocus energy as appropriate on different need areas.

Who Should Complete the Rubric?

- An outside consultant could apply the rubric by observing classrooms and interviewing personnel.
- Members of the leadership team could be released to perform these same activities.
- An administrator might complete the rubric as part of the observation process.

How Will the Results Be Shared?

- The leadership team reviews the completed rubric to decide if they will present the complete results or a summary of more critical items.
- At a faculty meeting, the rubric results are presented by highlighting trend information from each of the four components.

How Will Areas of Strengths and Weaknesses Be Identified?

- In small groups, faculty members discuss individual components to identify strengths of the present program and weaknesses that will need to be addressed.

- The products of the small groups are given to the leadership team for tabulation and are presented back to the faculty with the strengths displayed and a selected number of needs identified.

- The faculty as a whole will select the areas of need that the school community will address through a literacy initiative.

Support Structures for Embedded Literacy

Support structures must be aligned to implement any literacy initiative. Each step requires time and equal emphasis.

Step 1: Access to the Content for All Students

Know Lexile and Quantile Levels

It is important to know the Lexile levels of each adopted textbook and other prose materials that students use at your school. Then, it is important to know the Lexile level at which each student is working and to get this information into the hands of teachers. If the textbook presents material at a Lexile level that is too high for many of your at-risk students, how will teachers still provide students with access to the content?

The CCSS and Next Generation Assessments will require students to read far more informational material and literary nonfiction than before. Consider your school and classroom materials. Do students have access to that type of writing? Are teachers aware of the important differences between reading fiction with good comprehension and reading nonfiction with good comprehension? Can they communicate these differences to their students?

Merely having a good reading class or lab is not enough for students who are falling behind in reading and writing. While you are helping students catch up on needed literacy skills, how will they function in all of their other classes? If students do not have supplementary materials appropriate to their learning levels, schools will create a second form of discrimination, in effect, by not allowing them access to the content.

Most secondary schools in the United States have reference and resource databases that are Lexiled. These can be found at the following websites:

- EBSCO Information Services: http://www2.ebsco.com/en-us/Pages/index.aspx
- netTrekker: http://www.nettrekker.com/us
- Thomson Gale: http://www.gale.cengage.com/
- SIRS Researcher from ProQuest: www.proquest.com

Teachers who are in the habit of finding content material at various levels for each unit and creating digital libraries of those sources will help students at any literacy level access the content. For instance, students can be given the same questions and asked to read these Lexiled materials aloud in the class. Everyone can contribute, be successful, and acquire content knowledge and skills. Students need not know that the materials are designed for different levels unless that is a helpful part of each student's literacy goal or plan. Additional school literacy programs or courses will help them close the achievement gap.

The Quantile Framework® for Mathematics will help teachers locate students' skills and processing levels in math along a continuum of QTaxons, or skills and processes of math. If educators know the prerequisite and subsequent skills for a particular math concept, they can teach the right students the right concepts. If a teacher knows students are missing prerequisites, he or she can build background knowledge into a hands-on, interactive math class. Then, all students can access the current concept.

Use Embedded Literacy Materials to Supplement Traditional Texts

A major criterion for leadership in literacy is to ensure that students have access to a variety of resources beyond the standard textbook. Instead of using just one text, teachers will need access to software and electronic sources, as well as a variety of print materials. Fortunately, many types of embedded literacy materials are free on the Internet and in the community. It is important that teachers choose a variety of supplemental materials and electronic sources that match what they are teaching. The use of authentic documents in English and history, for instance, is well researched. The use of authentic lifestyle, workplace, and community documents and sources is also well researched outside the U.S. (Dickinson and DiGisi, 1998)

For struggling students, using authentic and relevant documents increases motivation and attention to the task. For all students, using relevant materials helps them dig deeper for the kind of creativity, problem solving, and action orientation they will need to succeed in their postsecondary education. Documents and electronic sources should form an essential part of supplemental or primary teaching materials and resources.

Step 2: Expand and Update Educator Toolkits

Students today are not the same as the ones who walked in the school doors twenty or even ten years ago. They are physiologically different from their predecessors. The exposure to television, electronic communication, and entertainment forms has increased the size and complexity of the visual portions of their brains. As a result, we need to use different practices and tools for teaching and learning to address the needs of this generation. (Restak, 2003; Zull, 2002)

Update Your Tools

At home, if you find that your pipe wrench has become rusty, you go to the hardware store for a new one. You find that the newest wrenches automatically adjust to the diameter of the pipe. Thinking this new idea is great, because you remember adjusting your old wrench in all types of tight places, you purchase this latest innovation in tool design. We need to apply the same principle to education. We should constantly be asking: What are the latest innovative tools for teaching and learning strategies that better meet the needs of today's students? Which tools automatically adjust for different types of learners? Which tools, in short, are the best power tools for a 21st-century education?

Our students interact with advances in multimedia every day. They will also utilize embedded literacy nearly every day of their lives. For these reasons, the sections in this kit will provide a much needed update to the teacher's pedagogical toolkit, and thus will both prepare students for global competition and increase their access to the lifestyle of the 21st century.

Step 3: Shift the Dialogue

Professional development has changed over the last decade. The old "sit and get" workshop delivered by an expert works well for motivational purposes, but unless the school leader allows time for dialogue and interaction around the topic or new skills, no transfer to real student understanding will occur. It is great for us to be inspired by leaders in education; it is another thing to cause change in our classrooms. Leaders need to use professional learning communities and other vehicles to provide teachers with the opportunities to share best practices, discuss problems with practices, review student work as an efficient and up-to-date data source, review rigorous and relevant learning plans, and seek to maintain and improve student-staff relationships.

Consider Workplace Needs

If we are to establish a more comprehensive literacy program at any secondary or post-secondary school, embedded literacy needs to be part of our awareness, discussion, and resource allocation to effect the change we need. An important rationale for this addition to our embedded staff development can be found in the needs described by our students' future employers. In workplaces across the country, changes have occurred in the human resource training programs. In mandatory and optional workplace offerings for retraining, technological skillfulness, in addition to career-based embedded literacy, is a major component. (Roth and Rapiller, 1998)

Given these realities, a focus on schoolwide or workplace literacy is incomplete without embedded literacy strategies. Content-area literacy and traditional intervention programs provide only part of the solution in preparing students for the world beyond school. Shifting the literacy dialogue to include a rationale, examples, and effective strategies will help educators achieve a more comprehensive literacy approach that is oriented to the future of our students.

Accountability for Embedded Literacy

Next Generation Assessment

Schools, teachers, and literacy initiatives cannot be considered successful unless students are successful, and that is precisely the point of the great changes that are rocking education at the present time. The CCSS are driving these changes and it is a time of great optimism and excitement in the educational community. It's about time that we set up national standards and began teaching young people skills they can use for a lifetime.

But how do we measure the success being achieved in the classroom? In the past, student achievement was typically measured by state or national tests built around multiple-choice or short or extended response answers. The exams tested students on what they knew but seldom measured how well they could *apply* what they knew to academic situations or, more rarely still, to real-world situations.

One of the much-needed changes being brought about by the CCSS is the development of the Next Generation Assessments. These assessments include process or product performance-based tasks that require students to demonstrate mastery of skills that are aligned to CCSS. Each task describes the context for student work and spells out expectations for student achievement that will be produced during a given time frame. All tasks require students to apply what they know to real-world situations.

The NGA are constructed for high levels of rigor and relevance, and typically require students to analyze, synthesize, or evaluate information while applying the information to predictable and unpredictable real-world situations. The tasks are based on situations in content areas ranging through the entire curriculum — language arts, math, science, art, career technology, social studies, music, and health.

It is important that teachers of all subjects at all levels understand their own responsibility for students' literacy. Because formal assessment will now involve so much reading, writing, listening, speaking, and language — outside of their typical place within ELA assessment — teachers in the content areas must be accountable for their students' literacy as well as for their grasp of the content.

Another, no less vital method of assessment involves focusing on what occurs each day and in each unit of study. Teachers in ELA and in the content areas should implement assessments that are rigorous and relevant enough so that students can themselves show you what they can *do* with what they have learned. If not, how can necessary adjustments to instruction be made?

School and Staff Accountability

On their own, the CCSS and NGA cannot prepare young people for their futures in college and the workplace. New curricula, new textbooks, and professional development likewise offer limited reach in raising achievement levels. These are only tools to be used by a school's most important resources: teachers in the classroom and the school administrators whose responsibility it is to guide students to succeed. More and more, voters and parents are demanding increased accountability from these people, and states are responding to these demands.

Some states are instituting methods for rating school and district performance. Systemized data-gathering, for example, is being used to measure achievement, which is often summarized in general performance classifications, such as A–F grades. The measurements are generally drawn from a range of indicators of student success, such as graduation rates, AP courses, achievement gaps, attendance, and performance on college entrance exams.

Besides simply reporting performance and giving grades, states are also developing methods for translating data into usable information that will enable stakeholders to understand which schools and districts are falling behind, which are making strides forward, and how schools can be helped and improved.

A growing number of states are making student performance part of teacher evaluations, which can then be used in making employment decisions. These student performance measurements are becoming increasingly powerful instruments for these decisions as CCSS and improved assessments like NGA provide a more accurate basis for comparing student performance from district to district and state to state. Salary and tenure, as well, appear to be headed toward performance-based criteria.

These changes provide state and local governments with methods for measuring teacher and administrative performance and for holding them accountable for student achievement. But what has not yet been made clear is how such changes will incentivize the system. Star teachers or schools with outstanding student achievement are not automatically rewarded. Indeed, during these times of budget shortfalls, the opposite is more nearly the case as any available financial incentives are steadily whittled away.

Penalties for poor and declining performance have also been slow to materialize. Some states and schools are attempting to address these issues. Some of the methods used to enhance school achievement include replacing ineffective teachers, converting failing schools to charter schools, implementing 3rd-grade reading requirements, reducing automatic grade advancement, and prohibiting participation in sports without legitimate academic performance. But it is difficult to change the inertia of a system, of course, and it takes strong organizational leadership to bring these changes about.

Communicating the Vision to Parents, Students, and Other Stakeholders

Implementing a literacy initiative can represent a significant shift in priorities, curriculum, assessment, instruction, and other aspects of the school routine. It cannot succeed unless all stakeholders — parents, students, and others — are brought on board. Getting the message across clearly to these various groups is one of the most important tasks the administration has, and it should be done in the earliest stages of implementing of the initiative.

Your decisions and the strategy you have planned will largely be based on student data sources (test data, graduation rates, or college entrance results) that can be used to explain the need for the planned changes. Additionally, providing a clear outline of DSEI can promote more rigorous and relevant instruction that will lay a second foundation for supporting change. Presenting an explanation of CCSS, which incorporates content-area literacy with ELA standards, and NGA, which provides a process for measuring and enhancing these rigorous standards, will further promote understanding and support.

After the data have been assembled and your methods and goals are defined into a coherent picture, the stage is set for a change process within the school. Your communication with outside stakeholders can proceed in two main stages: listening to stakeholders and then, based on the data, sharing the action plan.

Identifying the Concerns of "Outside" Stakeholders

Once school leaders have identified a need related to reading and an approach to address the need, they should involve other stakeholders such as parents, community representatives, local business leaders, district administrators, and students. Each of these groups has its own concerns, so it is necessary to address the needs of each group separately as well as collectively.

Generally, involving these groups requires listening to them and providing clear, coherent answers to their concerns. Commonly, these two overarching questions are raised:

- Why are schools turning toward a system of embedded literacy?
- How will this initiative benefit students and the community?

Beyond addressing these common concerns, leaders must recognize the unique perspective of each stakeholder group.

Parents and Caregivers

In general, what are the concerns and expectations of parents? Many are aware that their students are not reading as much as they would like, are having difficulty with homework, are not motivated by school in general, and may not be attaining the skills they need to succeed in college, vocational training, or business. At the middle and high school levels, parent involvement is frequently minimal, but administrators and teachers should not assume that parents lack interest. When given the opportunity, most parents will support activities that are designed to help students succeed.

An initiative aimed at advancing proficiency in embedded literacy offers the prospect of addressing several issues that concern parents about the future of their children. With the proper introduction, parents will support the training process as long as they see a direct positive impact on student learning within the classroom. In addition, parents will happily play a role in supporting student assignments at home if it helps "keep the peace."

Parents/caregivers may have some of the following key questions that should be addressed:

- Will my son/daughter be prepared for future learning and employment?
- Will the school provide an exciting and motivating place for my student to learn?
- How will an emphasis on embedded literacy help my child achieve greater learning and higher performance on high-stakes tests?

Colleges and Postgraduate Trainers

Colleges and other training institutions receive only transcripts listing grades and course titles. Admissions office staff hope, of course, that high grades signify the ability to do advanced work at their institution, but they are aware that some students lack skills, motivation, and interest in learning, despite having superior grades. Consequently, the reputation of the high school and a written description of curriculum can sometimes indicate to the admission staff whether a graduate is well prepared for learning after high school.

College staff may have some of the following questions that need to be addressed:

- Will graduates of this high school have acquired the literacy skills necessary to be successful in advanced learning?
- Have the applicants been involved in a curriculum that is rigorous and relevant to real-life tasks?
- Have the graduates developed the ability to learn independently and the desire to master course material appropriate for their career objectives?

Employers and Business Leaders

The Lexile Framework offers direct assistance to employers who are confronted with hiring decisions. Lexile measures can be reported, for instance, as part of the school record to assure employers that the student has demonstrated an ability to read and understand materials comparable to those used on the job. The Lexile Framework offers two benefits here from the employer's perspective. First, the employer can gauge the amount of training that will be necessary before the new hire can do the job. Second, the employer can use an independent readability scale to compare the reading skills of applicants.

In the late 1980s, the U.S. Department of Labor created the Labor Secretary's Commission on Achieving Necessary Skills (SCANS) to address the concerns of the business community. Business and industry leaders felt that a number of high school graduates did not possess the prerequisite skills to begin a productive work life or to succeed in the costly training programs provided by employers. Just like today, business leaders did not want to assume the expense and time necessary to provide new hires with basic skills in reading, writing, math, and problem solving.

Business leaders have long sought to have schools address skills that are workplace related. As school administrators now propose the use of this program for embedded literacy, some questions that might be in the minds of members of the business community may include:

- Will the graduates whom I hire require additional training in reading, writing, and speaking before I can train them in specific job skills?
- Will these students possess the attitude and enthusiasm that are needed to learn the new skills associated with a position in my organization?
- Do the applicants have experience in cooperative and collaborative learning activities that will allow them to work effectively with fellow employees and to follow directions?

Taxpayers and the Public-at-large

The taxpaying public appreciates information about how school personnel design educational programs that are cost efficient and effective. As community members, they take pride in the accomplishment of students and their schools. When they believe that their tax dollars are being well spent, they have "bragging rights" when discussing their school system. Many schools also make a special effort to involve the community's most senior citizens since, as a group, seniors exert considerable voting power and can use their clout to restrict spending unless they see, hear, and participate in a vibrant school environment. Administrators are wise to inform the general public about school activities throughout the year and not wait for budget time to communicate the good news about achievements and performance.

Questions in the minds of taxpayers might include:

- Why is it necessary to set aside staff development funds to train teachers to teach reading?
- How do I know that my tax dollars are being well spent?
- Is there a way that my skills can be used in the schools that would benefit students and me at the same time?
- Will building a more rigorous and relevant learning environment based on embedded literacy make my community an even better place to live?

Students

Since student performance and frustration with reading are the reasons why such a program is necessary, students should have information about the goals of the program and understand how it will help them be more successful in school. Students can be directly included in the planning activities, for example, by being asked to evaluate their textbooks and their own use of strategies and to set personal goals for improved performance.

Students might have the following questions about these activities:

- How will my course work be different? Will there be more or less work for me?
- Will I experience more success in my learning and grades?
- How will my efforts help me with college, employment, and other future learning?
- Will my teachers offer me more help if I have difficulty understanding how to use the reading strategies in my courses?
- Will this program single me out as a less-than-competent reader?

Crafting the Common Message

General Communication Instruments

Many schools already communicate regularly with parents and the community through a variety of instruments, such as newsletters, websites, and "principal's letters." Some schools employ annual reports, the media, and direct mail to inform constituencies. Secondary teachers gather additional support from parents by providing information about course content during open houses, mini-class schedules designed to introduce course outlines, class newsletters, homework expectations, and grading policies. Taken collectively over time, these opportunities will clarify what is happening within their classrooms. Messages from teachers reflect schoolwide attitudes about learning, aspirations, as well as modeling and shared responsibility.

In addition, there are opportunities to communicate with the community at large through sporting events, concerts, theater, community events, polling sites, and business meetings that invite the public into the schools. Each activity provides a chance to showcase the school's students, projects, and achievements and to instill a positive image of the school in the minds of those who attend. Schools can use all of their current communication activities to introduce, explain, update, and "sell" the embedded literacy initiative, and thereby secure ongoing support and enthusiasm. The following model message to stakeholders, for instance, would help them understand why the change is needed and what to expect as it proceeds.

Sample Message to Stakeholders

Our Literacy Challenge

- Currently, the reading and writing achievement of many students is lower than is desirable or acceptable. Yet outside of special education, little direct instruction in reading and writing skills and strategies is provided beyond the elementary grades.

- To be college and career ready, our students need to read and write at a higher level than they currently do. High-level reading and writing in history/social studies, science, and technical subjects are critical to success in college and career and will be tested on Next Generation Assessments.

- Matching readers to suitable print material in a systematic way is one key to reading success. Yet, until now, the district has not possessed a uniform, research-based readability framework to guide our selection of reading materials and reading-related instructional activities for students and teachers—especially beyond the elementary grades.

Opportunity to Improve Our Students' Literacy Skills
through an Embedded Literacy Initiative

- Students in all grades need direct instruction in reading and writing and other learning opportunities that will help them develop the skills and strategies they need for their courses, for assessments, and for college preparatory work, not to mention for their eventual employability and success as adults. To meet this challenge, the embedded literacy initiative provides instruction in reading and writing skills and strategies, even for middle and high school students.

- Because the new Common Core State Standards require students to be literate across all areas of the curriculum, we will need to establish literacy guidelines for content-area learning as well as for English language arts.

- The district can enhance student reading competencies by means of a readability framework system that teachers can use to match readers with reading at appropriate levels. As a result, we can ensure competence, confidence, and success. With this goal in mind, we will employ The Lexile Framework, a proven and easy-to-use readability scale that can be used to match readers with reading materials.

The reading competencies of students are enhanced when schools go beyond mere communication so as to invite the *participation* of parents and community members, thereby extending the boundaries of learning beyond the school. The invitation to participate can also be extended to tutors, role models, guest speakers, and committee members. Knuth and Jones (1991) outline several activities for parents, community organizations, and other groups that can enrich a school's initiatives:

1. Visit schools to participate in scheduled events and focus groups.
2. Sponsor field trips and reading groups.
3. Donate reading materials and tutoring time.
4. Provide opportunities for apprenticeships, visits to offices and businesses, mentoring programs, and student involvement in discussions.
5. Promote discussions within the community about educational issues through the local media, public forums, and use of community groups to gather information important for decision making.

When parents and community leaders participate in the reading initiative, both within and beyond the school, it becomes easier for students to recognize the importance of reading to their future success. The relevance of content learning is continually highlighted, and strategic reading engages students in an active pursuit of both gathering and processing information. By extending learning beyond the walls of the school, teachers open three avenues for reading to gather information and perform tasks: reading for understanding, talking about texts, and reading apprenticeships. Each type of activity can be extended into the home, inviting parents to reinforce learning (Shellard, 2001):

- **Reading for Understanding.** Developing *metacognition* skills (thinking about reading) and modeling a type of reading apprenticeship in which students talk about their reading/learning strategies.

- **Talking about Texts.** Improving the processing of text through discussions, questioning, reciprocal teaching, and study techniques.

- **Reading Apprenticeships.** Demonstrating the use of text aids, "talk alouds," and reflective journal writing, along with other techniques to encourage the thoughtful processing of content material.

Each of the three types of reading can also offer an opportunity for enlisting the in-school aid of volunteers to tutor or help high school students discuss their reading. Senior citizens, retired individuals, businesses and charitable organizations, and others, too, can be invited into the school for targeted work with students who have been selected based on needs or interests. The fringe benefit of such a program is that all volunteers will potentially serve as advocates for students and the schools as a result of their participation.

In summary, administrators at the building and district levels have a responsibility to communicate with the stakeholders, both within the schools and the community, in order to foster the success of the reading initiative. Parents, colleges, employers, media, teachers, and students, too, have questions and concerns that need to be addressed. Anticipating the questions and concerns of each group and then planning appropriate communication are all crucial to successful school improvement activities.

Summary

Evidence for Change

As the developers of the Common Core State Standards understood, evidence for the need to change our educational system is strong. Television programs, newspaper articles, and political debates abound on the subject. Consider reading *Time* magazine's 2006 cover stories "Is America Flunking Science?" and "How to Build a Student for the 21st Century." These articles point to the dire circumstances in which our educational system finds itself with respect to the rest of the world. *Training and Development* magazine frequently publishes stories about the changing nature of the job market. The National Center on Adult Literacy at the University of Pennsylvania cites key shifts in how learning systems are designed. Our colleges and universities report that our students lack complex, life-oriented literacy skills. *Scientific American* magazine, the Dana Foundation, and numerous other sources report monthly on the latest research in the changing physiology of our students. Still, our schools are slow to change.

Other nations have not been slow to see the need for change, nor have they been slow to act. Canada, for instance, has developed one of the major workplace literacy and numeracy initiatives in the world, along with Australia and Switzerland. In Singapore, likewise, the Workforce Development Agency actively seeks to provide students with skills that will continue to be vital in the 21st century: workplace literacy and numeracy, information and communications technology, problem solving, initiative and enterprise communication and relationship management, lifelong learning, global mindsets, self-management, workplace-related life skills, and health and workplace safety. Unfortunately, U.S. curriculum guides and courses for our middle schools and high schools do not look like those found in Singapore, not to mention China or India, where 21st-century skills have been placed at the top of the priority list. (Singapore Workforce Development Agency, 2006)

In the past, it has been easy for us to ignore the evidence or advances of others, but how can we ignore the future? The future is quite literally sitting in our classroom today, and it is time for change. Not to tend to the future of our students is to commit an act of unconscionable neglect and malpractice. Courageous leaders and educators all over the country and the world are demonstrating that it is, in fact, possible to focus on our students' future. However, examples of success in this country are isolated, and our goal must be to reach a critical mass of success, using up-to-date methods.

The challenge for all educators, taken up by CCSS, is to redefine literacy in schools and in the workplace. The future will require students to function in multiple jobs in a global economy filled with diverse workers and as of now unimagined work and lifestyles. This shift requires a foundation in literacy that is different from the literacy of the last century. The 21st century demands people who can read, write, speak, and listen in order to *do* and to *create*, not just to *understand*. We deserve schools with the courage to focus on today's definition of literacy and the future of our students.

It is within our grasp to implement a program that can turn the bad news about our educational system into good news by giving our students the tools they need for success in the years ahead. The CCSS provide the means for producing a rigorous and relevant instructional program that will embed literacy in the minds and the lives of our young people. By assessing our schools, establishing our goals and methods, and then communicating our initiatives to parents, students, and other stakeholders, we will be taking positive steps in the right direction.

Does every step and piece of advice offered in this chapter have to be carried out to the letter? Absolutely not, but overall planning and a proactive approach will always net better results than a "let's try it and see" reactive approach. A systemic plan, in which everyone knows and understands his or her role, and in which all stakeholders are fully informed of the process, will build success and sustain teams through the inevitable not-so-successful bumps in the road.

Questions to Consider

- How can you structure your system to promote and support embedded literacy?
- What benefits can you see in assessing the current level of embedded literacy in your school or your program?
- What particular issues might represent obstacles to beginning an embedded literacy initiative? How can those issues be resolved?

References

Dickinson, D.K. and DiGisi, L. "The Many Rewards of a Literacy-Rich Classroom." *Educational Leadership,* 55: 23–26, 1998.

Knuth, R. and Jones, B. *What Does Research Say about Reading?* Oak Brook, IL: North Central Research in Education Lab, 1991.

McNulty, R. "Using the Learning Criteria to Support 21st Century Learners." Paper presented at Model Schools Conference, 2009.

Restak, R. *The New Brain: How the Modern Age Is Rewiring Your Mind.* Emmaus, PA: Rodale Publishing, 2003.

Roth, G. and Rapiller, E. "A Partnership for Integrating Work and Learning," in Rothwell, W., Ed., *Action: Linking HRD Programs with Organizational Strategy.* Alexandria, VA: ASCD, 1998.

Shellard, Elizabeth. "Critical Issues in Developing a High Quality Reading Program." *Spectrum* (Fall): 4–11, 2001.

Singapore Workforce Development Agency. "Singapore Workforce Skills Qualifications," 2006.

Zull, J.E. "The Art of the Changing Brain," *New Horizons for Learning,* 2003. Online: http://education.jhu.edu/newhorizons/Neurosciences/articles/The%20Art%20of%20the%20Changing%20Brain/index.html

Zull, J.E. *The Art of Changing the Brain: Enriching the Practice of Teaching by Exploring the Biology of Learning.* Sterling, VA: Stylus Publishing, 2002.

 **Chapter 4**

Instructional Leadership for Embedded Literacy

The framework that the DSEI recommends for implementing an embedded literacy initiative requires leadership and effective teamwork. The research included in Chapter 3 indicates the urgency with which we must address our literacy gaps with other nations. It is up to leadership to communicate that urgency and to empower staff to meet the challenge of new standards with higher expectations.

Use Research to Establish Urgency for Higher Expectations

There is a gap between what we teach (or fail to teach altogether) in reading programs within the school setting and much of what students will do as adult readers — as parents, citizens, consumers, and household managers. We need to address this disconnect through a reexamination of what we provide in K–12. A growing body of research underscores the problem, and the CCSS has given us a clear framework within which to work. It is left up to districts to decide how to make instruction happen.

The development of CCSS has provided educational leaders with a reset button. As we build instructional programs to meet these new higher standards, we can begin fashioning an instructional program that will produce real-world literacy among our young people.

Reading Skills in the Workplace

Leadership can begin by expressing the reasons for the change. For decades, employers have complained that high school and college graduates lack the skill sets that the American economy needs to maintain its world-leading standards. The findings of several other groups, across several perspectives, suggest that this concern about the workforce population is, indeed, well founded. The following trends have attracted particular attention.

- **Low Workplace Readiness Levels.** Only about half of the U.S. adult population 16–65 years of age reached a minimum standard (Level 3) of workplace literacy proficiency, as defined by a number of national and state organizations, including the National Governors Association. Occupational literacy requirements were sorted according to five levels, with Level 5 representing jobs with the highest levels of literacy. The fact that such a significant segment of the adult population fell below Level 3 is an alarming indicator.

- **Uneven Distribution of Levels of Literacy.** In terms of distribution, the United States ranked third highest (tied with Finland) in the International Adult Literacy Survey (IALS) when it came to the percentage of workers who scored in the lowest segment, Level 1. Similarly, the United States tied for 6th place with respect to the percentage of its workers who scored in the highest levels, Levels 4 and 5. This dispersion would suggest a high degree of unevenness and inequality in terms of literacy rates across the United States. Our most literate workers are very literate, while our least literate are far too numerous. We are top- and bottom-heavy at both extremes, suggesting that Americans are not benefiting equally from educational opportunities and that a large gulf exists between our literacy "haves" and "have-nots."

- **Uneven Literacy Distribution Among Age Groups.** Younger adults in the United States, in general, ranked lower than their counterparts in other countries. Those 25 and under, for example, ranked 14th among 19 countries, and those aged 26–35 ranked as low as 16th. Generally, the older American age groups (46–55 and 56–65) ranked much higher against their counterparts in other nations than younger Americans. This does not speak well for the younger workers who will have to form the basis of our adult workforce as these older American workers retire.

- **Grim Outlook.** If we project current age group literacy rates for Americans into the future, the United States is faced with a future workforce that will be less literate compared to the rest of the world. Our younger workers and graduates are falling behind their global competitors. Moreover, the shifting demographic makeup of the United States is changing in ways that are not likely to increase literacy levels. Unless literacy levels rise in native-born Black and Hispanic groups and immigrants, the future workforce will likely be less literate overall, less homogeneously skilled and educated, and less globally competitive.

Employers express concerns about student literacy because they recognize that the futures of their businesses are at risk as the worlds of employment and education get further and further out of sync. According to job projections by the Bureau of Labor Statistics for the decade from 2010 to 2020, the fastest job growth will occur in jobs requiring some type of postsecondary education. (Bureau of Labor Statistics, 2012)

- Occupations requiring a master's degree are expected to grow by 21.7 percent.
- Occupations requiring a Ph.D. or professional degree are expected to grow by 19.9 percent.
- Occupations requiring an associate's degree are expected to grow by 18 percent.
- Among the 30 fastest growing occupations overall, 17 typically require a postsecondary education.
- Meanwhile, only three percent of the occupations expected to experience the largest employment decline require a postsecondary education.

As the sheer load of information in the workplace increases at all levels and for all workers, literacy will assume greater and greater importance. Content-loaded reading and informational literacy, in particular, will also become increasingly important. Literacy and content-reading skills are crucial, among other reasons, because they enable proficiencies that underpin, support, and develop other key workplace and employability competencies, including technological skills.

In the past, business leaders and educators have argued that current K–12 language arts and English standards as well as instructional practices (including the neglect of instruction in content reading and informational literacy altogether, at least, at the post-elementary level) should be rethought to address 21st-century adult and workplace literacy needs. That is exactly what the CCSS address and why we are encouraged to use them as we frame our instructional discourse from this point forward.

The International Center's research in employment-related reading content readability levels shows that another disconnect also exists: as it turns out, the readability levels of workplace documents, forms, and text sources are higher than many would have imagined — higher, in fact, than much of the reading material that students are generally asked to focus on in educational settings. The International Center's analysis and research have yielded data illustrating the comparative readability levels of a wide variety of workplace reading materials. The materials analyzed include "on-the-job" text sources, such as handbooks, manuals, forms, reports, memos, directives, and other must-have/must-use reading material. Reading these types of materials, as it turns out, constitutes a key element of many employees' core job responsibilities. In addition to materials that employees must read on the job, the researchers also analyzed reading materials and text sources that would be considered discretionary rather than mandatory. This type of material might include professional development reading material that most occupational practitioners would want to read or be expected to read to stay current and informed in their profession or areas of expertise. Lexile measures of occupational reading materials are shown in the following table.

Lexile Measures of Occupational Reading Materials

Occupational Reading Material	Career Cluster	Strand	Occupation	Lexile Readability Measure
"Flood Control"	Architecture and Construction	Surveying and Drafting	Surveyor	1370L
Cadence article: "Liberté, Égalité, Fraternité"	Architecture and Construction	Surveying and Drafting	Draftsperson	1480L
Computer TRAK 250 Monitor Instructions	Agriculture and Natural Resources	Agriculture Production	Farm Machinery Mechanic	1010L
"Weed Control for Small Grains, Pastures, and Forages"	Agriculture and Natural Resources	Agriculture Production	Agronomist	1220L
1998 Farm Leasing Survey	Agriculture and Natural Resources	Agriculture Production	Agri-Business Manager/Farmer	1210L
Employment Applications Forms	Hospitality and Tourism	Lodging	Hotel Manager	1230L
Housekeeping Survey	Hospitality and Tourism	Lodging	Housekeeper	910L
Front Desk Information	Hospitality and Tourism	Lodging	Desk Clerk	870L
Room Types/Price Sheet	Hospitality and Tourism	Lodging	Hotel Manager	1180L

From this wealth of information, the International Center's researchers derived several key findings:

- **The reading requirements of individual occupations are varied, and workers read and use a wide variety of content sources and formats.** Workers are required to read, use, and work with documents as diverse as employee handbooks, on-screen reports and files, emails, newsletters, instruction manuals, training booklets and handbooks, questionnaires, order forms, human resources forms, the complete range of inter- and intra-office business letters, memos, reports, proposals, slide-format presentations, informational databases, and so on.

- **Workplace reading requirements are high.** For example, using actual workplace documents read by employees in the Lodging and Food strands of the Hospitality and Tourism cluster, the International Center determined that the following workers were routinely required to read materials with these Lexile measures:

  - Hotel Manager: 1180–1230L

  - Waiter: 850–1150L

  - Chef: 1150–1530L

  - Hotel Desk Clerk: 850L

  - Housekeeper: 910L

By comparison, the readability of Tom Clancy's best-selling novel, *Patriot Games*, is 770L, and *Jurassic Park* is 710L. *War and Peace* measures 1200L, probably somewhere on the slightly high-average side compared to the reading tasks required of these mid- to entry-level occupations. The average high school graduate, by comparison, reads at a Lexile measure of 1150L. Based on this measure, many high school graduates cannot read well enough to work as hotel managers or chefs and are more nearly qualified for jobs as waiters, housekeepers, and desk clerks. Are these the careers we aspire to for our students?

Given the kinds of literacies required for work and for life, the CCSS expand the required Lexile levels for grade-level reading to prepare students more realistically for college and career. These increased readabilities may seem daunting to students and teachers alike, but they are based on the realities of the workplace.

Common Core Expectations

The Common Core State Standards are available at www.corestandards.org. Leadership needs to provide time for all teachers and staff to review the standards and to compare and contrast them to existing state standards.

In the words of the Common Core State Standards Initiative (2010):

> Students who meet the Standards . . . habitually perform the critical reading necessary to pick carefully through the staggering amount of information available today in print and digitally. They actively seek the wide, deep, and thoughtful engagement with high-quality literacy and informational texts that builds knowledge, enlarges experience, and broadens worldviews. They reflexively demonstrate the cogent reasoning and use of evidence that is essential to both private deliberation and responsible citizenship in a democratic republic. In short, students who meet the Standards develop the skills in reading, writing, speaking, and listening that are the foundation for any creative and purposeful expression in language.

Dissecting a few of the new standards in a group setting may help to focus attention on the changes and the potential requirements for change in instruction. Begin by looking at the major shifts in direction that have to do with literacy:

- text complexity
- high-quality, text-dependent questions and tasks
- a range and quality of texts
- a focus on academic and domain-specific vocabulary
- writing and research that analyze sources and deploy evidence

Consider what is happening in the district now and what might need to change to accommodate these shifts.

Reviewing Student Work

With teachers and staff, review the expectations for students who are college and career ready in reading, writing, speaking, listening, and language (page 7 of the Common Core State Standards for English Language Arts & Literacy in History/Social Studies, Science, and Technical Subjects). The following questions can help align faculty and staff around a common set of expectations.

- **Do students demonstrate independence?** Do they comprehend and evaluate complex texts without significant scaffolding? Do they construct effective written or oral arguments? Do they seek out and use resources as needed, whether from teachers and peers or from print and digital materials?

- **Do students build strong content knowledge?** Are they becoming proficient in new content areas through the research and study of high-quality works?

- **Do students respond to the demands of audience, task, purpose, and discipline?** Do they adjust their purpose as warranted by the task? Do they respond to nuance and tone in language?

- **Do students comprehend as well as critique?** Do they question assumptions and premises? Can they assess claims and reasoning?

- **Do students value evidence?** Do they cite specifics as they interpret texts and construct arguments?

- **Do students use technology and digital media strategically and capably?** Can they employ technology efficiently both to acquire information and to enhance communication?

- **Do students understand other perspectives and cultures?** Do they read materials representing a variety of world views? Can they communicate with people of diverse backgrounds? Do they listen to and respond appropriately to divergent opinions?

Before teachers can address where to go instructionally, they need to observe where their students are now in light of the new expectations. With this goal in mind, a serious review of student work for deficits in reading, writing, and literacy must be part of any new literacy initiative.

Set against this dramatic need for changes in education to improve literacy are some dramatic changes in the student population of our schools. Teachers and administrators are realizing that "things are changing" in education, and not for the better. While most teachers continue to believe that they are doing a good job in the classroom, the lack of improvement in test scores serves to highlight the many conditions beyond their control. Educators often cite the following factors that contribute to low student performance:

- declining parental support for education
- a drop in funding for programs
- increasing class size
- a lack of student motivation for learning
- increasing levels of poverty, students with special needs, and students whose primary language is not English
- increasing accountability, paperwork, and classroom disruptions
- a lack of support for professional development

Critics of the system deem such explanations as "excuse making." One fact, however, is incontrovertible: a focus on conditions outside the control of educators has a negative impact on the culture and climate of classrooms. Do teachers believe that they can make a difference in the lives of their students? Can teachers be motivated to change if they do not truly believe that all their students can learn? Will teachers commit to school improvement? The concept of efficacy is predicated on the belief that one does, in fact, have control over the conditions that lead to the successful accomplishment of a task. Too often, though, collective self-efficacy among teachers is negative. In short, teachers often do not feel in control of the conditions that lead to job effectiveness. Without self-efficacy, teachers and administrators harbor the feeling that "We can work hard, but the results will not reflect our efforts." This is precisely where strong leadership from districts, schools, department chairs, and leadership teams can make a difference.

The 2008 *MetLife Survey of the American Teacher* reported the following findings:

- Teachers in 2008 are twice as likely as in 1992 to believe that the language skill of their students is a barrier to learning for at least 25 percent of students.
- An increasing number of teachers (49 percent) in 2008 said that poverty is a hindrance for at least 25 percent of their students, compared to 41 percent of teachers who said that in 1992.
- An increasing number of teachers (43 percent) in 2008 said that the wide range of abilities and interests of students hindered their instructional skills, compared to 39 percent who said that in 1992.

Although the tendency to focus on things beyond school control may be increasing overall within individual schools, strong school leaders can, with thoughtfulness, shift the focus back to what can, in fact, be controlled or improved. The challenge is clear for administrators and teacher leaders alike: How do you build a coordinated, comprehensive whole-school reform process? Such a process begins by building teachers' self-efficacy through a common vision and by sharing the successes of best literacy practices. Leaders wishing to move the focus away from a self-defeating mindset would do well to consult the work of Megan Tschannen-Moran (2001), who has identified four sources of self-efficacy and how to affect them:

- **Verbal persuasion:** giving pep talks, providing encouragement, and celebrating achievements
- **Vicarious experiences:** observing good teaching, modeling strategy teaching, and providing embedded staff development
- **Physiological awareness:** reducing excessive stress levels and helping teachers to become comfortable with their instruction
- **Mastery experiences:** recognizing changes in student achievement, celebrating good practices, and learning achievements

Typically, when teachers feel that they can and are making a difference in the achievement levels of their students, it is easier to construct a common vision and articulate the goals of whole-school reform. In sum, what results from improving levels of self-efficacy is an unleashing of a new, positive culture of continuous improvement. When this happens, the whole faculty will be ready to investigate what it is that converts a merely promising school into a school of demonstrated excellence.

Align Curriculum to Standards

One critical step in preparing the district for the CCSS and Next Generation Assessments is to ensure that the curriculum matches the new expectations.

An Action Plan

For one recent white paper, Achieve3000 interviewed a variety of curriculum experts and used what they learned to develop an action plan for adapting a current curriculum to the CCSS:

1. **Identify and engage stakeholders**. Include administrators, teachers, staff, and parents in the process. Offer multiple means of getting information into the community, from PTO meetings to webinars.

2. **Perform a gap analysis**. You must know where you are to know how far you need to go. Start with the state standards that you have used for years, and allow teams to compare them closely to the CCSS to see what will need to change. Remember that the new Lexile levels of reading materials are one important change.

3. **Provide professional development**. Determine which of the shifts in standards will be most daunting for teachers — argument-based writing and speaking? complex texts? performance tasks? — and plan professional development opportunities accordingly. All professional development surrounding the CCSS must be rigorous, practical, and relevant to the daily work of teachers in the classroom.

4. **Visualize the standards' full "trajectory."** By this, Achieve means that observing one grade level or strand of the CCSS is not enough. Teachers and leaders need to be familiar with how the plan will move up the grades in order to prepare students for college and career. At the very least, teachers need to evaluate what students will need to know as they enter the classroom and what the next grade level will expect of those students. Looking at the continuum of skills will help everyone better plan the curriculum to match the standards.

5. **Think about how the CCSS cross traditional curricular disciplines.** This is crucial to your embedded literacy initiative. Consider the kind of collaborative teamwork you will need to allow all students to make literacy gains across the curriculum. This will affect staff meetings and the structure of your internal teams.

6. **Create a repository of lesson plans and other resources.** Look at what you already have across the school or district. What is usable? What might be shared? How can teachers get together to share best practices? Can technology help?

7. **Consider *all* students' needs.** Make sure that teachers throughout the district are familiar with the CCSS documents *Application of Common Core Standards for English Language Learners* as well as *Application to Students with Disabilities*. Get teachers together with special education specialists to discuss how the CCSS will affect and perhaps alter existing IEPs.

8. **Follow the leading assessment consortia.** Most states are signed up to receive Next Generation Assessments from one of two consortia, the Partnership for the Assessment of Readiness for College and Careers (PARCC) or the SMARTER Balanced Assessment Consortium. Each of these offers materials and resources that can help you plan your preparation for Next Generation Assessments.

9. **Provide CCSS information in many formats.** State departments of education provide a variety of resources, so check these first before you create your own. Consider linking to important and valuable resources via the school website or creating webinars for teachers who need help.

10. **Step back and reflect.** Think clearly and critically about where you stand right now. Differentiate between what needs to happen now and what might be a long-term adjustment.

Any consideration of how to implement an embedded literacy initiative must involve all of these steps. Which steps are more important than others will depend on where your district stands right now in terms of literacy instruction across the curriculum.

Crosswalking Standards

Crosswalking state standards to the CCSS may have already been done by your state department of education. Correlations are also available from Next Navigator through the International Center for Leadership in Education. Before you engage in a lengthy crosswalking exercise, consult the resources that are already available.

The International Center recommends a crosswalk that uses their Next Navigator as well as the Rigor/Relevance Framework to compare current standards and assessments to the new CCSS and Next Generation Assessments. The matrix also takes into consideration performance indicators from the National Essential Skills Study (NESS), which addresses "real-world" skills. The matrix might look something like this:

A		C		D
State Standards	State Tests	NESS	Common Core State Standards	Next Generation Assessments

Letters A, C, and D correspond to rigor and relevance levels on the Rigor/Relevance Framework, where D is the highest level of rigor and relevance. Column 1 lists the current state standards. Column 2 indicates the priority ranking (Low, Medium, or High) of each standard relative to the state test. Column 3 indicates the priority ranking (Low, Medium, or High) of each standard relative to NESS. Skills with a high priority in columns 2 and 3 should be retained and taught. You may consider eliminating skills with a low priority, as long as they do not correlate directly with anything in column 4.

Column 4 crosswalks the standards in column 1 to the CCSS. Column 5 shows the items on the upcoming Next Generation Assessments that link to those Common Core State Standards. The completed crosswalk will show you at a glance those skills that are important to teach and those you can drop from your existing curriculum.

Curriculum Mapping

Curriculum maps are the best tools to use to identify and fill in gaps in instruction. If your district is using a mapping system that works for you, it should be easy enough to adapt it to take into account CCSS expectations. Keep in mind that the CCSS are based on the concept of learning progressions, where learning is a continuum that contains a sequence of subskills that must be mastered before the standard is achieved.

The International Center suggests a format for mapping that might look like this:

CCSS Anchor Standard:				
Grade-Level Standard	Content *What I Teach*	Process *How I Teach*	Type of Measure *How I Assess*	Student Work *Evidence of Student Learning*

(Daggett, Gendron, and Heller, 2010)

Because it encourages collective ownership of the learning progressions within and across grades, curriculum mapping can help you develop the interdisciplinary instruction needed to achieve an authentic embedded literacy initiative.

Technology Considerations

In addition to collaborative curriculum mapping, districts need to look closely at their technological capabilities. Next Generation Assessments will all be computer-based, probably cloud-based, and the CCSS require that media be intertwined with reading, writing, speaking, listening, and language. Districts need to consider their existing bandwidth, available hardware, and student comfort levels with technology.

Integrate Literacy and Math Across All Content Areas

The Need for Numeracy

So far, we have been talking about reading literacy, but an equally pressing issue is quantitative literacy. Over the last few decades, the attempt to define quantitative literacy has been associated with national and international assessments such as the National Assessment of Educational Progress, the National Assessment of Adult Literacy, and the International Assessment of Adult Literacy. Nations such as Switzerland, Canada, and Australia started defining quantitative literacy in the mid-1980s, after the first major assessment of workplace, lifestyle, and community literacy was given to adults in 20 countries. Underlying these assessments is a growing concentration on numeracy in U.S. public schools for grades K–12.

Numeracy implies not only the deep understanding of — and thinking needed for — mathematical concepts and processes, but also the use of mathematical processes in any context. Quantitative literacy involves the use of required numeracy skills when dealing with any document or source that requires mathematical problem solving. The International Adult Literacy Survey (IALS) of 2003 defines quantitative literacy as "the knowledge and skills required to apply arithmetic operations, either alone or sequentially, to numbers embedded in printed materials, such as balancing a checkbook, calculating a tip, completing an order form, or determining the amount of interest on a loan from an advertisement."

No current research indicates the effectiveness of mathematics when it is taught in discrete mathematical subjects comprised of chapters that isolate particular calculation skills. Research does, however, show interesting gains in adult numeracy when instruction focuses on workplace skills.

The Intersection of Numeracy with Literacy

One hallmark of mathematical understanding is the ability to justify, in a way appropriate to the student's mathematical maturity, why a particular mathematical statement is true or where a mathematical rule comes from. There is a world of difference between a student who can summon a mnemonic device to expand a product such as $(a + b)(x + y)$ and a student who can explain where the mnemonic comes from. The student who can explain the rule understands the mathematics, and may have a better chance to succeed at a less familiar task such as expanding $(a + b + c)$ $(x + y)$. Mathematical understanding and procedural skill are equally important, and both are assessable using mathematical tasks of sufficient richness. (CCSSI, 2010)

The Common Core State Standards include eight Standards for Mathematical Practice that focus on process. They also include grade-specific Standards for Mathematical Content that encompass both proficiency and understanding. The intersection where the new focuses on process and understanding meet is a perfect place to introduce of literacy skills. Consider the opportunities for reading, writing, listening, speaking, and language in these examples of CCSS Standards for Mathematical Content.

Grade 2 Number and Operations in Base Ten

- 2.NBT.9. Explain why addition and subtraction strategies work, using place value and the properties of operations.

Grade 5 Operations & Algebraic Thinking

- 5.OA.3. Generate two numerical patterns using two given rules. Identify apparent relationships between corresponding terms. Form ordered pairs consisting of corresponding terms from the two patterns, and graph the ordered pairs on a coordinate plane. For example, given the rule "Add 3" and the starting number 0, and given the rule "Add 6" and the starting number 0, generate terms in the resulting sequences, and observe that the terms in one sequence are twice the corresponding terms in the other sequence. Explain informally why this is so.

Grade 8 Geometry

- 8.G.6. Explain a proof of the Pythagorean Theorem and its converse.

High School Statistics & Probability

- S-MD.7. (+) Analyze decisions and strategies using probability concepts (e.g., product testing, medical testing, pulling a hockey goalie at the end of a game).

As these examples illustrate, mathematics problems often involve a significant language component, and the student who hopes to explain mathematical strategies, rules, proofs, and decisions will need the ability to speak or write in coherent English. The CCSS Mathematics Standards offer many possibilities for the incorporation of literacy skills and strategies.

A useful exercise might be to establish interdisciplinary teams of teachers who are responsible for mathematics and other content, including ELA. Consider having all teachers on each team first review the CCSS Mathematics Standards for the grade levels they teach and then respond to the following questions:

- Which math standards clearly involve reading, writing, listening, speaking, and/or language skills?
- (For teachers of content other than mathematics) Which math standards could I easily infuse into my own curriculum?

We will discuss teamwork in more detail later in this chapter.

Reviewing Student Work

Just as is the case for ELA and content-area literacy, it is important to evaluate where students in the district stand in terms of numeracy skills. For such purposes, MetaMetrics has created the Quantile Framework® for Mathematics, a tool that helps educators understand where a student is functioning mathematically. MetaMetrics experts explain (2011):

> The Quantile Framework for Mathematics is a scientific approach to measurement that locates a student's ability to think "mathematically" in a taxonomy of math skills, concepts, and applications. The Quantile Framework measures student mathematical achievement and concept/application solvability on the same scale, enabling educators to use Quantile measures to monitor a student's development in math and forecast performance on end-of-year tests.

> Quantiles take the guesswork out of determining which mathematics skills a developing mathematician has mastered and which ones require further instruction.

Because the Quantile Framework uses a common, developmental scale to measure both student mathematical achievement and task difficulty, educators can accurately determine a student's readiness to learn more advanced mathematics skills and solve more complex problems with targeted instruction.

Quantiles provide diagnostic information that can form the basis for instructional material or skill level selection, just as Lexile levels allow teachers to select reading materials at the right level for the student. If we truly are going to make progress in mathematics in the United States, it is imperative that we know what students can do mathematically and what understanding they may need next. The first factor in effective instruction is to determine the level at which students can currently perform with a degree of competence. Then we can differentiate our instruction with the right types of materials, homework, assessments, technology, manipulatives, and strategies. Quantiles help us understand the likelihood that students will be able to solve a given problem in a specific mathematical area, concept, or skill.

The MetaMetrics model calls a mathematical skill or task a QTaxon. QTaxons align along the content strands per the organization of math content recommended by the National Council of Teachers of Mathematics (NCTM). These strands include:

- numbers and operations
- geometry
- measurement
- algebra/patterns and functions
- data analysis and probability

QTaxons are divided into three groups:

1. **Foundational Group:** This group has no particular prerequisites, and forms the base on which other QTaxons are built.
2. **Supportive QTaxons:** These skills should be taught at the same time as the main QTaxon.
3. **Precursory QTaxons:** These are prerequisite skills and concepts that should be mastered before beginning instruction of the main QTaxon.

MetaMetrics' Quantiles website is a useful resource for looking up skills that must be taught and understood and for identifying the precursory and supporting QTaxons associated with them. The site also contains a valuable vocabulary section with definitions of the terms necessary for mathematical understanding. New QTaxons are added to the website each week, and a helpful search feature allows users to search the QTaxons for specific skills, strands, or state standards. Once all the state standards are loaded and correlated to the QTaxons, math and science teachers will able to view the precursory skills as well as supportive and stand-alone skills in a format that is organized by specific state standards and grade-level indictors.

It is important to keep in mind that Quantiles and grade levels differ substantially. *Grade level* simply describes what average students should know at a certain point in their education. *Quantiles*, on the other hand, detail what a particular student knows and understands to a level of competence so that decisions can be made for that student instructionally in math.

This level of individualized detail helps teachers know what, precisely, to teach. For example, a student who moves from school to school is prone to problems in math, since one skill builds upon another. Merely knowing that the student is performing below grade level is insufficient. Instead, if educators know the student's competence in certain skills and concepts within an area of math, they can use that information to create the right combination of classes, daily support, labs, and other supporting programs. School and team leaders can then do much more to provide and support instruction that is targeted to specific student needs.

In addition, Quantiles help educators forecast a student's likely ability to pass a state assessment or other benchmark tests. Again, leadership can provide supporting programs and assistance that can be identified for the student with greater precision. The more precise we are in understanding what a student can do, the more precise we can be in selecting the right instructional package for that student.

Facilitate Data-Driven Decision Making to Inform Instruction

Useful Data to Collect

Change must be data-driven, but determining which data to use is an important first step. Not all data are of equal importance. Some of the data sources that are probably most relevant as you prepare to incorporate an embedded literacy initiative include the following:

- student performance on state tests from previous years
- gaps between current state standards and the CCSS
- the number of students with special needs who may need additional support
- the number of ELLs who may need additional support
- the number of ELA and content-area teachers and aides who will be impacted by CCSS
- similar schools in the state for possible collaboration on best practices
- budget limitations

Poll content-area teachers to determine which ones are using literacy skills and strategies right now in the classroom. This can give you useful information as you consider establishing leadership teams.

In addition, do not forget to collect data from students. Simple questionnaires can garner data on how students feel their literacy skills measure up. The International Center's handbook entitled *Transforming Schools Through Comprehensive Literacy Initiatives K12* (2012) contains one questionnaire for current students and one for graduates that can show you where students think your school stands in addressing overall literacy.

Using Data Effectively

While most schools are rich in data, many are poor in their use of data to impact decision making and instruction. Often, teachers complain that too much instructional time is devoted to administering tests with little feedback to refine instructional practices.

The Learning Criteria provide a format for schools to arrange data in ways that facilitate a timely interpretation. In particular, schools are able to cluster data in four dimensions: Foundation Learning, Stretch Learning, Learner Engagement, and Personal Skill Development for all students. Districts using the Learning Criteria can allow teachers to share data, collect additional data if needed, and judge the desired outcomes for student achievement. Districts and schools equipped with the Learning Criteria are not only rich in data, but also rich in their ability to use data effectively.

There are several models for converting standards-driven data into good teaching. Wagner and Kegan, for instance, offer practical suggestions for how to create more standards-driven and rich instructional practices in schools by using their Seven Disciplines for Strengthening Instruction. Schools with strong instructional practices possess (Wagner and Kegan, 2006):

1. urgency for instructional improvement using data
2. a shared vision of good teaching
3. meetings to address the craft of teaching
4. a shared vision of quality student work
5. effective supervision techniques
6. modeling on site of quality professional development
7. the application of diagnostic data collaboratively

A review of the characteristics of high-performance schools and districts can also provide valuable lessons. At the 2009 Model Schools Conference, Willard R. Daggett shared five characteristics of high-performing schools that are based on the International Center's research initiative, which was funded in part by the Bill & Melinda Gates Foundation. He stated that high-performing schools:

- understand and own a core mission with a common language
- have a laser-like focus on their mission
- minimize the "them versus us" mentality in the school culture
- analyze their work using data, student work samples, teachers' lessons, and outcome measures
- do more of what works and less of what does not work

High-performance schools have also changed the negative aspects of their culture so that everyone is moving in the same direction to pursue common goals, which could, just to take one example, state:

- We will improve student academic achievement in ways that are under our control.
- We will personalize the education experience of all students in our school.

At the beginning of the transformation of both the vision and culture, teachers may feel under-appreciated, overworked, lacking in opportunities for collaboration, and disrespected by the administration and parents. As a result, many teachers may resist efforts to change until data are presented to show that student performance is hovering at indisputable and unacceptably low levels.

Use of Data

Questions to Consider
• Why is the use of data important to the kind of change involved in an embedded literacy initiative?
• What do data "tell" teachers, administrators, and parents?
• What types of data are important to gather and display?
• How much data should be gathered in the four dimensions of the Learning Criteria?
• How should data be used, analyzed, and highlighted?
• What role could a leadership team play in presenting data to identify what is and is not working right now in the area of content-area literacy?
• Does the school have too little or too much data in the four dimensions of the Learning Criteria?

In considering these questions, assumptions about the effective use of data in schools include the following convictions (Love, Stites, Mundry, and DiRanna, 2008):

- Making progress in improving student learning and closing the achievement gap is a moral responsibility and a real possibility.

- Data in and of themselves have no meaning. Meaning is imposed through interpretations that are framed by how we see the world (culture).

- Collaborative inquiry, a process of constructing an understanding of learning problems, unleashes the resourcefulness to improve instruction.

- A school culture of shared responsibility and trust is the foundation for collaborative inquiry.

- Using data does not improve teaching. Teachers need to implement sound teaching practices grounded in knowledge of subject matter.

- Every member of the school community can act as a leader in impacting relationships and students' learning proficiencies.

School leaders need to stand at the forefront in guiding the interpretation of data and in using the derived meaning of the data to support changes in school culture. The meaning of data cannot be imposed from the top but must be derived, and bought into, by all stakeholders — in particular, by teachers who will base their instruction on a deep understanding of what the data mean.

The importance of data and its importance for considering how to increase student achievement can form the discussion points on several levels at the school. Such discussions can involve having:

- schoolwide faculty study and implement the literacy initiative
- departments discuss instructional strategies and individual students
- a restructuring committee and an administrative team review test results
- guidance counselors evaluate student progress
- students review graduation progress and career goals

Since each group operates independently, efforts must be made to communicate the findings and suggestions among these groups to ensure a "family atmosphere" of working together for common objectives.

The Basics of RTI

Organizing data around essential questions of student performance can serve as a critical strategy to achieve "data literacy":

- How do student outcomes differ by demographics, programs, and levels?
- To what extent have specific programs, interventions, and services improved student performances?
- What is the evidence of longitudinal progress of student cohorts?
- What are the characteristics of students who achieve proficiency and of those who do not?
- Where are we making the most progress in closing achievement gaps?
- How do absence, second languages, and mobility affect assessment results?
- How do student grades correlate with state assessment results?

An important tool for responding to many of these questions can be found in the Response to Intervention (RTI) framework. Response to Intervention (RTI) is a multi-tiered approach to the support of students with learning needs. A student's RTI is now part of the evaluation procedure to determine which students are identified with learning disabilities, but it is also a useful means of differentiating instruction. The object of the RTI framework is to supply struggling learners with interventions that match their needs, accelerating and intensifying instruction until they are on a par with their peers.

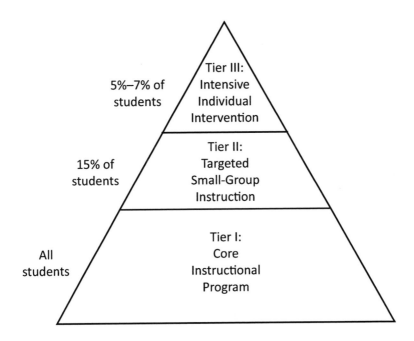

Students who fall into the 20 percent or so of Tier II and III students on the RTI model require scaffolding interventions that enable them to succeed. Use the RTI model to produce data on the needs of struggling students as you implement an embedded literacy initiative.

Linking Differentiated Instruction to Embedded Literacy

Differentiated instruction and embedded literacy are two evidence-based strategies that can target the needs of at-risk students in your district population. Either strategy can improve student outcomes; when linked together, they are a powerful engine for growth.

Screen students to determine their literacy capabilities and use that data to decide when to intervene. Struggling readers and writers may then receive differentiated instruction within their content-area classrooms. To differentiate instruction, teachers might opt to use flexible grouping or leveled tasks.

Students who score high on literacy assessments may not need to work intensively with literacy strategies in content-area classrooms. Nonetheless, those students should have the opportunity to work on other meaningful tasks while their classmates receive small-group instruction. Teachers of students who require intervention should receive regular assistance from the district's or school's literacy coach.

Provide Opportunities for Focused Professional Collaboration and Growth

Preparing the teaching staff for change through their active involvement in an assessment of school reading and learning skills, needs, and benefits is an essential first step in a literacy initiative. Once the group that will largely carry out the plan has been effectively engaged, a well-planned program of professional development is a requisite part of making the initiative successful where it really matters — in delivering instruction to students.

First Priority: A Leadership Team

One of the first steps in developing an initiative is to create a leadership team, which should, at the very least, consist of an administrator, a literacy coach, and teacher leaders from as many content areas as possible. While parents, community members, and even students can be assets to the team, the administrator, literacy coach, and teacher leaders should form the core group. Creating a team is important for several reasons:

- The team can help to assess, plan, implement, and sustain the initiative so the work does not rest on the shoulders of one or two individuals.

- A team that cuts across content areas can give a strong signal that literacy truly matters to all, and it can help promote a broad-based buy-in by all staff members.

- A team ensures that an initiative will not only get started, but that it will sustain itself. If an initiative only works because of a strong administrator and/or literacy coach, the initiative may fall apart if those individuals leave the school or district.

Team Leader

The team leader is not the most important person on the team, but one of many. However, the team leader is crucial to the team's success.

A good team leader has two important priorities. First, obviously, is the literacy initiative; the leader must push it forward, finding the best, most effective and efficient methods to reach that goal. Team members will do most of the actual work in gathering research and data and interpreting it. They will plan strategies, teach the strategies to staff, and follow up to assess each stage to determine how the initiative is working. The team leader will also coordinate all of these efforts.

Second, the leader must prioritize managing the team. Individuals must be massaged, encouraged, reassured, contained, and melded into an efficient and productive team. Everyone should be made to understand that the initiative is a team effort. Team-building can be difficult and time consuming. To this end, the team leader must:

- **Communicate with the group and with individuals.** Each person needs to understand that his or her role is vital to the team's success. Each assignment needs to be accompanied by a clear explanation of the how, what, and why of the task. No one should be left in the dark about why the task is important.

- **Instill a common vision and mindset for the team.** Initially, the leader should develop a mission statement that encompasses the overarching goals of the team. A general map outlining the project's scope and how the team will proceed should be introduced, and the leader should ensure that each member of the group, at this point, is fully invested in the team's vision.

- **Create a climate of risk-taking and innovation.** Team members should be encouraged to offer fresh ideas and new approaches; mistakes should be regarded as opportunities for learning.

- **Let roles evolve naturally.** While every team member will bring particular skills and experience to the team, other less-well-known skills or interests may emerge during the life of the team. Allowing those skills to drive roles on the team can enhance overall team effectiveness.

- **Incorporate a sense of camaraderie and fun.** The initiative is important. Pressure to succeed can be significant, the stress of working through problems and obstacles can be intense, and members of the team may be putting in many extra hours to see the initiative through. To keep everyone functioning at a high level, it's important to lighten the mood when possible.

Effective Team Members

To participate on the leadership team, the team members must have the requisite skills and experience, but even more than that, each member must understand the goals of the initiative and take ownership of them. That means that each team member must be a great listener who is willing to consider, thoughtfully and fairly, the ideas of all team members as well as the input of staff, administrators, and other stakeholders — whether or not they are on the leadership team. All of this input is vital to gathering information that can be used to develop and implement the best possible literacy program.

Trust must also exist among all team members. They must trust that other members will do their share, present ideas objectively and honestly, and do what they say they're going to do. That, of course, also implies that team members must be reliable and straightforward. It's a two-way street, but both trust and responsibility are critical to the effectiveness of the team.

The Literacy Coach

Typically, a literacy coach at the secondary level is an experienced middle school or high school teacher with expertise in literacy instruction, a talent for communicating with peers, and the ability to be a liaison across and among groups. Putting the right literacy coach in charge of this area of professional development can help both the administrative team and the teachers who are striving to incorporate Common Core State Standards in content-area literacy into an already crowded curriculum.

Team Meetings

Most people don't like meetings, but there's no way to avoid them as you plan and implement a literacy initiative. There are several key factors that can ensure the success of those meetings: keep them as short as possible, address the issues that need to be discussed, make necessary decisions, delegate tasks as required, and end the meeting on time. *Efficient*, *effective*, and *over* — that's the recipe.

The number of meetings should also be kept to a minimum. If information can be covered effectively via email, by all means send an email. When meetings are necessary, however, plan ahead for them. Build an agenda and share it with team members, allowing sufficient time for members to comment on it or add to it and do any necessary reading or preparation beforehand. When the meeting takes place, follow the agenda. Also, don't forget to set a time limit for the meeting, which should be included in the memo sent out with the agenda so that everyone knows what to expect and can build their lives around it. Then, stick to the time limit.

One of the first agenda items during the first team meeting should be to establish general rules for meetings. At the top of the list should be the rule that the meetings are the responsibility of all who attend. Furthermore, meetings should not be dominated by one or two people; everyone should participate. The team leader or meeting facilitator should enforce these rules, but team members should be responsible as well.

All meetings should be conducted with a whiteboard, flip chart, or similar device for recording problems, options, decisions, and schedules.

When a decision needs to be made, it can help to develop a decision-making structure that everyone can become familiar with and proceed through automatically. Following a procedure has the advantage of organizing the discussion so that everyone knows when to present alternatives, voice objections, and raise questions. It reduces the occurrence of back and forth discussions that can slow down meetings and thus cause frustration and impatience. What follows is a sample decision-making sequence. Of course, it may not be the one that works best for your team. What's most important is that you adopt one and follow it as a predictable process.

1. Define the problem, issue, or opportunity.
2. Brainstorm and list alternatives.
3. Evaluate each alternative.
4. Choose a solution.
5. Identify an implementation plan of action.
6. List methods of measuring the success of the action.

Sometimes, frequent but brief meetings may be useful. They may involve the whole team, or simply teams or individuals committed to certain projects. These meetings may be especially useful when events are happening quickly or when crucial deadlines are approaching. Rather than having everyone wait a week to get together, a short meeting can help people check in, discuss an issue that may be holding up progress, or get advice or ask needed questions. Although these meetings may occasionally be useful, avoid them as much as possible; meetings quickly become tiresome and can keep the real work from getting done.

Setting Goals and a Climate for Training

The challenge for principals and other administrative leaders is to organize training that includes support, choice, clearly stated outcomes, and opportunities to buy into the process. The group charged with the responsibility of designing the training should discuss several questions in making their decisions.

- How does the brain function when students are reading and learning content material?
- How and when can learning best take place in classrooms?
- What types of learning does the content area require?
- How will developing a repertoire of reading, writing, and learning strategies increase content learning and workplace readiness?
- What does this information imply for instructional practices in the classroom?

Few high schools have reading teachers assigned to that level, and fewer still have reading specialists whose main responsibility is to address content-reading issues. When middle and high schools do have reading specialists, these experts work mainly in remedial education programs. When such specialists are not available, the English teachers frequently include some elements of reading improvement, study skills, and reading comprehension in their curriculum. Because of this lack of reading support at the middle school and high school, many districts create a new position for a literacy coach to lead the literacy initiative.

Whatever the case in your district, the English department staff and the reading teacher, if available, should play a leading role in implementing the literacy initiative, since they may be the first to recognize the need for change. These staff members should join the organizing team and lend their expertise to the initiative, although it is essential that content-area teachers are well represented too. The team should:

1. Survey the entire staff to determine their perceptions of student needs in the area of content reading.
2. Define a training schedule and identify a facilitator.
3. Select the topics, strategies, and materials that best reflect the needs within the building.
4. Design an evaluation instrument.

128

Team members would include administrators, teaching staff, and special area teachers, such as reading teachers or curriculum specialists, plus the literacy coach, if there is one. The team might also ask the building administrator for help in arranging the location and the hospitality necessary for good training sessions.

The team would be charged with the responsibility of ensuring that buy-in from the staff occurs from the beginning of the process and on through the evaluation or follow-up activities. Here are several suggestions for helping teachers gain the sense that they really own the initiative.

- Have teachers discuss students' reading and writing difficulties in the staff room, lunchroom, over coffee, or at faculty meetings. Informal opportunities to identify problems exist in schools whose culture supports a proactive approach to improvement. Yet, even in schools where an open discussion of problems is not the norm, teachers can identify this issue as one appropriate for collaborative planning with a school leader. At some point, the issue of student reading and writing difficulties will need to reach the level of formal discussion if there is to be an attempt at resolution.

- Have teachers attend district or regional in-service programs that deal with literacy-related learning.

- Make test results the starting point of the discussions.

Creating a Literacy Initiative

Once a team or work group is given the responsibility of outlining steps to accomplish the objective of the initiative and to locate the resources necessary for success, managing the project follows some general stages.

Stage 1. Assess Needs

While every school or district should consider its own DNA when determining a course of action, the following objectives will start to drive the improvement process.

- **Assess the school culture**. The team must consider how receptive the staff will be and plan accordingly. If this is perceived as just the latest initiative in a long line of failed initiatives, the team will need to take the staff's reluctance into consideration. If this is another initiative demanded on top of several other new initiatives, the team must help the staff to see how literacy fits into the "big picture" along with the other new initiatives.

- **Look at data**. What are the greatest needs? The team must look at the data that they (or their district) consider to be most important and use that information as a starting point. Your district data may even lead you to determine that a literacy initiative should supersede or subsume existing initiatives.

- **Get the strongest people on board**. With luck, the strongest people are already on the planning team! There are others who can be assets as well; in every building, there are strong individuals who can support the initiative, try strategies, and share their experiences with others.

- **Envision the stumbling blocks**. Consider what problems may surface and how the team might deal with these potential setbacks:
  - Will the union create roadblocks?
  - Will the students react negatively?
  - Will the teachers feel that strategies take too much time?
  - Will some teachers resist trying new approaches?
  - Will content teachers resist taking time away from content to teach literacy?

Every school has its unique culture, but an effective leadership team should anticipate potential problems and plan accordingly.

As schools transition to the Common Core State Standards and PARCC or Smarter Balance assessments, this assessment becomes even more important, especially with the implementation of the Literacy Standards.

Stage 2. Plan for Change and Improvement

Change can and does happen. If a team wants positive change, planning makes all the difference. Objectives might include the following:

- **Create a plan determining *who* will do *what* and *when* they will do it**. While this objective seems obvious, a specified plan helps a team to determine the roles and responsibilities of various team members and keeps everyone on a timeline. Most importantly, a plan keeps the team from doing too much. While it seems more would be better, that is not the case. Starting small and building on success can happen only if the team has a clear focus. A plan keeps a team from adding on too much too soon.

- **Determine the job descriptions/roles for each team member.** Every member of the team should know his or her responsibility. Teacher leaders, specifically, should know how much time they will need to contribute toward meetings and professional development. If they will be piloting strategies, how many strategies will they be expected to manage? Remember:
  - A literacy coach is not an administrator and should not be expected to act in an evaluative capacity. A coach's available time for any task will be impacted by whether he or she still has teaching responsibilities or other duties.
  - The team needs to know and understand the role that the administrator(s) will play in the initiative. Will they be curriculum leaders or will they offer behind-the-scenes support? The administrator(s) need to make clear to the team — and to the rest of the staff — the difference between suggestions, expectations, and actual requirements.

- **Create a timeline.** Do not expect everything to happen in one year, especially if there is a history of failed initiatives; the staff will think they can simply "ride out the storm" and that nothing will actually change. Success may not be evident in the first year, or even in the second or third year, but giving up only reinforces to the staff that there is no reason to change. So create a timeline for implementation that covers what your team decides is a reasonable time frame, and stick to it. Adjustments in the program will have to be made as things move forward, but expect to follow the timeline regardless of any initially discouraging results. While there may be a temptation to "rush the initiative" as they transition to the Common Core State Standards, schools must be cautious and not try to implement too much at once and risk having too many plans and not enough resources.

- **Decide which assessments will be used.** The team should determine which data would give them the most valuable information. For example, some schools use their state assessment test data to influence student placement decisions. Other schools use Lexile levels, either through state test data or through specific Lexile testing programs such as the *Scholastic Reading Inventory*. Without reading data, most staff members will have no idea whether a student merely *won't* read or actually *can't* read. It is hard to deny that a student needs help, though, if the student's Lexile level is 400L and the textbook is 1100L. Data provide immediate credibility for the effort to push forward with change.

- **Elementary teachers will be very comfortable with assessing reading levels, but middle and high school teachers usually have very little experience with reading assessments and using such data to differentiate their curriculum.** The data, along with professional development on how to use the data, are crucial for staff understanding, especially as teachers across all subject areas implement the Common Core Literacy Standards.

- **Look closely at the rubrics teachers are using to teach writing.** Is there a school-wide or districtwide consensus on how to evaluate writing? Should there be? Does what you now have translate readily into evaluating writing in the content areas?

Stage 3. Implement Action Steps

Stage 3 may seem like the most difficult stage, but if the team has accurately assessed its needs and developed a strong plan, it is actually the most exciting stage.

- **Use the leadership team to "test drive" strategies.** The leadership team is an invaluable asset to the initiative. Team members can try strategies in their classrooms *before* introducing them to the rest of the staff to determine what works well and what does not. Team members will also build their comfort and confidence in using strategies as they become authentic teacher leaders to others.

- **Use the leadership team to cheerlead.** The leadership team members need to become marketing experts. If they can be positive about the initiative when talking with their departments or teams, if they can speak excitedly about using strategies, and if they can assure others that the initiative is not just a "flavor of the week," then the more reluctant members of the staff will see the initiative in a more positive light.

- **Design professional development opportunities.** A professional development timeline should already be built into the plan. Here is where the leadership team can prove the efficacy of literacy strategies by becoming part of the professional development program for the school. While the literacy coach will most likely be responsible for ongoing professional development, the team can and should be part of the initial training.

One way to introduce strategies to the staff initially is by setting up a round-robin system whereby a pair of teachers from the literacy team introduces one or two strategies to staff and the staff rotates through a certain number of pairs. Here is an example of how that might work with reading strategies:

- Pair One: The orchestra director and the technology education teacher introduce *Give One/Get One* and the *Concept Definition Map* (pre-reading strategies).

- Pair Two: The social studies teacher and the literacy coach introduce *ABC Boxes* and the *Vocabulary Knowledge Rating Sheet* (pre- and post-reading strategies).

- Pair Three: The English teacher and the family and consumer education teacher introduce *INSERT* and *Q-Notes* (during-reading strategies).

- Pair Four: The science teacher and the math teacher introduce *RAFT* and *Rock Around the Clock* (post-reading strategies).

In one morning or afternoon, every staff member would learn eight strategies from teachers in almost every content area. It is much less intimidating to use the *Give One/Get One* strategy, for instance, once the orchestra director and the technology education teacher have already both demonstrated how this strategy is used in their classrooms. Remember, though, that the most effective approach to introducing these strategies involves letting the staff *practice* the strategy so they can feel comfortable using it the next day in their own classrooms. Simply telling the staff about the strategy is not enough.

- **Provide support for staff as they introduce strategies into their classrooms**. Once the strategies are introduced, the literacy coach will be a valuable resource to the staff. The literacy coach can model strategies in the classroom or be a sounding board for teachers who want to try the strategies themselves. Depending on the literacy plan, the coach can provide additional strategies through either individual classroom efforts or ongoing professional development.

The team should continue to be utilized — they are the school's strategy experts. Create an "expert list" and ask staff members who are comfortable with a strategy to sign up to be an expert. Then the rest of the staff knows they can approach that person(s) if they have questions or want further information. If a teacher cannot get immediate help from the literacy coach, he or she might ask the math teacher expert for advice about a strategy. The wider the circle of influence, the more strategies will be used.

- **Make things as easy as possible for staff**. Teachers are deluged with informational sheets, forms, announcements, and so on. It can be overwhelming for teachers to keep track of everything that crosses their desk or goes into their mailbox. One small way to help teachers organize their literacy materials is to provide each person with a tabbed binder. Tabs could be used for articles, Lexile information, pre-reading strategies, during-reading strategies, and post-reading strategies. Everything that is handed to teachers should be three-hole punched with an indication of the appropriate tab. The International Center's literacy materials provide all strategies in binders for ease of use. Strategies could also be posted on the school's hard drive to make it easier for teachers to access the appropriate materials. But even with access to the hard drive, many teachers appreciate having a "hard copy" at their fingertips.

- **Leave stacks of graphic organizers or strategy sheets in the teachers' work/copy room.** Let teachers know that if they want to use a strategy that has been introduced, they can simply go to the work/copy room and grab a stack of blank strategy sheets for immediate use. The literacy coach could be responsible for keeping the stacks replenished. The key is to minimize or eliminate any reason or excuse a teacher might have for not using a strategy. Again, while these templates should be available on the school or district hard drive, putting templates in front of teachers where they photocopy materials or check their mailboxes is a quick, subtle reminder that strategy materials are readily available and easy to use.

- **Start successful ideas in small doses.** It is better to:
  - introduce and use eight solid strategies well than to work ineffectively with 20 strategies
  - assess the Lexile levels of one class of students and actually put those data to use than to assess all students and do nothing with the data
  - try DEAR (Drop Everything And Read) once a month and have the school community ask for more than to insist on silent reading every day if teachers are not valuing or modeling reading with their students

Remember that there will be time next year (or the next, or the next) to grow and change the initiative. But if the implementation does not go well at first, it is difficult to convince staff that the initiative is worthwhile.

- **Involve the community and parents.** These groups can be a tremendous help, if schools just remember to ask them. A community group might provide books or donate prizes for reading contests; parents might volunteer their time to read with students, run book fairs, or organize classroom libraries. Often, schools assume that parents and the community do not want to be involved when instead they are simply waiting to be asked.

Stage 4. Sustain Improved Performance

As the initiative progresses, the team can start to feel that its work is done. But this stage represents only the beginning.

- **Continue to meet as a team to monitor progress and adjust as necessary.** Not every step of the plan will go well. When a step does not go well, the team has to decide if it should "stay the course" or adapt. For example, if teachers do not understand how to use the Lexile data, does the team provide additional professional development to the entire group or does the literacy coach meet with individuals or small groups of teachers? The plan may have to change to ensure progress.

- **Use data to monitor progress.** Whatever data are being used — whether they be Lexiles, state tests, or something else — the data must drive the plan. For example, if strategies are implemented and Lexile scores do not rise, the team must determine how to proceed. Numbers do not lie; they should be used to convince staff who may see the literacy initiative as unnecessary.

- **Survey the staff.** About halfway through the first year, survey the staff about how they use the strategies and ask about any other appropriate aspects of the plan. For example, the staff could complete a short survey indicating what strategies they have used. The survey gives the team an indication of how many teachers are using strategies and which ones are most (and least!) popular. These data will help plan future professional development. Survey the staff at the end of the year as well.

- **Revisit and expand the plan.** As the first year progresses, the team can start looking toward the second year and beyond, determining the needs for the future. The team should look at its assessment to see if it is working and decide what additions or changes need to be made. It can then determine what strategies to introduce next year. Perhaps the team wants to focus on strategies based on skills such as note taking or summarizing. The team can also determine if it wants to try anything else in the next year, such as book clubs or contests. Continuing to follow and grow the plan keeps everyone on track.

- **Celebrate successes.** Successes are probably the most important aspect of the entire plan. The team needs to celebrate successes, big or small. If 12 percent of the staff are using strategies by February and 14 percent by May, celebrate the 2 percent increase!

Find ways to celebrate the staff, too. If the school has a monthly staff meeting, the week before the meeting the literacy coach can ask staff to let him or her know what strategy was tried and how it worked. Each response can go into a basket and two names can be drawn at the staff meeting to receive gift certificates. This simple idea allows staff to see that others are using strategies and that they are being rewarded for them. This is also an easy mechanism to gather informal feedback about strategy usage.

Use the local newspaper and TV stations as much as possible. If the school runs a book club, hires a visiting author, or tries anything new, alert the media! Ask the local newspaper to run a story on how the school is working to increase literacy levels for all students. Provide the newspaper with statistics regarding adolescent readers and then show them what the school is doing to counteract its challenges.

The more progress that is celebrated, the more confident the team (and the rest of the school) will feel about continuing the hard work.

Any improvement project takes time to plan, implement, and evaluate. Specific, visible outcomes should be set as objectives and then observed, since teachers like to see changes in student behavior and achievement commensurate with the time and effort they have spent. Teachers should have a sense that this is an ongoing process rather than a short-term fix. The horizon may be extended outward over time, but planning can focus on short to intermediate activities and goals, perhaps in six-month increments.

The literacy initiative should constitute part of an ongoing school and/or district staff development process. The activities, as well, should be part of a "continuous improvement" mentality that reflects a culture of renewal and self-reflection on best practices and research.

A Paradigm Shift in Professional Development

As staff development efforts are being planned, school leaders should consider what Dennis Sparks has described as a paradigm shift in staff development. In past years, an "expert" was asked to deliver information to faculty members without demonstration, participation, or feedback on the part of the staff. Staff trainings do not operate that way anymore. Sparks (1994) points to three ideas that have shaped current staff development efforts.

1. **Most training is now results-driven.** The desired outcomes are identified as part of the planning, and the success of the training is measured by the achievement of those outcomes.

2. **Training is now viewed as part of a total system approach** rather than a stand-alone piece limited to narrow objectives.

3. **Training reflects a constructivist point of view,** in which teachers believe that the learner is building knowledge rather than simply receiving information from the teacher.

Such a shift in staff development invites teachers to design their own program and to become actively involved in the gathering of information, in experimenting with approaches through action research, in conversing with colleagues, reflective practices, and other activities that signal teacher empowerment and ownership. This is especially critical in relation to content-area, informational, and functional reading since, as a general competency, it impacts all teachers and all students.

Sparks lists the changes in staff development that result from such shifts in mindset:

- from teacher development to teacher and system development
- from fragmented efforts to a coherent strategic plan of training
- from a district to a school focus
- from a focus on adult needs to student needs
- from training that takes place away from the teaching to "job-embedded" training
- from the transmittal of information to the teacher's active study of the teaching and learning process
- from generic skills to content-specific skills
- from trainers who develop skills to ones who consult and facilitate services
- from staff development as a "frill" to an indispensable process essential for effective instruction.

Several opportunities exist for district and building staff to design effective staff development programs. First, the material for this training is taken from and focused on individual classroom material and is thus "job-embedded" and hence, highly relevant to the staff. Second, since all teachers are working toward the same outcomes of student improvements in both reading and their use of learning strategies, the staff is focusing on schoolwide needs and student needs; therefore, the material represents a fantastic opportunity to develop both teachers and the system within which they work in ways that also promote team and vision building. Finally, the initiative needs to be content specific and must reflect a process that focuses on the teaching and learning process. The training support provided should be designed in ways that factor in the reality of where we now are in terms of the professional development paradigm shift.

Making Use of Professional Development Time

Many districts are fortunate enough to have professional development time built into their calendars in the form of early release or late starts, which allow for ongoing professional development during the school year. Other districts are not so fortunate and struggle to find enough time to keep a literacy initiative going. Rather than giving up and thinking professional development cannot happen, such schools can creatively approach whatever time is available.

Brown Bag Lunches

Some districts and schools cannot start students late or send them home early. For example, contract negotiations can make it difficult, if not impossible, to require teachers to implement literacy strategies. But sometimes a grassroots effort can yield positive results. If that is the case, then brown bag lunches can help to fit professional development into the school day. Asking teachers to come together at lunch is a low-key approach. The time constraints make it impossible to cover "too much," so teachers are not overwhelmed with information. A monthly lunch throughout the year would create an average of nine learning opportunities for the staff. A literacy coach or teacher leader could facilitate each session. Some possible formats include:

- **Strategy of the month:** one strategy is introduced each month with the intention that teachers try the strategy before the next session and "report out" their experiences before learning a new strategy. More than one strategy could be covered in subsequent months, depending on the comfort level of the participants. Teachers from each department could take turns sharing successful strategies in their classrooms.

- **Skill of the month:** the literacy coach or teacher leaders could share strategies on a particular skill each month. For example, if note-taking was the skill of the month, Q-Notes, Cornell Notes, and Outline Notes could be shared. If summarizing was the skill of the month, Rock Around the Clock, HIP, and the Minute Paper could be shared. This approach can help teachers to conceptualize a strategy's use and value rather than just viewing strategies as things that have to replace what they do.

Since teachers are very busy, these lunches should make these volunteers feel they are gaining something, not giving up something. Regardless of the content, making the time enticing is half the battle. Good food cannot be overestimated! Teachers at Kaukauna High School, for example, came to expect homemade brownies at every strategy lunch. It was a simple thing that was a treat for those who gave up their duty-free lunch to take advantage of a professional learning opportunity. Perhaps a small budget could be set up for treats or teachers could take turns providing them. Everyone appreciates rewards, big or small. Finding ways to express appreciation to teachers can go a long way.

Academic Resource Time

Referred to as resource time, advisee time, contact time, or intervention time, many schools have incorporated time within or at the end of the school day for teachers to tutor individual students or for clubs to meet. These timeframes are usually short, maybe less than an hour, but they can be opportunities for literacy coaches to meet with individuals or departments on a rotating schedule.

Board Credit at Other Times

While a school or district may not be able to require participants to attend, after-school or Saturday classes or workshops can still build momentum for a literacy initiative. Those participants who are most enthusiastic about literacy would most likely attend; they in turn could become teacher leaders and resources in their building(s). District and school leaders need to introduce these classes and workshops as opportunities for those members of the staff who are motivated to foster changes in classroom instruction and who can see the potential for improving student achievement.

Summary

The *de facto* reading and writing standards that reflect the realities of employment and other adult roles are rigorous — higher, even, than would have been expected by individuals who routinely focus on state academic standards. Regrettably, American adult literacy levels are low compared to those demands. Our general level of literacy underperformance is real, both relative to the actual demands of adult activities and relative to those of adults in other industrialized nations.

Essentially the same set of problems is apparent in quantitative literacy. Accordingly, students must be able to read and understand words in mathematics, science, economics and other math-infused courses. Students must also be able to complete and understand mathematical processes in a real-world context.

These challenges are great, but the cost of failure is even greater. To start the process of implementing an embedded literacy initiative, instructional leaders can use these DSEI steps:

- Use research to establish urgency for higher expectations, infusing staff with the clear understanding of the importance of improved literacy.
- Align curriculum to the new CCSS to see where gaps exist between expectations for literacy and current levels of instruction.
- Integrate literacy and math across all content areas to improve students' ability to use strategies and skills to solve real-world problems.
- Facilitate data-driven decision-making to inform instruction and to use facts to strengthen the instructional design of the literacy initiative.
- Provide opportunities for focused professional collaboration and growth so that all teachers achieve a level of comfort and expertise in teaching literacy strategies and skills.

Questions to Consider

- What are your biggest concerns about implementing a literacy initiative in your school?
- What is the view of your school's content-area teachers toward a literacy initiative?
- How can your school improve its use of data for decision-making?

References

Achieve3000. *10 Steps for Migrating Your Curriculum to the Common Core*. White Paper. Online: http://www.achieve3000.com/achieve3000-resources/white-papers/gated/31

Bureau of Labor Statistics. "Employment Projections: 2010–2020 Summary," 2012. Online: http://www.bls.gov/news.release/ecopro.nr0.htm

Common Core State Standards Initiative, 2010. Online: http://www.corestandards.org/

International Adult Literacy Survey. *Literacy Skills for the Knowledge Society*, 2003.

Love, N., Stites, K., Mundry, S., and DiRanna, K. "Passion and Principle Ground Effective Data Use." *Journal of Staff Development* 20: 10–14, 2008.

MetaMetrics, Inc. "The Quantile Framework for Mathematics," 2011. Online: www. quantiles.com

MetLife Survey of the American Teacher: Past, Present and Future. New York: MetLife Corporation, October 2008.

National Council of Teachers of Mathematics (NCTM). "Principles & Standards for School Mathematics," 2004. Online: http://standards.nctm.org/ document/appendix/ process.htm

Sparks, Dennis. "A Paradigm Shift in Staff Development." *Journal of Staff Development* 26: 26–29, 1994.

Tschannen-Moran, M. "Teacher Efficacy: Capturing an Elusive Construct." *Teaching and Teacher Education Journal* 17: 783–805, 2001.

Wagner, T. and Kegan, R. *Change Leadership: A Practical Guide to Transforming Our Schools.* San Francisco: Jossey-Bass, 2006.

Chapter 5

Teaching Embedded Literacy

If organizational leadership establishes the overarching vision for your embedded literacy initiative, and instructional leadership ensures that the data, tools, and support necessary are available for teachers, then teaching can proceed. The DSEI encourages teachers to embrace rigorous and relevant expectations, to build strong teacher-student relationships, to draw on a comprehensive repertoire of rigorous and relevant instructional strategies, to substantiate and grow their own content knowledge, and to use assessments to inform instruction rather than simply to compare students.

Embrace Rigorous and Relevant Expectations for All Students

The Common Core State Standards' focus on rigor and relevance means that all teachers must take the time to ask themselves these questions about their current instruction:

1. Does my lesson plan require students to use higher-level thinking (application, analysis, synthesis, evaluation)?

2. Is my lesson plan interdisciplinary and practical? Does it engage students in real-world problem solving?

The object is to prepare students for college and career. If students do little more than paraphrase texts, answer basic comprehension questions, or write personal narratives, they will not be sufficiently versed in the skills and strategies they need for adult life.

Supporting Active Learning and Independence

Explicit teaching is all about explaining the "what" students will learn, "how" they will learn it, and "why" they will learn it — its importance and value to them. Explicit teaching is a process, one designed to prepare students for learning, help them understand the steps of their learning, and lead them to the metacognitive state of knowing how they have learned so that they can repeat it. This final stage gives them the independence to proceed with learning on their own. Explicit teaching can be used with equal efficiency in math or science, social studies or physical education, ELA or music. It is often presented as a four-step process, as indicated here:

1. **Set a purpose.** The teacher finds a way to motivate students so that they buy in to the learning process. To achieve this, a teacher needs to know his or her students — what they know and what interests them. With this knowledge in hand, it is then possible to build their background knowledge by presenting new information, as necessary, and stimulating students to recall what they already know, based on facts and experiences they have already accumulated.

2. **Explain the topic.** The teacher then moves on to explaining the new topic or skill. In literacy, this might entail explaining how to analyze an author's purpose or how to identify the central idea of a text. Again, this is primarily the teacher's work.

3. **Model the skill.** Next, the teacher models the task or provides an example and helps students work through it. For example, the teacher might examine a text with students, pointing out clues that indicate the author's purpose.

4. **Provide practice.** At this point, the teacher begins to cut the students loose so they can explore, learn, build knowledge, and become independent learners.

One more step might be included here: reflection. This step involves prompting students to think about the process they have completed and helping them understand both what they've learned and how they learned it. Reflection can lead students to realize that they can duplicate this process on their own to become active, independent learners.

Some experts refer to this process as Gradual Release. The teacher focuses the lesson by explaining the skill or topic and showing how it is done. This is the "I do it" stage of learning in which all the work is done by the teacher. Then the teacher provides guided instruction — the "we do it" stage — by prompting, questioning, and guiding students through the completion of a task to develop their understanding of the skill. Next comes collaborative learning, the "You do it together" stage, which further releases students to do their own learning. During this stage, students work together to analyze a problem, discuss it, and figure out a solution by working with their peers. Finally, students are cut free and challenged to learn independently by taking on a task and completing it on their own. This is the "you do it alone" stage. No matter what term you use, however, this process is effective in moving students from directed learning to independent learning.

Engaging Students in Active Learning

Often, the most difficult parts to implement in this process are the final stages — the ones that shift students toward independent learning, or Quadrant D learning. Nonetheless, moving students into Quadrant D work reflects more closely what the Common Core State Standards require of them. Whether students will need to take the SMARTER Balanced or PARCC Assessment, they will have to think more deeply and demonstrate their knowledge and abilities at a higher level than was required in the past.

Too often, students are accustomed to thinking of themselves as sponges who are in class to absorb what the teacher tells them and then hold on to that knowledge until it is wrung out of them on a test. Students with this mindset regard themselves as passive learners whose only goal is to regurgitate what they have absorbed before they quickly forget it. The key to making students independent learners, though, is to change their mindset about their role. To determine how you can make students more active learners, consider the following questions:

- Are students passive learners who allow teachers to do the "heavy lifting" that ensures learning?

- Do students have a sense that they are responsible for their own learning with the assistance of teachers?

- Are students compliant workers who follow directions and produce factual material presented by teachers?

- What is necessary to shift toward a learning partnership between students and teachers in which students take on a greater role in their own learning?

According to Allison Zmuda (2008), the following beliefs prevent students from assuming a more active role in their learning:

1. Rules of a classroom and a content area are based on what the teacher wants.
2. What teachers want me to say is more important than what I want to say.
3. The point of the assignment is to get it done.
4. Once an assignment is done, it is off the to-do list.
5. If I make a mistake, my job is to replace it with the right answer.
6. I feel proud of my work only if I receive a good grade.
7. Speed is synonymous with intelligence.
8. Once I get too far behind, I will never catch up or pass the course.
9. What I am learning in school doesn't have much to do with my life — but it is not supposed to because this is school.

One clear challenge for teachers is to move students from being passive to active learners. However, teachers need to review their own instructional and classroom practices to determine what role they play in creating passive learners in the first place. The International Center's *WE™ Survey Suite* is designed to collect data on student and staff perceptions regarding both learning and relationships in their school. These data are crucial for helping teachers know what students really think about the teaching and learning that goes on in the classroom.

Working with ELL and Special Education Students

When working with ELL (or culturally and linguistically diverse students) and special education students in a regular education classroom, consider applying the following practical tips:

- **Model the strategies.** While modeling is important for all students, for ELL and special education students it is crucial. While most students use graphic organizers and strategies to learn content more effectively, for ELL and special education students, the graphic organizer or strategy can be just as difficult to learn as the content.

- **Lower the affective filter, or "fear factor," with peer tutoring.** Having to read aloud or answer comprehension questions in front of classmates often creates a great deal of stress for ELL students, but the affective filter drops when students are allowed to work together in a comfortable and caring one-on-one environment. With appropriately trained student tutors — who may themselves be ELL students — English language learners have more opportunities for purposeful conversation and make more progress than they otherwise can in the classroom.

- **Use students' Lexile levels to differentiate content and staircase texts.** By using a Lexile level, a teacher can find trade books at a student's reading level, ensuring that he or she can decode and comprehend the subject matter. For example, if a freshman English class is reading *Romeo and Juliet*, which is measured at 1260L, a student with a Lexile level of 600L cannot comprehend the text. Yet this same student could successfully read Sharon Draper's *Romiette and Julio*, a 620L book with a similar story line in a modern setting. Use Lexiles to staircase texts so that students grow across the course of a year, keeping in mind that the CCSS Lexile ranges are higher than before.

- **Begin with articles at a student's Lexile level.** Search engines such as Ebscohost or SIRS post articles that can be sorted by Lexile levels. For example, if a teacher wants students to read about automobile transmissions, but the automotive text-book is written at a Lexile level of 1400L, few students in the class may be able to comprehend the text. Instead, the teacher could find three articles at three different Lexile levels (e.g., 400L, 750L, and 1000L). The students could read their own articles, form groups, and share the information they learn. Later, they can transition to reading at the higher levels required by the CCSS.

Many resources, such as the International Center's handbooks entitled *Supporting English Language Learners Systemwide* and *Reinventing Special Education — K12*, offer research-based advice for helping all students to succeed.

Making Use of Peer Tutoring

Having a peer role model — or being asked to become a peer role model — can help integrate high school students into their environment, engage them throughout their high school years, and motivate them to stay in school. Consider supplementing classroom instruction with multi-age peer tutoring, which, when properly implemented, has been shown to produce one of the most powerful results of any intervention. (Hattie, 2009)

The Learning Together Company, for example, offers a high school peer tutoring model based on its highly effective Reading Together elementary program. As much a dropout prevention program as a literacy initiative, Learning Together High School targets at-risk 9th graders, supporting them throughout their high school years without the stigma often associated with adolescent intervention programs.

Each 9th grader is assigned to work with a struggling middle school student and is also paired with an 11th- or 12th-grade mentor. Mentors reinforce reading strategies using a structured, scripted curriculum based on high-interest trade books and related career-pathway modules. Mentors are also trained to model positive behaviors.

As tutor and protege simultaneously, each 9th grader thus receives the academic benefits that come from practicing reading comprehension skills with a middle school tutee, plus the social and emotional benefits that grow out of having a long-term relationship with an older, more motivated mentor.

After this first exposure to Learning Together High School, 9th graders graduate into a training program that supports their academic gains and prepares them to serve in leadership positions as mentors in 11th and 12th grades. Tutors and mentors are prepared for their roles by a program coordinator who has undergone extensive professional development.

Build Strong Relationships with Students

Research literature, professional experience, and visits to the classroom have all revealed that strong relationships between teachers and their students positively influence student achievement levels. Extraordinary teachers always demonstrate this ability to connect with students, and the classroom results for these teachers are undeniable.

As our schools change gears, refocusing to implement CCSS and to engage students with more rigorous instruction for embedded literacy, we need to find better ways to motivate students. Fortunately, many classroom-tested resources are available to help teachers and administrators ensure that each classroom builds academic achievement on a foundation of productive relationships between teachers and all students. This section outlines the rationale for this approach to academic achievement and provides an array of ready-to-use activities designed with these goals in mind.

Mutual Respect and a Caring Attitude

One of the teacher's primary goals is to create an atmosphere of mutual respect in which the students and the teacher participate together in the learning process. All students should believe the teacher cares about them and wants them to succeed, and it is often a learner-centered approach to teaching that helps create that atmosphere.

For example, in one middle school, a music teacher noticed that a group of students not noted for their academic accomplishments enjoyed writing songs for an impromptu band they had put together. Impressed by their enthusiasm, she worked with an ELA teacher to find poetry and lyric websites to share with the students and even located a songwriting contest for the group to enter. Acknowledging and encouraging interests is one way to build relationships.

In another high school, students in an English class were entrusted with the responsibility of conducting Socratic seminars. One student skillfully led a Socratic seminar discussion of Richard Wright's *Black Boy*. The student had read the assigned chapters near the end of the book and had prepared discussion questions. In order to invest the student-leader with full responsibility, the teacher sat in a chair among the students during the class activity. The discussion, which served as a culminating activity, was lively, informed, and supplemented by several students' examples of prejudice that they had personally experienced. The honesty and conviction of the student responses in this multiethnic school were impressive.

Engaged students do not create discipline problems, in part because they feel supported by the teacher and the class. In fact, the best teachers often describe the class as a family. They engender the sense that "We're all in this together." They say things like, "I can get you through this." "You know more than you think you know." They walk around the room and are not afraid to use positive reinforcement that is also descriptive: "I love the way you've introduced these characters with a description of their clothing!" "Your plan for solving that word problem seems to include all the steps we talked about!" "Clara's statement about the author's intent is even clearer — and a lot less wordy — than mine!" They laugh with students. If a student's attention is flagging, the teacher is likely to warn without missing a beat — "I need your attention up here, please" — and immediately move on. If discipline issues develop, the teacher never deals with them in front of the class but always alone and after class.

Another example of how to build positive student relationships occurred in a large urban high school. The English teacher, after five years of experience, noted that students needed a place to gather and socialize on weekends. Soon afterward, the teacher made arrangements for the school gym to be open on Friday evenings from 7 until 10 for shooting hoops, listening to music, playing ping pong, and dancing. Individual tutoring was also provided if a student needed help. Under the voluntary supervision of two dedicated teachers, more than 200 students per week participated in this activity.

Another high school teacher with 10 years of experience makes the extra effort to build relationships with students by taking them each year to Germany to study abroad. He also bought a house in the school community and makes a point of shopping at the local stores. He finds it helpful to live in the community and to interact with parents and business people. One of his students says of him, "We don't ever want to see him go away. He has field trips. He works at summer training camps. He coaches girls' and guys' tennis. I could never be a teacher like that. I don't have the patience."

Close relationships with students may seem difficult to achieve in a typical high school or middle school. After all, math, science, English language arts, and social studies teachers may lead five classes daily with 20 or more students in each class. How does one teacher establish relationships with so many students? One exceptional forensics teacher explained that he looks for opportunities to interact informally with students. If someone appears sad, he asks privately, "Is everything OK?" Conversely, if a student looks happy, he may comment on that as well. Other exceptional teachers find opportunities, for instance, to compliment the soccer player after the big game or the musician who performed in a school concert. Sometimes, just exchanging a word or two at lunch can improve a relationship. Often, such small, informal gestures convey to students that the teacher sees them as individuals and cares about them.

Activities for Getting to Know One Another

Many of the activities and tasks used for CCSS instruction involve paired or team activities. If students know one another and have experience working together, those activities will proceed more effectively. Any of the following activities can be used to break the ice and provide students with a level of familiarity that will make learning more fun and more productive. Each involves one or more literacy skills — reading, writing, listening, speaking, or language.

Alike and Different

Randomly assign students to pairs. Give student pairs two minutes to see who can list the most items in common (number of siblings, street they live on, favorite sport, favorite meal, etc.). Give a small prize to the winning team. As another option, you can repeat this with one or two additional pairs. Then have pairs of students indicate how individuals in the pair differ. (Ask that they not use physical appearance characteristics in their comparisons and contrasts.) Finally, ask students to reflect on the many similarities and differences among all people.

The Story of Your Name

Ask students to turn to a partner and explain what their name means and where it comes from (if they know). Most students reveal a surprising amount of interesting information. After partners have worked together, ask students to introduce their partner to the larger group and explain what his or her name means and where it comes from. The greater the ethnic and cultural diversity in the group, the better this exercise tends to work.

Get with the Beat

Assemble students into a big circle. Say your name with a motion for each syllable. The entire group then says your name with the motions. The next person says his or her name with a motion for each syllable. The entire group says your name with the motions, then the second person's name with the motions so that all names are repeated. Continue around the circle.

Balloon Toss

Have each student answer these three questions on a small sheet of paper:

- What is something *personal* about you that people do not know?
- What is something you are *proud* of?
- What is something *peculiar* about you?

Have students roll the paper small enough to fit in a balloon. Have students blow up and tie off balloons with their note inside. Then have students toss the balloons in the air, keeping all balloons aloft. After a minute, have each student grab a balloon, pop it, and remove the paper. Each student tries to find the student who wrote the responses.

Syllable Matchup

When forming teams, rather than just assigning groups, make it fun to discover partners. Write two-, three-, and four-syllable words on individual strips of paper and have each student choose one strip. Then ask students to find their partners by matching strips.

Activities for Building Strong Teams

Many CCSS assessments involve collaborative activities that require students to coordinate their work to achieve shared success. Helping them develop team-building skills early in the semester can yield positive results throughout the year. These activities, which are great for students at all grade levels and in all content areas, take only a few minutes and go a long way toward helping students learn about teamwork. Each activity involves one or more literacy skills — reading, writing, listening, speaking, or language.

Birthday Lineup

Have students line up in order of the month and day of their birthdays *without talking at all.* You'll find that they resort to sign language, nudges, or taps. Afterward, reflect on the communication difficulties that occur when people do not share a common language.

Encouraging Responses

Give a piece of paper to every student in the class. Have students write their names in the center of the page. Pass the sheet to another student. Everyone has 30 seconds to write one positive thing on each student's sheet. (Every 30 seconds, pass the sheets.) At the end, each student goes home with a sheet containing many encouraging statements.

Blind Obstacle Course

Set up a simple obstacle course that involves items to walk around, step over, and duck under. Working in pairs, one member of each team is blindfolded and must rely on their partners to direct them through the course. Students leading the blindfolded ones must give clear, specific directions. Followers must rely solely on their listening skills to gather information about how to navigate the course.

Puzzle Tag

Divide a group into teams of at least six people. Give each team an easy children's picture puzzle of at least 15 pieces. Mix up each puzzle and place it on the floor or a table a few feet from the team. The team sends one person to put two pieces of the puzzle together. That person then returns to the team and tags another person to put two more pieces together. Each team member must participate in order. Team members may coach and give directions to their other members. The first team to finish its puzzle wins.

Effective Communication

To build relationships with students, often it is not *what* you do but *how* you do it that has the greatest impact. To this end, communication strategies are important for assigning work and giving feedback to students in a manner that builds relationships. The following are suggestions on how to communicate in a way that helps build student relationships.

Timely Talking

The first component of effective communication involves deciding to talk at all. Sometimes the decision to engage in a conversation has more impact on building positive relationships than the actual conversation. For example, by asking a question, giving a compliment, or simply greeting a student in the hallway or upon entering a classroom, a teacher can initiate a conversation that helps to build positive relationships with the student.

Good timing is essential. When a student exhibits frustration, shows lack of interest, or feels isolated, a teacher must act quickly. Also, negative behavior is best corrected with an immediate, direct response. If a teacher fails to speak and acknowledge this inappropriate behavior, then the students may assume it is acceptable. Teachers should constantly be aware of how timeliness matters to take advantage of opportunities to build positive relationships, show interest, and assist students in engaging learning situations.

Tactful Honesty

Poor communication occurs any time a teacher provides inaccurate information, tries to cover up negative events, or shares only part of the "story" with students. Often this is done in trying to "protect" students. This lack of full honesty acts as a roadblock to the building of high-quality learning relationships. Students often indicate that they value teachers who are open and honest with them, and that means sharing good news and bad.

Still, being honest often can be a significant burden, and full disclosure can be brutal to students. So while it is important to be honest in talking with students, it is also important for teachers to use tact. One way to improve tactfulness in conversations is for teachers to be precise in their observations. For example, a teacher observes that a student is frequently late to class. Rather than commenting that the student is lazy, irresponsible, or disorganized, it is far more tactful to say to the student, "You've been late four times this week. That negatively affects your learning and postpones learning for the rest of the students in this class." This comment is still accurate, but less judgmental.

Active Listening

Active listening means to focus on the person with whom you are having a conversation, whether in a group or one-on-one, in order to understand what he or she is saying. It is essential for teachers to practice both focusing on students one-on-one and engaging in the conversation. Two important aspects of active listening are looking directly at a student and removing other distractions in order to become more aware of the student's nonverbal cues. Verbal clues and other observations can help a teacher decode the student's message.

Also, be sure to give students time to complete their thoughts. Express appreciation when students share information and encourage them to engage in future conversations. Sometimes it may be helpful to restate key points to affirm your understanding. Asking additional questions as part of the conversation helps to build this understanding. Avoid making snap judgments. Reflect on what has been said and respond appropriately.

Consistent Body Language

Body language consists of the unspoken communication that occurs in nearly every encounter with another human being. We all have acquired many innate and learned physical characteristics that reveal a great deal about our unspoken thoughts and emotions. Having the ability to read and understand a student's body language can make a significant difference in helping a teacher decide what communication strategies to undertake. Teachers should learn to read student body language and recognize the important characteristics that indicate students' feelings. Teachers also should reflect on their own mannerisms, posture, and gestures that might convey hidden meanings to students. Below are several tips on how to use one's body effectively in conversations.

- **Eye contact** is critically important. While there are cultural exceptions, good conversation in general requires making eye contact. Eye contact is essential to conveying interest in a conversation.

- **Posture** also conveys a great deal about emotions. Walking around with slumping shoulders or head down conveys a lack of confidence or interest and a generally weak attitude. Students are not likely to approach teachers who exhibit such negative posture.

- **Head position** is also an important indication of confidence. When we are confident, we keep our heads level, both horizontally and vertically. To be more authoritative, keep the head straight and level. Conversely, to be friendly and receptive, tilt the head just a little to one side or the other.

- **Hand gestures and arm movements** also provide valuable clues. In general, the more outgoing a person is, the more they tend to use their arms with big movements in conversations. The quieter the person, the less they will move their arms away from the body. Try to strike a balance of arm movements that conveys friendliness and enthusiasm.

- **Distance** from others is crucial to give the right signals. Standing too close labels a person as "pushy" or "too in your face." Standing too far away and keeping a distance indicates a lack of interest.

Possess Depth of Content Knowledge and Make It Relevant to Students

To develop high-quality instruction focused on reading, writing, listening, speaking, and language, teachers must know their own content areas and be well-versed in the elements of the CCSS that will have the greatest impact on content-area literacy.

Understanding Text Complexity

To implement the Common Core State Standards, teachers must choose texts that warrant rereading — texts with well-rounded, meaningful content. The CCSS suggest using a variety of texts on a single topic, allowing students to study that topic for a sustained period of time. Students in the upper elementary grades and beyond are expected to read these texts independently and respond in writing. Students in the early primary grades may participate in structured conversations with the teacher, orally comparing and contrasting as well as analyzing and synthesizing in response to texts that are read aloud.

The CCSS provide a backward-mapped staircase of text complexity, working from the expectations of college and the workplace down through the grades. The CCSS use three criteria — qualitative measures, quantitative measures, and reader and task considerations — to define text complexity.

Qualitative Measures

The qualitative portion of text complexity includes these measures:

- levels of meaning
- levels of purpose
- structure
- organization
- language conventionality
- language clarity
- prior language demands

Quantitative Measures

The quantitative portion of text complexity includes these measures:

- word length
- word frequency
- word difficulty
- sentence length
- text length
- text cohesion

Reader and Task Considerations

The third part of text complexity looks at reader and task, considering these factors:

- knowledge and experience
- purpose for reading
- complexity of text-based tasks
- complexity of text-based questions

All three measures are described in more detail in Appendix A of the Common Core State Standards for ELA & Literacy (www.corestandards.org/assets/Appendix_A.pdf).

Developing Text-Dependent Questions and Tasks

Text-dependent questions and tasks require students to revisit a text and show a deep understanding of its content. Students must demonstrate an understanding of the text before sharing points of view and interpretations.

Here are some characteristics of high quality text-dependent questions.

- They can be answered only with reference to the text.
- They ask students to focus on unique qualities of the text.
- They require students to draw evidence from the text.
- They may ask students to follow the logic of an author's argument.
- They expect students to return to the text to check their own interpretations.

Sample Questions: ELA

From . . .	To . . .
How does Douglass feel about moving to Baltimore? Describe a time you moved or visited someplace new.	Summarize Douglass's view on the role of education. Provide examples from different periods in Douglass's life to show how he conveys this view.

The first question does not require close reading of the text, *Narrative of the Life of Frederick Douglass*. It also asks students to connect to personal experience without showing a deep understanding of the text. The second question requires students to synthesize information and to find specific examples to support a theory.

Sample Questions: Science

From . . .	To . . .
Name three early supporters of the wave theory of light.	In your opinion, which experiments by early scientists best corroborated wave theory? Use evidence from at least three sources read in class.

The first question from a science unit requires only that students skim to find names in the text. The second question requires a deep understanding of a variety of texts and an application of what students have read. The second is a far better example of embedded literacy — it requires deep reading and writing as well as an understanding of content.

Selecting a Range and Quality of Texts

In college and the workplace, people read informational texts — almost exclusively. While the CCSS support a range and quality of texts, there is an increased emphasis on informational texts starting in the lower grades and gradually increasing through high school — in both English language arts and content-area classes.

CCSS Reading Genres

Grade	Literary Texts	Informational Texts
4	50%	50%
8	45%	55%
12	30%	70%

Content-area teachers must achieve some proficiency in selecting quality texts for students to read in depth. According to the CCSS, a quality text has one or more of these distinctions:

- literary merit
- cultural significance
- rich content
- rich language
- complex structure

Examples of quality literature appear in Appendix B of the Common Core State Standards for ELA & Literacy (www.corestandards.org/assets/Appendix_B.pdf).

Focusing on Academic Vocabulary

Common Core State Standards and their corresponding Next Generation Assessments focus on the kind of vocabulary found in complex texts, especially words that may be generalized across a wide range of texts and disciplines. It is important that content-area teachers understand this kind of vocabulary and teach it along with the domain-specific words that they may be used to teaching.

Domain-specific words might include *geology, microbe, divisor, bisect, longitude,* and *archaeologist.* Each of those words corresponds to a specific content area, and teachers probably already provide some initial instruction on words of this kind. In contrast, academic vocabulary is far more general, and teachers often bypass such words instead of presenting them via direct instruction. The CCSS recommend direct instruction of academic vocabulary where possible. The following are examples of academic vocabulary:

accumulate	forthcoming	likewise	qualitative
benefit	guideline	modify	reinforce
comprehensive	hypothesis	neutral	significant
duration	inherent	objective	temporary
evaluate	justify	phenomenon	unify

Teachers should use their own judgment about their students' needs and their own teaching plans to select academic vocabulary to teach directly. The following questions can help them to decide whether given words are appropriate for instruction.

- Does the word derive organically from the text?
- Is the word important to the text, precise, and generally useful?
- Does the word provide instructional potential?
- Can the word be explained in a way that students will grasp?
- Can I point out something interesting about the author's choice of this word over others?
- Does the word match the definition of academic vocabulary?

Writing Evidence-Based Arguments and Research

CCSS and related Next Generation Assignments require students to analyze and synthesize sources and to present well-supported claims. They focus strongly on argument writing — referred to as opinion writing at grades K–5 — since this is a critical skill for college and career readiness.

CCSS Modes of Discourse

Level	Argument Writing	Explanatory/ Informational Writing	Narrative Writing
Elementary	30%	35%	35%
Middle School	35%	35%	30%
High School	40%	40%	20%

This new focus on argument gives content-area teachers a chance to get their students involved in real-world, relevant problem-solving. Students at all grades should conduct week-long research projects as well as shorter writing assignments. Such projects offer a great opportunity for cross-disciplinary team teaching.

Facilitate Rigorous and Relevant Instruction Based on How Students Learn

In *How People Learn*, John Bransford and his colleagues (2003) synthesized a large store of recent brain research to develop some basic tenets for 21st-century instruction. Their key findings are summarized in the following graphic:

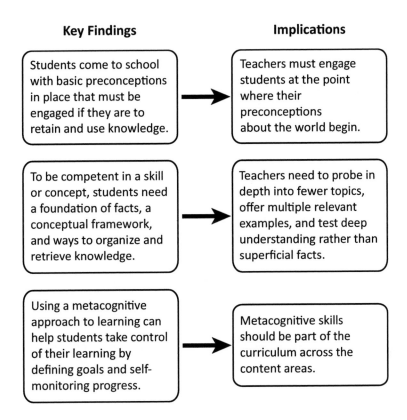

Key Findings	Implications
Students come to school with basic preconceptions in place that must be engaged if they are to retain and use knowledge.	Teachers must engage students at the point where their preconceptions about the world begin.
To be competent in a skill or concept, students need a foundation of facts, a conceptual framework, and ways to organize and retrieve knowledge.	Teachers need to probe in depth into fewer topics, offer multiple relevant examples, and test deep understanding rather than superficial facts.
Using a metacognitive approach to learning can help students take control of their learning by defining goals and self-monitoring progress.	Metacognitive skills should be part of the curriculum across the content areas.

Successful teachers, then, are experienced in their disciplines and have a strong grasp of students' understanding of concepts and the development of their thinking. Approaching students where their preconceptions begin and allowing them to monitor their own growth and understanding leads to increased student achievement.

Basic Elements of Embedded Literacy

The strategies that follow are designed to help teach the skills needed for embedded literacy. These approaches also work well in any content area that requires a significant amount of mathematics, information in multiple forms (including documents, charts, tables, graphs, and maps), or technology use. Notice that the strategies build upon the implications for instruction derived from brain research as described above.

Previewing the Document or Source

Skill #1: Understanding the Structural Complexity. Structural complexity includes recognizing the type and form of documents involved. Fully understanding the relationship between form and purpose is a key to this skill.

Components for Student Success

- Students know how to categorize particular documents according to class and can describe uses for the information contained in these classes.

- Using correct technical terminology, students can articulate the various components of a particular document's structure and type.

- Students can link purpose to structure.

Strategies to Teach This Skill

1. Use classification charts and graphic organizers, such as semantic feature analysis.

2. Use environmental imprinting methods by pairing a picture or example of a form with the correct terminology. Environmental imprinting is an association method that uses strong visual inclinations to create meaning and memory. For instance, young children naturally use this process when they begin to recognize that restaurant signs and logos represent a place to eat something they like. The brain absorbs information in the environment.

3. Have students turn a simple list into a combined, intersected, or nested list. This task helps them understand the concepts of the different types of lists.

4. Match the purpose or action needed with the likely type of list for information.

5. Relate the type of document to the workplace, lifestyle, or community-based interactions and encounters in which it would be used.

6. Build on students' base knowledge of graphs, charts, maps, and other visuals from their mathematics and social studies courses.

Skill #2: Understanding the Organization. The organization of a document is a crucial factor in understanding the purpose of a document as well as the information contained in it. All sets of documents have key features that students should recognize and be able to relate to that document's purpose or use. Understanding how a document or source is organized will make searching it more efficient and more productive.

Components for Student Success

- Students can relate the purpose of the format to the purpose of the document or site.

- Students can find basic and less obvious structural elements, such as links, fill-ins, subtitles, or nested list labels.

- Students can articulate how and why features such as pictures, graphics, graphical features, and color are used.

- Students can identify major and minor characteristics so that they will be able to search for information rapidly, using the major features without being distracted by the minor characteristics.

Strategies to Teach This Skill

1. The use of color highlighting for a printed document works well to alert students to critical features of a document. Color highlighting can be done online with the right type of browser tools, many of which are free and can be downloaded safely on school and home computers.

2. Semantic feature analysis also works well for this skill. Students can be given various examples of lists and asked to check the features of each type on a chart.

3. Use a scavenger-hunt approach to locate the various parts of a text and evidence of the document's purpose.

4. Create a chart identifying the parts of a document or source as well as the information that will likely be contained in such a document.

5. For each type of document, have students find an icon or symbol that indicates its purpose.

Skill #3: Understanding the Amount of Information. The amount of information in a document is determined by that document's structure, including type or array and the document density, and also including labels and items, all of which contribute to the varying levels of complexity. Students also need to know how to use conventional and nonconventional components of documents and how to use these elements accurately and efficiently.

Components for Student Success

- Students understand elements of the document in terms of the conventions used for various types.

- Students understand the amount of information that those elements represent (a simple list versus a two-axis chart that contains more information).

- Students can determine the conventional and nonconventional components of documents.

- Students can describe how these components interact to help readers find information.

- Students use components to understand the document or its sources of data and information.

Strategies to Teach This Skill

1. Highlight and explain the titles and labels on a graph. Note surprises versus expected components with respect to this type of document or source.

2. Guess and check. Have students guess, then check what type of information (and how much of it) may be represented by a particular type of document or source.

3. Note components that help determine sources of information and apply measures to ensure authenticity, especially of web-based sources.

4. Understanding the vocabulary in the labels well enough to locate items and describe their use is critical. Use great strategies to support this process, including use of real-world documents, pictures, or symbols. Always pair a concrete experience and some visual tool to teach this type of technical vocabulary. A definition alone is almost useless in developing this skill. It is better to offer a concrete experience that illustrates the vocabulary or concept and then give students the opportunity to develop a definition or guide using a more constructivist approach.

Understanding the Task

Skill #4: Determining the Relationship between Task and Document. Once you understand what the document contains, you have to know what the task is and how it relates to the document. For example, a graph may rely on two intersecting data sources, so readers need to ask: Is the task about one source? If so, which one? Is it about both? Readers need to know what information or action is required by the request, prompt, or question. They also need to predict whether or not that information will be contained in the document or source.

Components for Student Success

- Students can determine what the request, prompt, or question requires by reading and understanding the structure of the task.

- Students can locate key words within the document or source that help identify the task.

- After reviewing the document or task, students can predict whether the information will exist in that source.

Strategies to Teach This Skill

1. The first step in understanding the task is to find the words in the prompt that are similar to the document or source. Coding the key words that have common characteristics — such as color, for instance — helps students understand the level of congruence between the prompt, request, or question and the document itself.

2. Teach students to look at the question words in the request or prompt to help identify what is being asked. (Adapted from Mosenthal, 1996.)

    - **Level 1:** Who? What?

      Requires the identification of persons, animals, or things.

    - **Level 2:** How much? How many? Where?

      Requires the identification or use of amounts, times, attributes, actions, types, or locations.

    - **Level 3:** How? Why?

      Requires the identification or use of manner, goal, purpose, alternative, attempts, or conditions.

    - **Level 4:** Why? What for? What if?

      Requires the identification or use of cause and effect, reason, result, evidence, similarity, and extrapolation of information or other data.

    - **Level 5:** With what? If/then, so what?

      Requires identification or use of equivalency, difference, creativity, and theme or main idea.

These five types of questions or prompts help teachers understand the difficulty level of what is asked. Level 1 is the easiest form of question and Level 5 is the hardest.

3. Read the question or request and predict the type of document in which you might find the answer or the type of document or source that would be best for locating the information. Students could compare and contrast which source turned out to be the best match for the task and explain why. They also could describe what source they would be most likely to turn to the next time they have to take a similar action.

Skill #5: Comprehending the Question, Purpose, or Prompt to Initiate the Task. Complete comprehension of a question or prompt is basic to document, technological, and quantitative literacies. The level of understanding related to the task will determine the success of any search or action using that document or source of information. Questions, purposes, and prompts for this type of literacy are different from those used for prose. Such task requests require the reader to do something as a result of this comprehension. These questions must be answered by the student:

1. What answer or action is being sought?
2. What words give the reader that information?

This kind of thinking requires a high level of critical-thinking skills, such as prediction, summarization, restating intent or requirements, and inferential thinking.

Components for Student Success

- Students can restate the requests in the question or prompt.
- Students can determine the type of information or action needed to respond to the question or prompt.
- Students can predict one or more actions that may need to be taken to respond to the question or prompt.

Strategies to Teach This Skill

1. It is essential that students gain a clear understanding of how to predict types of actions needed or required. Build this understanding by:

- using the document as a source for predicting what the question or prompt might ask

- identifying the intended audience

- brainstorming about the document before reading the question or prompt to help students appreciate the context of the question or prompt

- asking students if they have seen this type of document or source before and asking them to identify its typical purpose

2. Restating the question or prompt in another familiar form — such as a text message, tweet, bumper sticker, or advertising slogan — helps students to summarize the essential elements of the request.

3. Have students underline or highlight the section of the question or prompt that contains the request for information or action. Then have students compare the logic of what they highlighted to the actual document. Does it match?

Skill #6: Identifying Given and Requested Information. Documents and other sources often contain information that is unrelated to the task or action that needs to be accomplished. On the Internet, irrelevant material may consist of a pop-up ad or part of the Web page. A document may have many purposes, so in order to perform the action requested, readers will need to distinguish what is essential from what is peripheral. In addition, some prompts will be directive and easy to understand while others must be inferred to fully understand the task.

For example, the request "What is the average?" asks the reader to calculate or find the average of several data points. On the other hand, the phrase "Find the best . . . " tells the reader to compare more than one thing and to make inferences about the items that are being compared.

Components for Student Success

- Students can clearly state the action or answer to a prompt or question.

- Students can distinguish between the information that is given in a question or prompt and that which is requested.

- Students can sort irrelevant from relevant information, both in the document or source and in the prompt or question.

Strategies to Teach This Skill

1. The cross-out method works well to help students eliminate unnecessary information in the question or prompt and focus on the essential words that convey the intended action.

2. Ask students to restate the problem or request in their own words.

3. Another way to help students understand questions is to give them practice in developing their own questions and prompts. Helpful activities include creating a hypothesis to test, solving a sample math problem, or making up questions for a chart or graph.

4. Remembering that events and actions require processes and procedures can help students comprehend questions or prompts. Ask students, "What did you do the last time you found a question like that, and how could you use the same actions this time?" Have students write a process or procedure for any familiar task or action and then develop questions based on sequence, consequences, predictions, and basic information. Most documents require students to have knowledge of sequence and patterns as well as a recognition of repeating information or events

Skill #7: Setting an Action Goal. Reading to act, or "to do," requires planning. It is also essential to set an action goal when looking for an answer, completing a task, taking an action, or making a decision. Using an Internet search to book a flight, for example, requires us to perform multiple actions, such as finding the best fare and the best times and finding the right airports and dates. Repeating these tasks many times may make the actions seem automatic, but we still are setting goals each time we complete a task. Likewise, successfully completing a tax form requires us to have the end result in mind *before* we proceed.

Action goal setting with the aid of document, technological, and quantitative materials is not a static process. We need to use what we learn and revise our goals continually, as needed. For example, we may start out with a goal of seeking the cheapest product or airline flight. But when we find the cheapest product, it may contain a feature or flaw that we do not like. A cheap airline fare may require a very early morning departure, for instance, or a cheap computer may not have enough hard-drive capacity. Information revealed in a chart, map, or graph may cause us to rethink our original action plan. Given new information, we often revise our goal or add variables to our search to get closer to a desirable result. This type of fluid and adaptable goal setting and planning is an essential 21st century skill.

Components for Student Success

- Students can identify what results will indicate the successful completion of the task.

- Students can formulate a question, hypothesis, or goal so that the actions needed to complete the task are clearly articulated.

- Students can devise a plan based on the question, hypothesis, or goal.

- Students can revise the original question or hypothesis, or they can test when new data indicate that a better result may be possible with an adjusted action goal and plan.

Strategies to Teach This Skill

1. Use relevant or real-world tasks to teach this essential set of skills.

   - Choose an Internet search task based on consumer needs, music, current events, or some other topic that motivates students. These are among the easiest kinds of tasks for teaching these skills.

   - Use real-world documents such as newspapers, magazines, and direct mail as another source of easily accessible material to start teaching this skill.

   - Use job-related documents, personal finance, or community-notice materials as other relevant sources.

2. Use a graphic organizer to help students develop a plan based on a goal or action to be taken.

3. Use simulations and mock rehearsals to teach the metacognition behind this skill. This type of reflection helps student think about their thinking. Mock rehearsals activate an adolescent's brain and take advantage of their natural tendency to learn from rehearsal, from seeing others do a task, from trying out a new skill in a simulation, or from other types of real-life applications.

Completing the Process

Skill #8: Locating Information. This essential skill requires readers to use what they know about a document or source to take the actions necessary to find information. Using labels, taglines, and other features of the document or source with the goal in mind will help readers locate information efficiently and accurately. In an auto lease or credit card application, for instance, this may require a reader to "read the fine print" or even locate where the "fine print" or essential information is located in the document, site, or source.

A credit card application, for instance, may contain bold, colorful displays of current interest rates, but where does it state what the rate is *after* the introductory period? This information is critical if the goal is to find the best credit card, but the reader may have to work hard to find it. In other contexts, locating information may be as simple as finding the intersection of two labels on a chart or as complex as going through an auto lease agreement or a government tax website.

Components for Student Success

- Students can locate information with both the goal and the nature of the document in mind.

- Students can use what is known about online sites and documents to find information efficiently.

- Students can locate information using both simple and complex documents as well as online sites.

- Students can locate information using multiple documents or sources.

Strategies to Teach This Skill

1. Assign a series of questions for students to answer by locating facts on the Internet such as "Who was the President of the United States in 1872?" or "What is the chemical symbol for mercury?" Discuss with students the shortcuts they found and the methods they used to save time. Also, balance the emphasis on swift location with a discussion of the site's quality. The point of this exercise is for students to recognize the importance of using reliable search engines and effective search strategies (such as adding and subtracting key terms to widen and narrow searches). Several commercials are available with a humorous twist on Internet search services that would help students see the lesson's purpose and underscore the relevance of what they are learning.

2. Ask students to compare two government documents, determine which one is easier to find information on, and explain why. Also, try doing the same activity by using a print or online fill-in form. Filling in the form correctly for the desired purpose is the goal.

3. Practice using labeled charts, maps, graphs, and tables to find information. Start with the phonebook or newspaper, since widely used everyday sources usually are less complicated than government, mathematical, or institutional formats.

4. Practice locating information that requires using multiple documents or websites. This is a more difficult skill and requires students to recognize key features while moving between documents to locate and keep track of pertinent information. Among the most complex examples are U.S. tax forms and tables. Simple searches can be done using an almanac or an online mapping program.

Skill #9: Cycling through the Document or Multiple Sources. Searching for information or completing a task within a document or source is rarely a single-action process. Usually, we move around within a document, looking for multiple pieces of information that may come from one source or multiple sources. Doing so requires persistence and judgment in knowing when a search is complete or having some perspective on how productive repeated attempts can be at finding information to complete a task.

Components for Student Success

- Students use the structural features of a source to efficiently and logically locate information or perform a task.

- Students demonstrate persistence in cycling through a document or multiple sources without confusion or frequent backtracking.

- Students can judge when that cycling is or is not producing the desired results and then adjust the goal or plan as needed.

- Students can explain the cycling process they used and assess how effective it was in getting results.

Strategies to Teach This Skill

1. This skill is best learned on an individual basis rather than as a group activity. To learn effective search methods and persistence, you must do it yourself. Practice in searching for information that requires several cycles of going back to the source is the best way to teach this skill. Use scenarios that are motivating and can be applied in the real world to help students see the purpose and value of persistence. Some examples include asking students to:

- Use several websites to find the best deal on an MP3 player.
- Compare home loan agreements to find the best deal using two or three variables, such as interest rate, closing costs, and required down payment.
- Use sales or stock market charts to predict the next quarter's results (incorporate charts from three previous quarters or years to help make the prediction).

2. Use a tally chart to have students determine how many times they had to return to a site or a data source. This helps them see the need for cycling. Give students a real-world task using both common and uncommon documents for this practice. A common document might be a bank application form. An uncommon document (for students) might be a hospital admission form.

3. Give students variables that are hard or impossible to find within a document or source. Ask students to reflect upon how and when they determined that the information was not present in the source. How many cycles did it take, and what conclusions helped students determine that searching was not productive? Web-based searches are great for teaching this aspect of cycling.

Skill #10: Integrating Information. Integrating information requires skill in comparing and contrasting data and understanding cause and effect. This includes the ability to understand parts-to-whole relationships, similarities and differences, agreeing and conflicting information, and answering questions that include stated or implied variables.

Students can complete a search for the best product, for example, only after understanding the variables that govern "best" for this particular product. Then the students compare sources for the product in terms of the variables and in terms of how easily one can find information about the product variables. Therefore, the students integrate product information and the criteria for determining which product is "best" for completing the task.

One source may give all the information one needs to make comparisons to the criteria while another may lack complete information. All the documents might contain the same information but they might not be consistent in terms of variable features such as size, quantity, cost, and other factors. Both of these comparisons require an integration of the task and the results in order to take action. In this case, the action is to purchase the "best" product, that is, the one that meets the most criteria or variables.

Components for Student Success

- Students can determine what data are similar and dissimilar and then, given the results, restructure information or actions as needed. Students can also determine which elements of the document are in agreement with the prompt or task and then combine elements into a pattern to make a decision, solve a problem, or take the required action.

- Students can compare data and information from multiple searches (cycles) and put together the elements of documents to reformulate a plan or determine a new action, if needed.

- Students can answer questions about the document and the prompt. Such questions include:

  ○ What?

  ○ How?

  ○ How would you . . . ?

  ○ How would you test . . . ?

  ○ What if . . . ?

  ○ How would you create an alternative . . . ?

Strategies to Teach This Skill

1. Integrating information is a form of analysis, synthesis, and evaluation combined. Teaching the basics of thinking strategies with the aid of real-life examples works well. Graphic organizers, for instance, may require much in the way of thinking skills. Sometimes the variables must be inferred from the data set, working backward from the information given. This sophisticated skill must be explicitly taught and carefully practiced. Often, it is helpful to have students pose questions about possible causes when the effect is known from the information given.

   Students can also predict possible effects if causes are known. This type of thinking is similar to hypothesis formulation in science and is a highly valued life skill for problem solving, for preventing unwanted effects, and for developing creative solutions.

2. Integrating various thinking skills is taught easily through occupational examples. Think of fire fighters and arson investigators determining the cause of a fire, a construction company determining the factors that will put them in the best po-

sition in the bidding process to acquire a new client or job, or a server determining the conditions and actions needed for restaurant customers to provide good tips.

3. Role-play the investigation of an auto accident, the malfunction of equipment, a technology problem, or some other real-life problem. Have students write the effect and the causes in a graphic organizer. Invite guest speakers from various occupations to help students see the real-life applications of this type of thinking.

Many technological sources and quantitative documents require integrated thinking with two types of causes for most effects. This process is known in industry as being amenable to the insights of a current theory called "Apollo Root Cause Analysis" problem-solving methodology. This methodology involves a process developed by Dean Gano and published in 1999 by Apollo Associated Services. It is based, in turn, on the psychology of problem solving (and cause-and-effect analysis) and has been well researched in multiple industries. Robert Latino of Reliability Industries also uses a form of "root cause" analysis in his company. Both companies train workers to understand and solve problems and create better solutions by understanding causes and developing prevention plans. All of their work, and the work of those like them, is grounded in the idea that workplace skill requires a thorough integration of facts before deciding on solutions or taking actions to change something or to continue it. Interacting with facts requires, moreover, a high degree of document literacy.

4. Creating data charts to help gather and organize information is a great way for students to try solving the problem or resolving the issue by integrating the facts. Data charts are useful in such situations as science experiments, problem solving, and social interaction. The creation of charts requires both cause and effect analysis and asking good questions. The art of asking good questions about data and information is critical to integrative thinking.

5. Students need to learn to formulate questions that help them see patterns and determine causes for certain effects or results. This will necessitate rehearsal as well as frequent opportunities to interact with documents or sources that require such questioning. Consumer websites, periodicals, TV news broadcasts and commercials, and orientation materials for new students or employees are all great sources of documents and media that easily invite practice in the formulation of questions.

Skill #11: Generating Inferences. Embedded forms of literacy require a great deal of inferential thought. Inference is the ability to understand or state what is not written down, presented visually, or stated explicitly. In prose contexts, we often call this skill "reading between the lines." For the type of literacy that requires actions or task completion, though, inferential thinking can include making predictions, asking questions, justifying actions, and carefully evaluating criteria, data, and source characteristics. In document, technology, and quantitative literacies, readers must often move quickly from literal and easily found information to information that requires specialized or prior knowledge to complete the needed actions.

Components for Student Success

- Students can articulate the purpose for the document and speculate on unstated purposes.

- Students can articulate the unstated or missing information in a question or prompt.

- Students can draw conclusions based on both the organization of the document or source and the data it contains.

- Students can make predictions about the task to be completed or the action to be taken.

- Students can use background knowledge, previous experiences, and specialized information to infer unstated information, decisions that must be made, or actions that must be taken.

Strategies to Teach This Skill

1. Use a variety of sources, media, and documents to introduce inferential thinking such as:
   - humor in audio clips, video clips, or cartoons (humor always requires inference)
   - commercials (unstated messages abound) or print and web-based advertising
   - artwork
   - holiday or event greeting cards (infer what the sender and the receiver would be like, along with any intended messages)
   - photographs (from photographer's viewpoint and from viewer's)
   - short video clips from popular television shows or movies (the meaning of actions or the motives of people require inference)

- symbols and abstract representations
- social simulations or role-plays requiring judgment, problem solving, decision making, and humor

2. Teach the prerequisites to inferential thinking (listed in order of what needs to be scaffolded first, second, and so on):

- **Concept Attainment:** Make abstract ideas both concrete and visual.
- **Concept Development:** Use brain-friendly vocabulary acquisition strategies.
- **Pattern Recognition:** Consider parts to whole, categorizing, sorting.
- **Analogies:** Make comparisons that can be visual, verbal, data-based, information-based, graphical, and that require the recognition of congruence.
- **Extrapolate:** Find and use information that is directly stated from a variety of sources (locating information and cycling will be required).
- **Synthesis:** Restate in your own words, summarize, create, and design.

3. Justify your reasoning, plan of action, or approach to task completion, and develop criteria for a particular result or set of variables. Question assumptions, as well. This entire process is the process of "elaboration."

To become skillful, students need to practice inferential thought almost daily. This thinking skill is a fundamental life skill for employment, health and safety, and the establishment of relationships.

Often, inferences are based on assumptions or a predisposition to believe one way or another. It is important for students to test their assumptions in order to infer more accurately. Because assumptions are based on beliefs and experiences, we need evidence to justify our point of view.

Would we be justified, for example, in assuming that, in response to law suits, a safety checklist for an oil rig operation was designed to prevent problems because there were previous problems? Might the checklist be used simply because the nature of the work is dangerous? Whatever the case may be, assumptions would have to be verified through research or by interviewing employees in knowledgeable positions. A safety-process or interview-process checklist will take on different kinds of meaning to an employer depending on its origins or the current interpretation of why that document exists.

Using workplace documents from a variety of job clusters, compare safety checklists. What elements are the same and different? What patterns do you see? What seem to be some universal characteristics of job-site safety checklists?

Skill #12: Formulating and Calculating (for Quantitative Documents Only). Three additional applications that students need for interaction with quantitative documents are:

- determining the type of calculation needed
- understanding the quantitative density of a document
- matching the question or prompt with information in a quantitative document

Determining the type of calculation involves not only determining which problem-solving method to use, but also understanding how to combine operations, conversions, and transformations for multistep problems. The **quantitative density of a document** includes knowing the structure of the document and prompt or question and using specific mathematical and scientific terminology to infer the necessary actions. **Matching the question or prompt with the information in a quantitative document** requires a combination of hypothesis formation, testing, problem-solving, and calculation.

Components for Student Success

- Students can perform mathematical operations — addition, subtraction, multiplication, division, using fractions and percentages, making simple or complex conversions and transformations, and ordering multistep operations — to solve problems.
- Students can use mathematical labels, symbols, unit information, and other attributes of quantitative documents to perform the needed tasks or take appropriate actions.
- Students can see trends in data and verify them through calculation.
- Students can use multiple sources of information in quantitative documents and then use that information to formulate an answer or response.

Strategies to Teach This Skill

1. The use of real-life examples is the best way to teach quantitative literacy. As sources of examples, consider using occupational, government, and educational websites. Couple these types of sources with video clips of people using math in workplace or community situations. Research shows that most people do not always recognize the extent to which they use everyday math in the workplace or in their lifestyle activities.

   Showing how quadrant equations are used in engineering and computer optimization and topology, for example, can be a helpful way to show the relevance of math and to illustrate problems that these professions deal with regularly.

2. Major workplace math tasks fall into predictable categories. Frequently, these contexts for teaching quantitative literacy have been found to be fruitful:

   - financial math

   - time and cost math

   - measurement and calculation

   - data analysis

   - numerical estimation

3. Using manipulatives is an essential method of math instruction and can certainly be a powerful tool for developing quantitative literacy. If you couple photo journaling or math models with these types of problems, students can later describe their own mathematical thinking. For example, using real-world problems, students can create a model or drawing of a possible solution or design. They could also photograph each step and use that in a presentation. Moreover, students could design a project to clean up garbage around a school, including models or posters for a campaign, calculation of the recycling benefit (e.g., the yield of reimbursement per pound per type of recyclable) and other great charting and data opportunities. While any of these strategies would be effective on its own, combining approaches helps students create better, richer, longer-term connections in their brains, which increases their problem-solving abilities.

4. Strategies for teaching quantitative literacy have certain common elements:

   - Ask relevant questions:

     o What is the purpose of this document or source?

     o How does the configuration or layout of the document help you understand it?

     o What mathematical actions must be taken with the document, or what tasks must you perform?

     o Did your results make sense and help you accomplish the work?

   - Use real sources of materials.

   - Use math "manipulatives" for problem solving.

   - Use strategies such as simulation, inquiry, and problem- and project-based learning.

   - Never teach the mathematics of documents out of context; use the real thing.

5. Students need plenty of practice in formulating hypotheses and problems to develop quantitative literacy. In typical classroom texts, we tend to ask students to solve existing problems. In the workplace, we frequently have to develop our own hypothesis and test them or work backward from facts and information to discover an underlying problem. Students must be given time to practice this higher level workplace skill using real-world contexts. Try these methods:

    - Ask students to pose problems or suggest a line of inquiry.

    - Ask students to investigate whether particular cases can be generalized.

    - Have students seek counter-examples or identify exceptional cases.

    - Encourage students to consider alternative ways of representing problems and solutions in graphical or diagram form and to move from one form to another to gain a different perspective on a real-life problem.

Skill #13: Taking Action. Taking action is a life skill. It is important to have a plan and to formulate a goal, but implementing and carrying out that plan requires another set of abilities. All forms of document, technological, and quantitative literacy require some form of action. This requires the ability to initiate a task or action, follow through with a plan, make changes along the way, identify the motivation and purpose for acting, and self-monitor progress toward the goal.

Most workplace, lifestyle, and community interactions with literacy are not guided practice events. Even if we are merely seeking information, that is an action, just as performing a calculation or finding a website is an action. Independent action or collaborative action is required for document, technological, and quantitative forms of literacy.

Components for Student Success

- Students can initiate the actions needed to complete a task with document, technological, or quantitative literacies.

- Students can make decisions while taking actions with documents or sources that use information, inferences, or problem solving.

- Students can articulate the reasons for the actions.

- Students can reject actions or change them if needed to fit the current criteria for success or even change the criteria if new information shows the need for this course correction.

Strategies to Teach This Skill

1. Start by stating motivations and desired results. Motivation in embedded literacy tasks, just as in life or work, is a key issue in completing tasks:

    -   "I have to know how much money is in my bank account, so I need to balance my checkbook."

    -   "To finish my holiday shopping and stay within a budget, I need to search for online sales."

    -   "I don't want to go to jail, so I have to file my taxes."

    -   "My boss wants these sales figures to be analyzed and presented."

    -   "I need this job" or "I want this promotion."

    We all have different motivations for our actions, and most of the time these are more powerful than getting an "A" on a quiz. The good news for teachers is that interacting with documents and sources has a degree of inherent motivational appeal. However, it is important in teaching the initiation of action to encourage students to practice stating their motivations and/or the desired results. Doing so helps students focus their thinking at the start of a task or project when it may feel overwhelming. It also reinforces the value of finding or interacting with the document or source.

2. Build capacity through training to help sustain actions, especially when working on complex projects. The key contributors to this capacity building are:

    -   **Procedural practice,** which includes making certain students have and understand the background knowledge and experiences needed to complete the task. To build additional background, it also requires providing rehearsal. Filling in data on purchase fill-in forms online involves common procedures such as providing a credit card number and personal information. Two elements of background knowledge required for this task are knowing how to fill in the form and knowing when a website is secure enough to be given that information. In this case, the procedure is not simply a step-by-step series of actions; it also includes some important decision making along the way.

    -   **Specialized practice,** which involves making sure that students have the resources they need and access to any specialized vocabulary or skills required to complete the required actions. For example, reading a graph is a common skill, but reading a Bureau of Labor Statistics graph involves some language that we cannot assume students know.

- **Monitoring progress practice**, which is making sure that students can ask questions as they cycle through a multistep or complex process of consulting documents or sources. This may include data collection and reflection on that data. In some workplace examples or simulations, this may involve keeping a boss or supervisor up to date on progress. This also is a good way to evaluate decisions that have been made along the way.

3. Require students to identify the data sources as they take action and to pause long enough to reflect on the data. Do any changes in action need to be made? This "if-then" sort of thinking requires practice opportunities. Tracking and monitoring progress is essential to success in taking actions with documents or sources.

   For example, say you earn $75 per month doing odd jobs and your parents give you a small allowance. You are always short of money on the weekends for dates, excursions, and purchases you would like to make, so you track your spending habits for two months. Given the table you generate, you notice that bus/train fares (or gas prices) have gone up. You have to make decisions based on the following options: ask your parents for more allowance money, end the weekend purchases, or find additional work income to cover your desired expenses. Coding your data with "needed" versus "wanted" expenditures also may be helpful.

4. Simulations, project-based learning, problem-based learning, and inquiry methods are all great ways to provide practice in taking action. Combining these approaches with the right kind of document or sources will help students acquire this essential life skill. Explicitly teaching the need for identifying purpose and results, knowing the procedure, knowing specialized information, and monitoring progress to make good decisions — all of these skills are required of successful workers and citizens. Students should not have to wait until they graduate from school to use them.

Skill #14: Evaluating Results. When we evaluate the results of our interactions with embedded literacy, we need to consider three essential processes:

- measuring results
- reviewing the goal and plan
- determining the success of the actions taken

If we evaluate our literacy results, we can measure for future use the effectiveness of the plan, make informed decisions that impact current and future needs, celebrate accomplishments, and document the benefits of what we did. We can do this by means of a simple verbal reflection or in a more formal documentation of events and results, as is often done in businesses and governments.

Components for Student Success

- Students can articulate the results of the actions.
- Students can compare the result to the desired outcomes.
- Students can perform a cause-and-effect analysis of the results.
- Students can predict or state future actions based on evaluating the results for the task at hand.

Strategies to Teach This Skill

1. This evaluation process requires making a habit of asking good questions at the completion of a task. This is a life skill and helps us learn and change when we do not achieve expected or desired results. This also takes practice, so role-plays, mock review boards, simulations, debates, and written reviews are effective in teaching this skill. The following questions can guide students' process and thinking:

   - Was your result the one you wanted? Why or why not?
   - Review the data, forms, or documents you used to complete the task. How did they impact the results?
   - Was the method or strategy you chose effective and efficient?
   - Compare your performance to that of other team members. What can you learn from your team or other teams?
   - Did your goal and plan match the actions you took? Was that effective? Did you have to change the goal, plan, or actions along the way? Why or why not?
   - If you did make changes along the way, what caused you to do so? Were the changes effective? Why or why not?

2. A successful individual uses specific skills or steps when evaluating results. Teachers can watch for these behaviors and offer feedback or coaching as needed, based on the results. If students use these skills on their own as part of the evaluation, that is even better. Evaluation steps or factors may include:

   • reviewing feedback from the student about how the process went

   • gauging the awareness level of students in terms of minor or major changes that had to be made along the way; some students make intuitive corrections, without realizing that they have done so

   • identifying factors that contributed to students surpassing or missing targets

   • helping students to list or quantify the benefits of correctly completing a task

3. Action plan reviews have many advantages. Teaching students to design the review process before completing a task helps them develop a great life skill that is used frequently in business and government functions. This review can involve the formulation of a simple checklist or a more elaborate rubric for judging success in obtaining document, technological, and quantitative literacies.

   • Components of an elaborate evaluation plan (e.g., for completing taxes, planning a vacation, buying a car, completing a job or other application, or creating a will or other legal document) may include:

     ○ developing insights for new or future actions

     ○ avoiding failures or missed steps in the process

     ○ refining the process for greater efficiency

     ○ providing stories and examples of success

   • Components of a simple evaluation plan — such as making a consumer purchase of a small item, balancing a checkbook, developing a personal budget, losing weight, taking medication appropriately, choosing a charity, or finding the cheapest rental car — may include the following evaluations:

     ○ determining whether the desired results or intended information was achieved

     ○ identifying a strategy or plan that worked

     ○ noting actions that produced the result efficiently

     ○ assessing whether he result was accurate and/or complete

Demonstrate Expertise in the Use of Instructional Strategies, Technology, and Best Practices

As brain research indicates, teacher expertise is a critical building block to student achievement. As schools begin a literacy initiative to implement CCSS, strategy decisions usually take place early on in the process. It is not difficult to find good strategies, of course. Yet randomly selecting strategies from the Internet or any other source may not result in success. This can be especially true as teachers strive to embed literacy; so many of the tried and true strategies of the past were developed without a clear understanding of how students will use their reading and writing skills as adults or without a recognition that embedded literacy should be mandated rather than used haphazardly.

The following examples illustrate a handful of strategies that are effective for teaching embedded literacy in all content areas. For more ideas, see the International Center's publication *Effective Instructional Strategies for Content-Area Reading*.

Embedding Reading Strategies

The following road-tested reading strategies are particularly useful in helping students become more proficient in literacy skills. They can be adapted for any content area.

Vocabulary Knowledge Rating Sheet

A Vocabulary Knowledge Rating Sheet is an excellent strategy for determining how much students actually know before starting a lesson or a unit. By listing the words and asking students to rate their knowledge, a teacher can readily verify how many words students know and how well they know them. If all students indicate that they know the first word, then the teacher does not need to spend much time on that word. If few students know the word, then more time is spent. Ideally, students can monitor their learning as the year progresses and they move closer to the test. This strategy is also a helpful post-learning tool that students (and teachers) can use to determine how well the words have been learned and how extensively the student or the class needs to review. A math template follows.

Term	1. Do Not Know It *What? This is new to me. I need to be sure to study this one carefully because I have a long way to go!*	2. Heard It, Seen It *I am somewhat familiar with this term, but I need to review this because I am still not ready.*	3. Can Define It, Use It, Teach It *I would be comfortable explaining this to others.*	Definition, Example, or Diagram	Progress Check 1 Date:	Progress Check 2 Date:
Chapter X						
Intercepts						
Symmetry with respect to the y-axis, x-axis, and the origin						
Slope of a line						
Point-slope form						

Anticipation Guides

Anticipating the content of a passage can help build purpose, interest, and energy for reading. An anticipation guide features four or five key statements related to the topic of the reading. By asking students to agree or disagree with these statements, you can determine what students know and don't know about the topic. This strategy can help generate discussion on the topic, identify students' experiences with the topic, and uncover misconceptions. An anticipation guide works equally well in social studies, literature, science, and other content areas. Consider the following example, using the article "How a Bill Becomes a Law":

Learning the Strategy

Anticipating the content of a passage before you read can help build purpose, interest, and energy for reading. An anticipation guide features four or five key statements related to the topic of the reading. Do you know which statements are correct? Can you find proof to support your answers in the reading? This strategy will help you determine what you know (and don't know) about your topic.

Practicing the Strategy

Read each of the following statements. In the space next to each statement, write **A** for **agree** or **D** for **disagree**. If you are **not sure,** write **NS**.

_____1. A bill is passed either in the Senate or the House and then sent to the President for signing.

_____2. To "table" a bill essentially kills it.

_____3. If the House of Representatives changes a bill passed by the Senate, a joint committee must be appointed to reach a compromise.

_____4. If the President disapproves the bill, he may *veto* it.

_____5. It takes only a "50 percent plus one" vote to override a presidential veto.

Next, read the text, then go back and change any wrong responses to the correct ones.

How a Bill Becomes a Law

The process of law making at the federal level is complex and sometimes can be confusing. But it is important to know the many steps a piece of legislation must take before it becomes the law of the land.

The idea begins in the offices of the senators or representatives. Staff members write a working draft of the bill, and then the senator or representative introduces it in the House of Representatives or Senate. The person who introduces it is called the bill's "sponsor."

In the House or Senate, the bill is recorded and placed into the Congressional Record and onto the Internet site thomas.loc.gov. The bill is numbered for identification; in the House, bills have the initials H.R. If the bill originates in the Senate, it has the initial S.

Next the bill moves to the committee with responsibility for that particular topic. For instance, if an H.R. bill pertains to changes in education law, the bill will go to the House Education and Workforce Committee and then to a subcommittee that has specific expertise on the issue. The committee members of either the House or Senate study the bill, discuss it, amend it, and decide whether it should be "reported out" of the committee to the full legislative body.

Suppose a bill originates in the House of Representatives. The members may decide that the bill should go back to the committee for more work, or they may pass the bill and send it to the Senate for passage. A bill must pass both the House and the Senate in identical form before becoming law.

In the Senate, one of two things will happen to the bill. Senators will pass the bill as it is, or they will amend, or change, it and send it back to the House of Representatives. Sometimes the Senate passes a different version of the bill. In this case, a joint committee of the House and Senate meet to work out the differences in the two bills.

Once a bill passes both House and Senate, it is sent to the President, who has 10 days to sign it into law or veto it. Another option is to allow the bill to become law by not signing it within the 10-day period.

If the President vetoes the bill, it is sent back to the House or Senate, depending on where it originated. Members then have the option to override the veto, send it back to committee for revisions, or "table" the bill, a practice that essentially kills the bill. A veto override requires a two-thirds vote of the House or Senate.

INSERT

The INSERT strategy works for any learning situation that requires reading. A simple way to implement INSERT is to give all students "sticky notes" and a bookmark containing the INSERT "code." The codes are symbols to indicate ideas that confuse the reader, raise a question, seem important, and so on. Students can use the bookmark as a reference and write their thoughts on the sticky notes. This activity is helpful for several reasons:

- Students can track their thinking so that reading becomes a more interactive process between the student and the text. Instead of their eyes simply skimming over the page, students slow down enough to deliberate over the content as they mark the section or sentence with the given symbols.

- Student notes become a study guide for later use as a tool to review material.

- Student notes facilitate a richer class discussion since the students' thoughts are literally at their fingertips.

- Because highlighting or writing in reading material is generally not allowed, INSERT allows students to relate to the text without damaging the material. Even when highlighting is permitted, INSERT prevents students from getting "highlighter happy" and randomly highlighting whatever seems important. In addition, more thoughtful work is produced because students are required to ponder why they are confused or why they are making a connection, rather than simply coloring the page.

Double-Entry Diary

Students begin this exercise by dividing a sheet of paper in half vertically. In column 1, they record specific information from a text. This might include direct quotations or passages, specific facts or details, or a summary. The right column is for a student's reactions to the text in column 1. This might be a personal reflection, a reaction for or against an argument, a request for clarification, an inference, or a connection. (Tompkins, 2009) Teachers may need to model this exercise, which stimulates metacognition and the deep reading of text. Here is an example.

From Speech before the American Anti-Slavery Society, May 11, 1847 *by Frederick Douglass* *I am very glad to be here. I am very glad to be present at this Anniversary, glad again to mingle my voice with those with whom I have stood identified, with those with whom I have labored, for the last seven years, for the purpose of undoing the burdens of my brethren, and hastening the day of their emancipation.*	*This speech was given before the Civil War!* *We read a bit of his autobiography last year.* *He's talking to people he likes.* *I wonder what the "anniversary" is?* *He identifies with the American Anti-Slavery Society.* *He's been working toward emancipation since 1840. A lot has changed in 172 years.*

Embedding Writing Strategies

Like the reading strategies above, these writing strategies may be adapted to any content area. Remember that most CCSS writing involves responding to a complex text. For more ideas, see the International Center'spublication *Effective Instructional Strategies for Content-Area Writing.*

RAFT (Role-Audience-Format-Topic)

RAFT is a strategy that demonstrates student understanding in a more in-depth manner than chapter questions may. RAFT also allows for more student creativity in subject areas that are traditionally less imaginative. For example, imagining that they are a *plant* writing the *sun* a *thank-you note* explaining the sun's role in a plant's growth is probably more interesting for students than simply answering questions on a worksheet. A *square root* writing a *love letter* to a *whole number* explaining a relationship might seem silly, but it is actually much more challenging than filling in a blank or answering a multiple choice question. RAFT activities help teachers and students move out of Quadrant A learning and toward more rigorous and relevant experiences. RAFT's only limitation is the teacher's imagination.

Steps for Developing a RAFT Task

1. Give students a **role** that helps them apply the knowledge they just learned in class: "You are a _____ in a _____."

2. Give students a problem to solve as a professional that involves applying the concept or **topic** they just learned in class. The **audience** consists of whoever needs the information or has the problem. Outline the problem, including all details needed, so that students understand what is expected of them:

   - What is the situation at work?
   - Who are the others involved?
   - What is the background of the problem?
   - What person or group requires your solution?
   - To whom will you address the solution? etc.

3. Give students options for the solution that include skills they would need in their professional roles. There is no single correct solution. Set it up so that, as students respond in the role, they will apply the topic/concept just learned in class.

   - What do you, the professional, see as possible solutions?
   - What steps will the company or organization or group have to take?
   - What is the most efficient and most effective way to react/respond?
   - What will be the results? Will the problem be solved to the satisfaction of all parties?
   - What will it cost? Is it cost-effective?
   - Who will need convincing?

4. Give students options regarding products and **formats** to generate.

Minute Paper

The Minute Paper strategy works well for short readings. After a reading, students jot down significant points, unanswered questions, and ah-ha's (new information) for application. With that information in hand, students write a quick paper in a minute or two, pulling together all the information they had jotted down. This strategy gives students valuable practice in summarizing and determining key ideas.

Minute Paper

Significant Points
Unanswered Questions
Ah-ha's for Application
My Minute Paper

TFCN and Somebody Wanted But So

Sometimes asking students to write a summary can be an exercise in frustration — it seems that their summaries are longer than the reading itself! That is why TFCN and Somebody Wanted But So are such effective strategies. In fact, they can be so effective that some students consider them "cheat sheets" for summarizing.

TFCN works well for nonfiction readings. Start by giving students the "code": **Topic**, two **Fascinating** facts, **Connections** made, **New** understanding. A TFCN for a global warming article might look like this:

- **T**: Global warming
- **F**: 1. Alaska's average temperature has risen 4°F over the past 50 years.
    2. Ice is 40% thinner in some parts of the Arctic.

- **C:** Our textbook talked about global warming, but the statistics weren't so serious.
- **N:** I think global warming is getting worse.

The paragraph could then read:

> Global warming has caused the Earth's average temperature to rise. Alaska's average temperature has risen 4°F over the last 50 years. This has caused the ice to become 40% in some parts of the Arctic. Our textbook mentioned global warming, but it did not make it seem so bad. I think global warming will only continue to get worse unless we make changes to stop it.

As you can see, it is easy to take the statements from TFCN and pull them together into a one-paragraph summary. This activity gives students a structure to work from.

Somebody Wanted But So is an excellent strategy to use for works of fiction or for certain narrative nonfiction, such as a memoir or autobiography. Here is an example using *The Great Gatsby*:

- **Somebody:** Jay Gatsby.
- **Wanted:** Daisy to marry him.
- **But:** She had already married Tom Buchanan when Gatsby returned from the war.
- **So:** Gatsby built a mansion across the water from the Buchanans in an attempt to win her back.

This information can be compiled into a one- or two-sentence summary. For example, the summary might read thus:

> Jay Gatsby wanted Daisy to marry him, but she had already married Tom Buchanan when Gatsby returned from the war. So Gatsby built a mansion across the water from the Buchanans in an attempt to win her back.

Notice that the exercise does not give away the ending. Adding a "then" to the strategy will allow for the ending to be revealed. This strategy can work with short stories, children's stories, chapters, or entire novels.

What-Why-How

The What-Why-How chart is a good strategy to use for any sort of argument writing. The meaning of each category may vary depending on the task. (Adapted from Peha, 2003.)

Opinion Writing

What	Why	How
(What I believe)	(My reasons)	(Examples)

Responding to a Text

What	Why	How
(My inference)	(My reasons)	(Examples from the text)

Responding to a Writing Prompt

What	Why	How
(My thesis)	(My reasons)	(Evidence from multiple texts and bibliographic references)

Use Assessments to Guide and Differentiate Instruction

The two main assessment consortia — Partnership for Assessment of Readiness for College and Careers (PARCC) and SMARTER Balanced Assessment Consortium — propose assessment throughout the year to provide immediate, actionable data. The proposed systems of assessment are not just for accountability; they are meant to provide data that informs and guides instruction, intervention, and professional development planning.

Preparing for Next Generation Assessments

To prepare students for the new assessments, teachers should start now to make adjustments in instruction. Consider the following ideas to increase rigor and to align instruction with CCSS expectations.

- **Make time for extended reading.** The CCSS expect students to do sustained, independent reading of complex texts. ELA and content-area teachers should start to build in practice for extended reading, whether in the classroom or as homework.

- **Require performance tasks.** Long-term projects, problem solving, and reports based on evidence and research will need to be regular components of every class, at every level.

- **Make classroom tests more rigorous.** Multiple-choice-only tests will not prepare students for the rigor of the NGA. Teachers must learn to create test items that are multistep, have more than one solution, and require application and synthesis skills.

- **Design interdisciplinary lessons.** The CCSS encourage cross-curricular collaboration. Teachers may wish to work together to create interdisciplinary lessons or projects.

- **Shift the learning environment.** Involving all students, using media and technology across disciplines, and expecting more rigorous research projects may require teachers to rethink the design of their classrooms.

- **Consider technological capacity and skill.** Since NGAs will be given on computers, teachers need to ensure that their students are ready and capable of working with the hardware and devices available in your school.

The International Center's online Next Navigator offers digital tools to help teachers develop assessments aligned with the CCSS and NGAs.

Preparing for Performance Tasks

Teachers need to begin to incorporate long-term performance tasks into their classroom assessment of concepts and skills. A quality performance task is:

- **essential**, measuring a key concept or skill
- **valid**, effectively measuring a core standard

- **authentic**, connecting learning to the real world
- **integrative**, synthesizing different aspects of learning
- **engaging**, keeping students involved
- **structured**, with directions and understandable outcomes
- **equitable**, allowing for different learning styles
- **scorable**, using an agreed-upon rubric

There are no specific rules for writing performance tasks. Two examples are found in Chapter 2 on page 26. In those cases, notice that literacy is embedded into the math example, just as it is a key part of the ELA example.

Using Rubrics

Teachers in many content areas are not accustomed to assessing writing. It is essential to develop an easy-to-apply rubric that can be applied consistently by all teachers. Training in the rubric and in evaluating student writing is not a luxury — it is a necessary complement to the rubric. Creating a rubric that works for your district across the curriculum will be a useful step in the development of your literacy initiative.

Teachers might use this process as a guide to design effective rubrics to assess performance tasks.

1. Identify the learning outcome(s) that you are assessing.
2. Identify the types of work that you will evaluate (e.g., essay, drawing, model).
3. Identify the component dimensions of the learning outcome (e.g., organization, argument, vocabulary use).
4. Create descriptors for each dimension (e.g., best possible work, unacceptable work, in-between levels of work).
5. Share the rubric with students to set expectations prior to task completion.

Consider using the following sample rubric as a model.

Score of 6 (Outstanding)	Score of 4 (Competent)
A paper in this category is **outstanding**, demonstrating clear and consistent competence though it may contain occasional errors. Such a paper: • effectively and insightfully develops a point of view • is well organized and fully developed, using clearly appropriate examples to support ideas, reasons, and other evidence • displays consistent facility in the use of language, demonstrating variety in sentence structure and range of vocabulary, and is free of most errors in grammar, usage, and mechanics	A paper in this category is **competent**, demonstrating reasonably consistent mastery, although it will have occasional errors and lapses in quality. Such a paper: • develops a point of view and critical thinking skills • is generally organized and focused, using adequate examples and reasons to support the position • exhibits adequate but inconsistent facility in the use of language, using generally appropriate vocabulary • employs some effective sentence variety, but contains some errors in grammar, usage, and mechanics
Score of 5 (Effective)	**Score of 3 (Inadequate)**
A paper in this category is **effective**, demonstrating reasonably consistent mastery although it will contain occasional errors or lapses in quality. Such a paper: • effectively develops a point of view on the issue and demonstrates strong critical thinking, using examples, reasons, and other evidence • is well organized and focused, demonstrating coherence and a clear progression of ideas • exhibits facility in the use of language, vocabulary, and varied sentence structure • is generally free of errors in grammar, usage, and mechanics	A paper in this category is **inadequate**, but demonstrates developing mastery, and is marked by one or more of the following weaknesses. Such a paper: • develops a point of view on the issue, demonstrating some critical thinking, but may do so inconsistently or may lack adequate examples and support • is limited in its organization or focus and may demonstrate lapses in coherence or the progression of ideas • displays a developing facility in the use of language • lacks variety in sentence structure • contains an accumulation of errors in grammar, diction, or sentence structure

Score of 2 (Seriously Limited)	Score of 1 (Fundamentally Lacking)
An essay in this category is **seriously limited,** demonstrating little mastery, and is flawed by one or more of the following weaknesses. Such a paper contains: • a vague point of view, weak critical thinking • poor organization, inappropriate or limited support • inadequate or inappropriate detail to support ideas • little facility in the use of language (vocabulary, usage, mechanics) • frequent problems in sentence structure • errors in grammar, diction, and sentence structure so serious that meaning is obscured	An essay in this category is **fundamentally lacking,** demonstrating very little or no mastery, and is severely flawed by one or more of the following weaknesses. Such a paper: • develops no viable point of view • provides little or no evidence to support its position • is disorganized or unfocused, is incoherent • contains fundamental errors in vocabulary • contains severe flaws in sentence structure • displays pervasive errors in grammar, usage, or mechanics that persistently interfere with meaning

The Basics of Formative Assessment

The Common Core State Standards recognize the importance of formative as well as summative assessment. Both types of assessment are built into the Next Generation Assessment cycles being produced by state consortia. When teachers use formative assessment, they create formal and informal activities that give them information on whether or not students understand concepts. They give immediate feedback to improve students' achievement of given instructional outcomes.

Using Formative Feedback

The goal of formative feedback is to help students to improve their work in the future. Formative feedback should link to the learning goal, provide guidance for the learner, and describe in simple terms where and why the student has and has not reached the target of the assessment. The best formative feedback is simple, to the point, and directive. Feedback works in both directions. Students learn where their gaps are and how they might fill them in. Teachers learn what is and is not working in terms of their instructional approach to the learning goal.

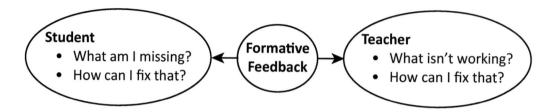

If instruction is not working for all students, teachers should differentiate instruction based on the results of the formative assessment they have used.

For more information on formative assessment and its use in the classroom, see the International Center's handbook *Leveraging Formative Assessment to Improve Instruction*.

Summary

Planning and implementing an embedded literacy initiative is a major undertaking that will include multiple elements. CCSS sets the standards for a much more rigorous curriculum, one that will challenge teachers and students to adjust and adapt to new changes. Teachers need to embrace the notion that all students can and must learn. There should also be an increased emphasis on building strong teacher-student relationships. Teachers who are strong in their content area must develop strength in embedded literacy as well, and they must seize the opportunity to use assessments not only to compare students or measure achievement but also to guide and differentiate instruction.

Questions to Consider

- What observations have you made about the effect of active, respectful student-teacher relationships on the success of students?

- How can teachers work together to incorporate argument writing across the curriculum?

- How might teachers share existing strategies to support a content-area literacy initiative?

References

Bransford, J., Brown, A., and Cocking, R. *How People Learn: Brain, Mind, Experience, and School.* Washington, DC: National Academy Press, 2003.
Online: http://siona.udea.edu.co/~jfduitam/curriculo/doc/How%20people%20learn.pdf

Hattie, John. *Visible Learning: A Synthesis of Over 800 Meta-Analyses Relating to Achievement.* New York: Routledge, 2009.

Mosenthal, P. "Understanding the Strategies of Document Literacy and Their Conditions of Use." *Journal of Educational Psychology* 88: 314–332, 1996.

Peha, S. "The Writing Teacher's Strategy Guide." Teaching That Makes Sense, 2003.
Online: http://www.ttms.org/PDFs/01%20Writing%20Strategy%20Guide%20v001%20 (Full).pdf

Tompkins, Gail E. *Literacy for the 21st Century,* 5th ed. Upper Saddle River, NJ: Prentice Hall, 2009.

Zmuda, A. "Springing into Active Learning," *Educational Leadership* 66: 32–37, 2008.

Chapter 6

Successful Practices

Since 1991, the International Center for Leadership in Education has observed and supported hundreds of schools as they have undertaken major transformations in literacy instruction. Every school has tackled the problem somewhat differently, and our conclusion is that there is no single right way to develop a rigorous, relevant, and dynamic literacy program. In fact, it may be the case that every school needs to find its own way, taking ideas and inspiration from programs that have already succeeded. In this chapter, we will examine some of the different approaches that have been successful.

The Brockton Literacy Initiative—Part I: Creating a Shared Vision

The shaping of Brockton High School's philosophy and vision can be traced to many factors: state education reform, a change in leadership, and faculty and community concerns about low student performance levels. While external mandates provided the original stimulus, the faculty and administration injected a new level of professional stimulus by establishing the restructuring committee to lead the change process within the school. This change across the school community was both structural and substantive, impacting instruction and assessment, which in turn significantly impacted the performance of students.

In the process of becoming a strong learning community, the school's stakeholders adopted a common vision, goals, language, and behaviors. Many teachers were themselves educated in the Brockton, Massachusetts, schools and are part of their long tradition of athletic champions. While that tradition continues, now — alongside the usual recognition of athletic accomplishments displayed throughout the buildings — visitors will find an equal number of banners, certificates, and trophies representing academic, vocational, and fine arts accomplishments. This widespread and fundamental change can be attributed to a literacy initiative that began in 1995 and was spearheaded by the administration and a restructuring committee.

The restructuring committee was charged with the two goals of increasing student achievement levels and personalizing the education experience. The outgrowth of the committee's work has necessitated a comprehensive, consistent, and sustained staff development program. Staff development, the committee determined, is critical to the continuing success of the school as it shifts to a culture that demands higher expectations for student achievement. With this vision in mind, professional development now focuses on student needs. Unified by their common vision, teachers identify schoolwide goals and results while still expressing pride in the achievement of individual departments.

Need for Action

The schoolwide literacy initiative has been the most significant factor in the academic success story of Brockton, a large, urban high school with a diverse student population. Despite challenging demographics, Brockton has transformed itself from an underperforming school into a model that has garnered awards and recognition at both state and national levels because of its literacy initiative.

State Requirements

When Massachusetts first instituted its high-stakes assessment, Brockton's scores on the Massachusetts Comprehensive Assessment System (MCAS), the statewide standards-based assessment program, were dismal. In English language arts, 44 percent of the students failed, and only 22 percent reached proficiency. In math, the story was even more disheartening. In the first year of the assessment's administration, 76 percent of Brockton students failed the math MCAS and only 7 percent reached proficiency.

Eight years later, the statistics tell a very different story. In English language arts, Brockton reduced its failure rate 39 percentage points, from 44 percent to only 5 percent, and dramatically increased the percentage of student reaching proficiency by 52 percentage points, from 22 percent to 74 percent. In math, the results were also impressive. The failure rate has been reduced by 60 percentage points, from 76 percent to 16 percent, and the percentage of students reaching proficiency increased by 47 percentage points, from 7 percent to 54 percent.

In Massachusetts, a student must pass the MCAS in order to earn a diploma; there are *no* exemptions. At Brockton High, the minority population is approximately 71 percent, over a third of the students do not speak English as their first language, and the poverty level is extremely high, with 72 percent of students receiving free or reduced-price lunch. Nevertheless, all students are expected to succeed.

Although many initiatives and reform efforts have contributed to Brockton's turnaround, the most important reform was the establishment of clearly defined literacy goals for the entire building. At Brockton, every faculty member in every discipline is held responsible for teaching literacy skills in reading, writing, speaking, and reasoning to every student. This effort was the school's core commitment and the rallying point for the entire staff of teachers, counselors, and administrators.

Defining Literacy for Brockton High School

Using state standards and teacher perceptions of what students should demonstrate in order to be successful for state testing, college applications, and career preparation, the restructuring committee defined literacy in four areas: reading, writing, speaking, and reasoning. Four charts were prepared to guide the next steps in the process.

The development of the charts was no easy task. The definition of literacy for each area needed to be clear, concise, and most importantly, understandable to teachers in every discipline. It was crucial for the four literacy skills to apply across disciplines and crucial that every teacher could see the skills as necessary for their students' success in each subject area.

Each literacy chart illustrates a literacy skill (reading, writing, speaking, or reasoning) at the center, with the content area disciplines that support the skill branching off from the center. Beneath each chart, the achievement goals for each area are listed in terms of the specific skills that students are expected to acquire.

Literacy Chart: Reading

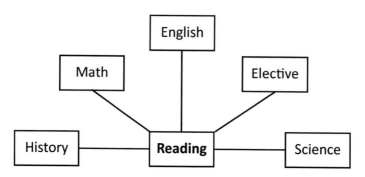

- to read for content (both literal and inferential)
- to apply pre-reading, during-reading, and post-reading strategies to all reading assignments, including determinations of pre-learning vocabulary and the text's purpose
- to research a topic
- to gather information
- to comprehend an argument
- to determine the main idea of a passage
- to understand a concept and construct meaning
- to expand one's experience

Literacy Chart: Writing

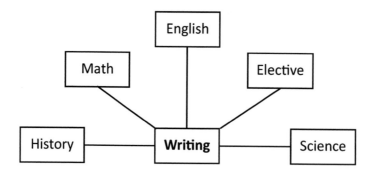

- to take notes
- to explain one's thinking
- to argue a thesis and support one's thinking
- to compare and contrast
- to write an open response
- to describe an experiment, report one's findings, and report one's conclusion
- to generate a response to what one has read, viewed, or heard
- to convey one's thinking in complete sentences
- to develop an expository essay with a formal structure

Literacy Chart: Speaking

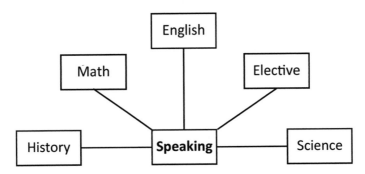

- to convey one's thinking in complete sentences
- to interpret a passage orally
- to debate an issue
- to participate in class discussion or a public forum
- to make an oral presentation to one's class, one's peers, one's community
- to present one's portfolio
- to respond to what one has read, viewed, or heard
- to communicate in a manner that allows one to be both heard and understood

Literacy Chart: Reasoning Skills

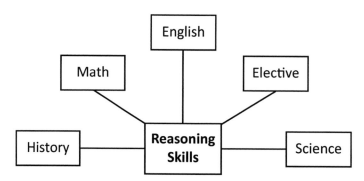

- to create, interpret, and explain a table, chart, or graph
- to compute, interpret, and explain numbers
- to read, break down, and solve a word problem
- to interpret and present statistics that support an argument or hypothesis
- to identify a pattern, explain a pattern, and/or make a prediction based on a pattern
- to detect the fallacy in an argument or a proof
- to explain the logic of an argument or solution
- to use analogies and/or evidence to support one's thinking
- to explain and/or interpret relationships of space and time

By having a central focus for all teachers, Brockton was able to achieve a dramatic change in the level of expectation for student success.

Like many high schools, Brockton had always been a traditional comprehensive high school with clearly defined departments and very little cross-disciplinary instruction or learning. Organizing instruction through literacy skills, however, marked a dramatic change in the culture of the school. Still, agreeing on the schoolwide concept in order to develop the restructuring committee's charts represented only the initial step. Much more work still needed to be done.

Gaining Cooperation

After numerous drafts, the restructuring committee was satisfied with the literacy charts and sought the input of the entire faculty. In small interdisciplinary faculty discussion groups facilitated by members of the restructuring committee, the faculty offered many suggestions.

After taking the input of the faculty as a whole, the restructuring committee again revised the charts. While the charts are specific to a literacy skill area, they are phrased to provide interdisciplinary applications for those particular literacy skills. The following examples demonstrate how the literacy skills are applicable to each content area:

- **Reading:** to read for content, to gather information, to comprehend an argument
- **Writing:** to take notes, to explain one's thinking, to generate a response to what one has read, viewed, or heard
- **Speaking:** to convey one's thinking in complete sentences, to interpret a passage orally, to debate an issue
- **Reasoning:** to create, interpret, and explain a table, chart, or graph; to interpret or present statistics that support an argument or hypothesis; to use analogies and/or evidence to support one's thinking

Before finalizing the literacy charts, the school council (composed of administration, faculty, students, parents, and members of the community) provided critical input. One member of the council, the chairman of the region's Chamber of Commerce, said that if students possessed these skills, they would be career as well as college ready. This was a powerful endorsement for the literacy initiative.

Once the literacy skills were finalized, the greater challenge lay ahead — namely, how to train a faculty of over 300 teachers representing every content area discipline on how to teach these skills. With the new vision in place, the literacy skills detailed in the literacy charts now represented the school's core learning goals. The following list suggests how to win the willing cooperation of your team for such an ambitious project.

Key Factors in Gaining Cooperation
- Analyzing the data
- Opening the discussion of "what is working and not working"

- Deciding to limit the focus to literacy
- Articulating the meaning and scope of literacy
- Selecting the application of reading, writing, speaking, and reasoning to all disciplines
- Continuing communications between the restructuring committee and the entire staff
- Granting the restructuring committee the decision-making power to guide the initiative

Train the Trainer: Faculty Meetings Become Literacy Workshops

The restructuring committee knew that its work was viewed with skepticism. Faculty members and members of the committee had encountered several negative attitudes that needed addressing:

- "We are not reading specialists."
- "What can we expect from our student with their backgrounds and lack of language skills?"
- "Our students do not have the skills necessary to do high school work."
- "We do not have the full support of teachers to try new things."
- "This is the latest 'flavor of the month' and we will be off to another project within a few short months."
- "We can't speak for all the teachers and staff."
- "We are doing the best job possible with what we have to work with."
- "I will be able to retire in a few years so I am holding tight."
- "I am working hard but getting few returns for my efforts."

Have you heard these concerns before? As the meetings began, when the members of the restructuring committee heard these concerns, they asked themselves, "What is possible for us to accomplish this year?"

At this point, Principal Szachowicz described the ongoing process of training and gaining faculty buy-in:

As difficult as it was to define literacy, far more challenging was training the faculty in how to teach these skills. As a former history teacher myself, I could identify with how difficult it would be; I had never been trained to teach reading and writing. The challenges were myriad. First the restructuring committee had to figure out where to begin. There were many skills identified in the four literacy areas of reading, writing, speaking, and reasoning. Student performance on the MCAS needed to be improved. There were no in-service days in the contract for training. And perhaps the greatest challenge of all would be in taking on the resistance of the faculty. Throughout the school there were negative undercurrents. Comments such as, "I'm a biology teacher, not an English teacher," and "It's not my job to teach reading and writing; I teach art" could be heard.

This is where the restructuring committee's examination of the data was critical. Because so much of the MCAS exam involved student writing, and because our students scored so low in every writing question, the restructuring committee selected writing as our first area of focus and targeted the skill "to write an open response." On the MCAS, students are asked to read a difficult passage, to answer multiple-choice questions on the reading, and then to complete an "open response" on the passage, which essentially asks the student to construct a response, essentially a short essay, to a question on the reading.

Writing Open-Response Questions

The restructuring committee next faced these questions:

- Which of the four areas of literacy (reading, writing, speaking, and reasoning) should we address first?
- Which area represents the greatest need based on the available data?
- Which area will teachers and counselors accept most readily?

The answer to these questions was indeed clearly writing with a specific focus on the open-response aspect of the MCAS English test. After the restructuring committee made this decision, the next faculty meeting was devoted to reviewing a copy of the writing test results and the test itself. Teachers quickly honed in on the low performance in the open-response section that challenged most students. As a result of the meeting, a general agreement emerged from the faculty to focus on improving the students' ability to complete the open-response portion of the writing test successfully.

Key to the success of the writing initiative was the implementation plan. The restructuring committee asked a small group of its members to produce a script to help train the trainers for the full faculty's training. This script is another key to the success of the initiative — trainers were trained using a common language that all faculty members followed. A common vision requires a common vocabulary. Each student would follow the same 10 steps in the open-response format:

1.   Read the question carefully.
2.   Circle or underline key words.
3.   Restate the question as a thesis.
4.   Read the passage carefully.
5.   Take notes that respond to the question, brainstorm, and then map out your answer.
6.   Complete your thesis.
7.   Write a response using your map carefully.
8.   Strategically repeat the key words from your thesis into the body and end sentences.
9.   Paragraph your response.
10.   Reread and edit your response.

Principal Szachowicz describes how the process unfolded:

A subcommittee of the restructuring committee met and drafted a script of a "literacy workshop" for the faculty on open-response writing. It seemed a daunting challenge because this workshop had to have a number of important components. First, the workshop needed to define what open-response writing means for teachers in every discipline. Next, every teacher needed to learn how to teach open-response writing in a specific step-by-step approach. Then and perhaps most importantly, every teacher needed to learn how to assess open responses according to a school-wide rubric.

Once the training script was developed, the subcommittee tried it out on the entire restructuring committee. We critiqued the workshop, revised it, and improved it until we felt it was ready to be presented to the entire faculty. Because there are no in-services or professional development days in our contract, we had to work within the constraints of the contract; we used the two faculty meetings per month, each one hour in length by contract, to accomplish this training. Members of the restructuring committee worked in training teams to present the "Literacy Workshop: Teaching Open-Response Writing."

In the first training session in October, the faculty was divided into interdisciplinary groups of approximately 25 teachers per group. Because the workshop was carefully scripted to model how teachers should teach open-response writing to their students, every teacher received exactly the same highly interactive presentation. Teachers were shown examples of open-response questions, they went through the writing process step-by-step, and they were shown an assessment process using the rubric.

Two weeks later, a follow-up literacy workshop was held with teachers in their specific departments. The purpose of this workshop was to plan the implementation of open-response writing within the content areas. Department heads were paired with restructuring committee members to run these meetings. Essentially, teachers had to ask themselves how to create an open-response writing lesson for their students that supported their content and followed the 10-step format. After these two literacy workshops, the school was ready to begin the implementation.

The script also provided training for teachers to work with students who were writing thesis statements, using active reading strategies, understanding key words in essay questions, and applying an assessment rubric. The training then cascaded from a small group who prepared the script to the entire faculty, according to this sequence:

- A subgroup of the restructuring committee prepared the script.
- The subgroup tried out the script by training a trainer from the restructuring committee.
- The script was revised based on comments and suggestions from the restructuring committee.
- The trainers presented open-response training for the faculty at the monthly meeting.
- The departments reviewed the material and for each discipline applied examples of open-response material as well as steps to follow.
- The principal prepared a schedule of open-response instruction.
- The assessment rubric followed the calendar of instruction.

Observations from Principal Szachowicz provide valuable insights on how the process unfolded at the school:

> After the training of the entire faculty in open-response writing was complete, I was in the position of Associate Principal for Curriculum and Instruction at the time and had the positional authority to ensure the implementation timeline. Because the restructuring committee believed that for this initiative to be successful (i.e., our students would improve their writing and MCAS scores), the students would have to practice open-response writing over and over again. The implementation plan would follow the schedule of the students.
>
> A calendar of implementation was created so that every couple of weeks the students would repeat the lesson in their different classes. Although the content of the open-response writing assignment would vary depending upon the subject, the format would be exactly the same. No department and no teacher were exempt. For example, the first week in November was assigned to the Science Department. Every science teacher during that week had to teach the open-response writing lesson using his or her content. The teacher could select the reading to be used; it needed to be a challenging nonfiction piece that supported the teacher's content for the lesson.
>
> The open-response writing format was prescribed. Students had to write using the specific open-response steps, and teachers had to assess the students' writing using the rubric. A couple of weeks later, another department was designated to do the same thing. For example, the History Department was designated to teach the open-response writing assignment in the last week in November. Every history teacher selected a difficult nonfiction passage that supported the student's content objective and used that reading to teach the open-response lesson — same format, same rubric, just different content.
>
> After another couple of weeks, the open-response lesson went to another department, then another, then another until every department had taught the open-response lesson. Each department followed the journey of the student as the year progressed. Over and over again, the student had an open-response lesson. How does a student master a difficult skill? Practice, practice, practice.

In retrospect, the success of the writing initiative was due to many elements, including:

- an effective implementation plan
- a small group of restructuring committee members producing a script to help train the trainers for the full faculty's training
- trainers using a common language so that all faculty members heard the same message
- no one being exempt — every teacher was trained and teachers in every content area participated
- students learning the writing process in several classes
- administrators monitoring the implementation process in classrooms
- student work being reviewed and critiqued in department meetings
- students practicing a skill many times over the course of the year in order to master it; by the time the testing occurred in the spring, the students were ready

Key Factors in the Training Model

- A small group prepared the script to ensure that everyone heard the same message.
- Scripts were tried, then revised based on reactions.
- Instruction on the target issue (i.e., open response) was expected in all classrooms over time and followed an implementation schedule.
- A common rubric was employed across the disciplines.
- A process of evaluation and feedback was used to determine the level of application in the classroom.
- Positive outcomes were celebrated as student performance increased.

Questions to Consider about the Training Process

- Who is best prepared to provide training for the faculty?
- How will the leadership team ensure the quality of training for all faculty members?
- What process will be used to determine the level of instruction in classrooms?
- How will new teachers receive training in the future?

Monitoring the Process

It was not sufficient to train the faculty to implement a writing method. Essential to the process was a method of monitoring that provided a measure of quality control. At this school, the monitoring came through a prescribed process for examining student work samples across all disciplines.

After teachers completed the writing lesson during their assigned week, student writing samples were collected and assessed using the schoolwide rubric developed by the restructuring committee. After teachers completed the assessment process, student work samples were sent to the department head. This step gave the department head an opportunity to examine the quality of the assignment and the quality of student work within each department. In many cases, the student work samples led to powerful conversations among members of the same department about expectations and grading procedures. The examination of student work was a key component in the success of this initiative, particularly in determining how to define, schoolwide, what constitutes acceptable levels of student work.

Once the department head examined student work samples, folders of student work were sent to the associate principal, who reviewed the samples to ensure attention to schoolwide standards. Although the rubric represented a schoolwide standard, the application and use of the rubric varied initially. This variation led to a meeting of the entire administrative team to discuss how to maintain consistency across disciplines and thus raise standards across the school. From this meeting, a literacy workshop on how to define proficiency was developed.

The associate principal not only reviewed the samples but, based on her observations, also provided individual feedback to teachers. For example, teachers were encouraged to ask higher level questions in their writing prompts and to provide higher quality feedback to the students. Essentially, the success of the open-response writing initiative has been due in large part to its well-structured, well-planned implementation followed by a careful monitoring process. Before and after teachers across content areas apply a rubric such as the following one, consider how your team will monitor progress.

Open-Response Assessment

Writer's Name:	Date:	
Content	**Form**	
8 • Response contains a clear thesis and insightfully answers all parts of the question. • Response provides relevant and specific textual evidence. • Explanations of evidence are clear and accurate, and demonstrate superior understanding of the material.	**4** • Response contains sophisticated and effective use of transitions and strategic repetition indicating complete control of the material. • Response is logically and effectively organized in its thesis, paragraphing, and sequencing of examples. • Response contains clear sentence structure with few or no errors.	
6 • Response contains a clear thesis and adequately answers all parts of the question. • Response provides relevant but general textual evidence. • Explanations of evidence are mostly clear and accurate and demonstrate good understanding of the material.	**3** • Response contains adequate but simplistic use of transitions and strategic repetition. • Response is organized in its thesis, paragraphing, and sequencing of examples. • Response contains clear sentence structure with no distracting errors.	**Legibility** **1** • Easy to read **0** • Difficult to read
4 • Response contains a thesis but only partially answers the question. • Response provides a mix of accurate and inaccurate textual evidence. • Explanations of evidence are vague and/or demonstrate limited understanding of the material.	**2** • Response contains some inappropriate use of transitions and strategic repetition. • Response demonstrates lapses in the organization of its thesis, paragraphing, and/or sequencing of examples. • Response contains lapses in sentence structure that interfere with the clarity of thought.	

Open-Response Assessment (Continued)

Writer's Name:	Date:	
Content	**Form**	
2 • Response contains a thesis but only minimally answers the question. • Response provides insufficient and/or largely inaccurate textual evidence. • Explanations of evidence are unclear and/or demonstrate minimal understanding of the material.	**1** • Response contains incorrect or inadequate use of transitions and strategic repetition. • Response reflects minimal organization of its thesis, paragraphing, and/or sequencing of examples. • Response contains major errors in sentence structure.	**Length** **1** • Sufficient **0** • Insufficient
0 • Response is incorrect. • Response contains insufficient evidence to show understanding of the material. • Response is off-topic and/or contains irrelevant content.	**0** • Response contains no evidence of transitions and strategic repetition. • Response reflects no organization. • Response contains little to no evidence of sentence structure.	

Evaluated by: (Circle One) Self Peer Teacher
Scoring 13–14 = Advanced 11–12 = Proficient 8–10 = Needs Improvement 0–7 = Failing Total Score: _____
Comments:

Brockton High School

Questions to Consider About Monitoring

- What role will departments play in applying learned skills for each subject area?
- Who will develop rubrics for each instructional activity?
- How is feedback provided to teachers?
- What role will the administration play in providing feedback to teachers?
- Will student work be reviewed across disciplines as part of the monitoring?

The Brockton Literacy Initiative—Part 2: Becoming Part of the Culture

Because of the success of the open-response training, the restructuring committee followed the same implementation plan for the other literacy skills (reading, speaking, and reasoning). The restructuring committee first examined the data to determine what would be the next literacy skill they should target. They followed the same training format and sequence:

- Create the script.
- Practice on each other.
- Use two faculty meetings consecutively for literacy workshops.
- Organize the first workshop in interdisciplinary groups to introduce the literacy skill and teach the process.
- Plan the second workshop two weeks later, and have faculty meet by department.
- Implement direct instruction using a calendar developed by departments.
- Assess student work using the newly developed rubric.
- Forward student work to the department heads and the associate principal.

The changing culture within the school led the teachers and staff to anticipate further training that could assist their efforts in producing higher levels of student learning. The more positive attitudes were the result of shared decision making along with the demonstrated success of the process. Students were succeeding at higher performance levels. Teachers felt that their hard work was having a greater impact on students. As one teacher commented, "I continue to work hard, but with the new skills and strategies available for my use through the workshops, I have a greater sense of my self-worth."

Based on the success of the initial literacy workshops, additional topics continue to be addressed. Successful training sequences include:

- Using Active Reading Strategies
- Analyzing Difficult Reading
- Difficult Reading/Responding to Challenging Questions
- Using Summarizing Strategies
- Previewing a Text Using the Table of Contents
- Using Visuals to Preview a Chapter
- Teaching the Text Backwards
- Decoding Vocabulary in Context
- Analyzing Graphs and Charts
- Teaching Multiple-Choice Strategies
- Helping English Language Learners to Achieve Academic Competence
- Developing Speaking Skills
- Connecting Literacy Activities
- Assessment: Checking for Understanding

The literacy workshops are a part of the literacy notebook, which each teacher owns. New teachers are trained every year in all of the literacy skills so they are ready to teach with a schoolwide focus.

After much hard work, the literacy initiative has become an integral part of the culture of the school. The literacy charts are not simply wall decorations; they are posted in every classroom, and teachers must use at least one literacy objective every day in their classes. The literacy objective(s) and the content objective must also be noted in daily lesson plans. Simply put, the literacy initiative forms the core of learning at Brockton High School.

Reading Comprehension Strategies

Based on its successful implementation of the open-response writing process across the school, the restructuring committee refocused its efforts on the second literacy area of reading. The teachers now understood how the literacy initiative fit into to their individual disciplines. Seeing for themselves its positive impact on student performance, they decided to use the same planning process as before, a choice that helped to move the teachers forward quickly.

Teachers appreciated how the hands-on approach of the training demonstrated practical applications and instructional strategies that could be incorporated immediately in their classrooms. An indirect but critical byproduct noted by staff was the improvement of student engagement and the reduction of discipline problems in classrooms. Students were beginning to take more responsibility for their own learning now that the steps in the writing process were posted in every room and were used in all disciplines. Students, in essence, were "getting it" because of repetition and direct teaching.

Active Reading Strategies

The restructuring committee began developing scripts and strategies to bring "active reading" into the everyday life of Brockton High. The members of the committee targeted research-based strategies that would help both struggling students and those students needing specific guidance with reading comprehension of nonfiction, textbooks, and other difficult content passages. A fact of life in the school was that many students, when faced with reading assignments beyond their ability or skills to "break open," simply shut down, gave up, and resorted to daydreaming or other off-task behaviors.

The committee decided to provide a base understanding among teachers about what reading is and to demonstrate some basic, active reading strategies that are designed to help students process texts independently. To accomplish these objectives, a subgroup of the committee prepared material for the training sessions that would:

- Establish an understanding of how students process information — *What is reading?*
- Demonstrate select strategies that are designed to engage students — *What are active reading strategies?*

- Outline specific direct teaching procedures — *What can we do in our classrooms?*
- Implement these reading techniques in different disciplines — *How will this align with my current teaching and materials?*

Literacy strategies that were used included the following:

Think-Pair-Share. The workshop training for teachers used the literacy strategy *Think-Pair-Share* to address the question, "What is your definition of reading?" Using this activity among themselves led teachers to understand its application to vocabulary development as critical for content comprehension, whatever the content. (Kagan, 1994*)*

Think-Pair-Share follows a four-step sequence:

1. Students define each word on their own.
2. Students share their definitions, either in pairs or small groups, to derive better definitions.
3. Each pair or group shares its definitions with the class.
4. The teacher facilitates the class in developing a class definition specific to the reading material.

Several teachers were already using this activity and could provide insights into its application to their own subject areas. The message delivered in the training was that as experts in a content area, they needed to show students which tools were most useful in accessing the content and to show them how to use these tools each day. Four essential elements were highlighted for the area of Comprehension Instruction:

1. **Assess** the text that students are expected to read.
   - Is the text interesting and pertinent to the instructional goal?
   - Is the text written at a reading level that is appropriate to students' skill levels?
2. **Model** your thinking process.
   - As an expert reader, identify what you do to make sense of text. (Read aloud.)
   - Share this information and demonstrate "how you process" texts.

- Help students understand how good readers and writers process texts and the interpretive options they have in working with a text.

- Provide information to struggling students about what they need and can do.

3. **Define** a purpose for the reading.

  - Help students find a clear reason for reading and an understanding of how information in the reading will be used.

  - Suggest how to vary their reading speed, as needed, and how to determine what needs to be remembered.

4. **Teach** students how to "hold" (retain and apply) their thinking.

  - Identify how students might respond *before, during,* and *after* reading a text.

  - Demonstrate active strategies for asking questions while reading, making connections to previous knowledge, giving an opinion, drawing a conclusion, making a summary statement, drawing a diagram, and creating a graphic organizer based on the reading of texts.

3-2-1 Strategy. At the end of the training session, teachers participated in one final strategy that also applied directly to the classroom, entitled 3-2-1. Teachers were asked to indicate the following information as a "pass to leave" the session:

- **3** things I have learned about teaching reading in my content area
- **2** things I could implement immediately in my classroom
- **1** question I still have and would like to discuss

Additional Active Reading Strategies

During the next two years, the teachers participated in training on strategies such as summarizing, previewing, using visuals and graphs, "teaching reading last," developing vocabulary, improving comprehension, writing multiple-choice questions, and developing listening skills. The same process was used that, at this stage of the initiative, was clearly established as an important part of the school's learning culture:

- Review data.
- Identify target skills.

- Develop scripts to guide training.
- Train all staff followed by department sessions.
- Apply training in all classrooms.
- Monitor use by the staff.

Summarizing is a difficult task to teach students because it involves reasoning skills and processing information. The teaching of summarization was described to staff as a process of helping students construct an overall understanding of the text by means of recalling and reorganizing only the most important pieces of information, thereby demonstrating a thorough comprehension of the material. Again, the teachers followed a series of steps to develop a summary statement:

- Define the purpose for reading by determining the main idea and the supporting details.
- Scan the text for repetitions of key vocabulary (nouns).
- Read the text actively, keeping the purpose in mind.
- Take notes using a graphic organizer to record phrases, your own words, and key vocabulary.
- Add the main ideas from your notes using established "criteria for summary." Criteria for a summary are:
  - including key vocabulary
  - using your own words
  - focusing only on the main ideas
  - developing the summary logically to show the sequence of the summarized text

Students receive a "Sum It Up" sheet to list the main ideas and supporting details, including space for their summary statement. Twenty blank lines at the bottom of the page encourage students to reduce the number of words to the most critical and important ones.

Students receive uniform instructions from each teacher about the use of a "Sum it Up" sheet:

- Obtain a "Sum it Up" sheet.
- Read the entire selection and as you read, list the main idea words on your sheet.
- Write a summary of the selection using as many main idea words as possible. Put one word in each blank at the bottom of the page. Imagine you have only $2.00 and that each word you use is worth 10 cents.
- Now, "sum it up" in 20 words.

Previewing was the next strategy presented. Teachers reviewed their own textbook and other printed material used for instruction. Reviewing the text, they highlighted features built into their texts that could help students process the information presented. Teachers discussed various ways of using the table of contents, glossary, summary paragraphs, highlighted vocabulary, key questions, charts and graphs, organizational patterns, and pictures. Teachers were asked, "Now, thinking about your own knowledge of the text's subject matter, your own interests, and your own strengths and weaknesses as a student, write your response to the following questions:

- What units would be the most difficult for you to learn? Why?
- Which unit do you feel most confident learning? Why?
- Which unit interests you the most? Why?
- Identify three ways you plan to help your students use the structure and organization of the textbook in your classroom.

Staff Development Moves on to Math (Reasoning) Strategies

The successful rollout of staff development by the restructuring committee can be characterized by the following important actions:

- taking a leadership role, but not without maintaining effective communication with the entire faculty and staff
- consistently returning to data analysis as the starting point for identifying needs within the instructional program

- proposing practical, hands-on suggestions (strategies) that could be used in all disciplines and by all teachers
- providing consistent training (scripts) and follow-up procedures (monitoring the use of the strategies in the classrooms)
- recognizing the improvements and efforts of the staff
- holding student needs as the prime force for continuing to change the culture

This direct instructional approach is evident in a statement from the training script provided at the beginning of the training:

> We know that we have had success when we are willing to take on a skill we know needs to be improved. As we review the results of the MCAS, we see improvements because students have been taught the steps in open response in all discipline areas. In math, we see the students leave many questions blank. This workshop responds to the many observations you made that reading may be difficult for our students. The active reading strategies that will be presented today will help our students break down and analyze questions they find confusing and overwhelming.

At this stage, all teachers had reviewed copies of previous math tests to identify what they felt were the skills needed for student success, what the state data indicated were strengths and weaknesses, and what could be done via a whole-school effort to improve performance. The faculty received feedback at the next meeting. The goal of the feedback was to ensure that they were invested in continuing to change the culture toward one of continuous learning, with the ultimate shared purpose of helping "our kids." Observations from the previous meeting were displayed for the staff's consideration:

Key observations from teachers:

1. The level of vocabulary on the test is difficult.
2. The test demands that students have strong reading skills.
3. Many problems and questions involve multiple steps.
4. Many visuals appear in the test, including graphs, charts, and drawings.

Frequently mentioned observations:

1. The test requires strategies for pulling out relevant information.
2. Estimation and approximation occur repeatedly.
3. Students do not know how to use the reference sheets.

To guide all teachers in applying active reading steps to math, the math department offered its expertise. At the end of two training sessions, all teachers were expected to include in their classrooms a six-step process for students to follow when answering questions based on an assigned reading:

1. Read the question carefully.
2. Circle key direction words such as *write, draw, explain,* and *compare.*
3. Underline important information. (Some information will be irrelevant to finding the correct answer.)
4. Write in your own words what the question is asking you to do.
5. Decide how you plan to address the question.
6. Answer the question.

The direct application in each classroom was stressed during training; emphasis was placed on the need to model the process using content material and direct teaching. The script used by the trainers read:

- Try these strategies by modeling them for your students. To do so, use test questions, homework assignments, or an example of writing in your content area(s).
- Remember that we are asking you to use readings and assignments in your own subject areas, not to create something new with your students in order to use these strategies.
- Give students credit for showing the reading process in their work.
- Make these strategies a regular expectation when students submit assignments.

Speaking and Civility

The staff also discussed ways to encourage civility among students and classrooms. They agreed to have students speak in complete sentences, cite the text rather than opinion, and raise their hands before speaking. Students accepted these requests since they had themselves identified the "trouble caused by some students who interrupt the rest of us." A schoolwide policy was put into effect that made students leave street language outside the school, maintain eye contact when speaking to an adult, and treat adults and fellow students with respect. Visitors to the school now frequently comment on the level of respect shown by students: they open doors, maintain eye contact, and speak in complete sentences.

Within classrooms, teachers increased the amount of group work as a means to increase rigor. With role models and uniform guidelines in all classrooms, the effectiveness of group work increased. For each group, the guidelines established the following roles and tasks. Each guideline served a useful purpose.

- Everyone is a Recorder (ensures all writing employs the complete sentence format)
- Voice Monitor (keeps the noise level down)
- Timer (makes sure the group completes the task on time)
- Spokesperson (reports the group's findings to the class)
- Participation Monitor (makes sure each member of the group participates)
- Writing Monitor (makes sure all members have the same material copied down in their notebooks)

Speaking Strategies

At this point, teachers asked for additional examples of methods to encourage speaking, full participation, and group interaction. To meet this request, the restructuring committee found simple, direct activities that all content area teachers would find acceptable and would use. As part of the program to teach the speaking area of literacy, the training focused on setting up classroom procedures for *Four Corners* and *Inner and Outer Circle/Full Class* discussions.

Four Corners. For this activity, students individually prepare responses to a topic question and then divide into four groups. Each group chooses a recorder and spokesperson and is sent to one corner to work and prepare a group response. These observations are listed on chart paper and are reported back to the full class for discussion.

Inner and Outer Circle/Full Class. Students are again directed to prepare their individual reactions to a question. Half of the class sits in the inner circle while the remaining students are arranged in the outer circle. The inner circle students speak for five minutes; the outer circle students take two minutes to discuss. The roles are then reversed for the discussion of the second question: five minutes for the new inner circle students and two minutes for the new outer circle group. In the full class format, students face each other, raise their hands to speak, speak in complete sentences, and respond to the previous speaker with "I agree," "I disagree," or "I would like to add."

Oral presentations add another dimension to the speaking literacy effort. An emphasis is placed on supporting shy students, encouraging full participation, listening respectfully, and using the following evaluation rubric to guide grading.

English Language Learners—Increasing Comprehensibility

The large number of ELL students in Brockton, as might be expected, demanded the careful attention of teachers. The literacy initiative addressed this issue with special training. The faculty worked with three principal needs: to increase comprehensibility, to increase interaction, and to increase thinking skills, all of which are crucial objectives that enable ELL students to perform well in the classroom. So that the message to the students was understandable, effective teachers adjusted their speech and classroom activities as necessary.

Three principles for instruction that were kept in mind were:

1. **Comprehensibility.** ELL students experience difficulty understanding new material if presented by lecture and text only. Teachers must provide multiple clues to meaning. (See the Oral Presentation Rubric that follows.)

2. **Interaction.** ELL students perform best in one-on-one interactions or small groups. Peer interaction is especially helpful. Because the language of peers is less complex it provides greater opportunities for interaction.

3. **Thinking Skills.** Language and processing skills need to be explicitly taught and modeled using strategies such as *think-aloud, graphic organizers,* and *questioning techniques.*

ORAL PRESENTATION RUBRIC

Presenter:_____ Evaluator:_____

Literacy in Speaking:
- **to make an oral presentation to one's class**
- **to communicate in a manner that allows one to be both heard and understood**
- **to convey one's thinking in complete sentences**

SPEAKING SKILLS	All elements present	Most elements present	Some elements present	No elements present
Delivery (Presenter doesn't rush, shows enthusiasm, avoids *likes, ums, kind ofs, you knows, etc.* Uses complete sentences.)	4	3	2	
Eye Contact (Presenter keeps head up, does not read, and speaks to whole audience.)	4	3	2	1
Posture (Presenter stands up straight, faces audience, and doesn't fidget.)	4	3	2	1
Volume (Presenter can be easily heard by all. No gum, etc.	4	3	2	1

CONTENT	All elements present	Most elements present	Some elements present	No elements present
Introduction Presentation begins with a clear focus/thesis.	4	3	2	1
Topic Development				
a. Presentation includes all elements previously determined by the teacher.	4	3	2	1
b. Presentation is clearly organized. (Material is logically sequenced, related to thesis, and not repetitive.)	4	3	2	1
c. Presentation shows full grasp and understanding of the material.	4	3	2	1
Conclusion				
a. Presentation highlights key ideas and concludes with a strong final statement.	4	3	2	1
b. Presenter fields questions easily.	4	3	2	1

TOTAL NUMBER OF POINTS:

35 – 40 = A	29 – 34 = B	23 – 28 = C	17 – 22 = D	10 – 16 = F

* Evaluator: Place comments beside each descriptor

Teaching the Text Backwards

Another training session applied to all students but contained special applications for ELL and special needs students. Teaching the text backwards asks teachers to:

- build background for the content material by accessing prior knowledge
- start from the concrete and progress to the abstract
- establish a purpose for reading
- identify criteria to indicate when a student has processed the information successfully

Teach the Text Backwards

Traditional Method	Backwards Method
Read the text.	Do selected applications based on concepts.
Do vocabulary activities.	Discuss concepts.
Answer the guiding questions.	Answer the guiding questions.
Discuss concepts.	Do vocabulary activities.
Do selected applications based on concepts.	Read the text.

This approach directs teachers to preview the text, use students' prior knowledge, build interest and motivation, set a purpose for reading, and then to identify key concepts, vocabulary, and guiding questions before reading the text. During the training, teachers discussed how the traditional approach to instruction using textbooks differs from using the "backwards" approach.

Achieving Successful Change

Several faculty meetings served as training sessions. To put the entire literacy process in focus, the essential question for these sessions was, "How would you integrate the literacy skills we studied as a faculty in your discipline?" Discussion, demonstrations, key strategies, and key classroom management techniques produced valuable practical examples for all teachers. Each classroom displayed the literacy charts and maintained a common set of procedures for group work, student behavior, and rubrics for assessment.

The faculty felt comfortable with the skills they had developed, the training support they had received, and the renewed vitality of teaching and learning at Brockton. The instructional climate had changed, but more work still needed to be done. Nonetheless, the faculty and staff now had a new, higher sense of efficacy — they had control over the instruction and procedures they needed to be successful, and they believed that they could succeed.

The process of literacy training has resulted in major changes at Brockton since 1995. Consequently, the school has been recognized at the state and national levels for its improvements in student performance. Most staff members attribute that improvement to the literacy initiative.

While this recognition is very important to this urban high school, perhaps the most important honor comes every year at graduation, when so many students are awarded diplomas that would not have been possible without the literacy initiative, the changed vision of both teachers and students, and the increased expectations for the success of every student.

Essential Factors of Literacy Instruction

- An effective leadership team (restructuring committee)
- Using data, communication, and feedback
- Using scripts and rubrics to unify training
- Efforts toward building capacity within the building
- Developing a common vision and language
- Supporting the administration for time and resources
- Recognizing success and celebration
- Emphasizing practice, consistency, and a whole-school approach

---

Questions to Consider About Literacy Instruction

- How would you demonstrate the literacy needs of your students?
- How would literacy skills/strategies best be displayed in classrooms?
- What training would be needed and who would best provide such training?
- What expectation would you have for the application of these skills within classrooms?
- What role would the leadership team play in identifying skills/strategies that are appropriate for all subject areas?
- What length of time would you devote to this effort?

Brockton High School has transformed itself from a school mired in low expectations, excuse making, and a culture of frustration. Now, the school celebrates athletic and academic achievements, holds high expectations for student success, makes no excuses, and demands high performance levels from teachers and students. Gone are the days when the administration could predict the number of students who would not pass the MCAS and when teachers lamented that the state tests were too challenging for their students. Now, thanks to the literacy initiative and their extraordinary work, they are able to celebrate the success of their instructional program, with its high graduation rates and its high numbers of students who are accepted into postsecondary institutions.

LaGrange High School: Literacy through Happenstance

LaGrange High School in Lake Charles, Louisiana, is part of the changing landscape of a city whose 76,500 citizens have experienced a building boom due to the growth of the aviation industry and casinos. Numerous vocational training programs are now available through Calcasieu Parrish Schools as well as dual enrollment opportunities at local community and four-year colleges. LaGrange is one of 11 high schools in Lake Charles and, up through 2001, it was one of the highest achieving high schools, even being named a "School of Excellence" by the State of Louisiana in that same year.

But for reasons that included demographics, test scores and performance had dropped by 2003. Nonetheless, with the advent of new leadership, revitalized efforts of a veteran staff of teachers, and support from Calcasieu Parish staff, literacy became a cornerstone of change. Today the school is considered a "hidden treasure" with outstanding programs, numerous interventions as safety nets, and high achievement levels.

While some schools form a team and create an extensive literacy plan, LaGrange could probably call its initiative "literacy through happenstance." It provides outstanding proof for the notion that there are many ways to create success around literacy without needing to follow a formula. As LaGrange lost funding and changed administrators, it still continued to put literacy at the forefront. As one administrator said, "For us, literacy is related to everything here at LaGrange."

The English teachers took the responsibility for beginning the literacy initiative. While this step made important inroads, it did not create the desired results and it was at this point that the initiative became a cross-curricular responsibility. When a new principal was hired, the retired English department chair came back to work as an assistant to the principal, which helped in the transition.

Graduation/Literacy Coach

LaGrange also hired a graduation/literacy coach who was charged with several responsibilities, such as working directly with teachers in classrooms. The coach follows the school's approach of *demonstrate-observe-return-refine*:

- **Demonstrate** a strategy.
- **Observe** the teacher using the strategy.
- **Return** to the classroom.
- **Refine** the use of the strategy.

The coach keeps a log of which classrooms she visits in order to keep track of who is using strategies and which strategies are being utilized. She says, "Circumstances often dictated what we could and could not do — money, time, and information." But she has persevered and continues to reach out to as many teachers as possible, saying, "Tell me your most challenging class. I'll be there!"

One approach the coach uses is to start with read-alouds. She explains, "Sometimes I begin by reading aloud with expression. Students have a preconceived notion of reading — dry, uninteresting. Frequently within a few days, students ask to read for the class. I respond, 'Only if you read with expression, like you feel.' It is an amazing difference in students now reading out loud."

The coach also identifies the reading levels of students. Lexile levels are measured in the 8th grade using the *Scholastic Reading Inventory*, which helps determine which students need *READ 180 Next Generation* or *Accelerated Reader* when the students reach 9th grade. Every library item also has a Lexile text measure. MetaMetrics, Inc. trained teachers on Lexiles so that the staff understand Lexile levels and can differentiate instruction for their students accordingly.

Building Blocks to Success

Another significant change involved the creation of the Freshman Academy. The original plan was for all students to participate in the academy. However, due to a loss of funding, only about 75 percent of the students could participate. Yet all freshmen receive "Gator 101," a training program on study and time management skills, financial literacy, and career orientation. Similar to Brockton's Road to Success, LaGrange provides a Survival Guide, a folder with a checklist outlining what students need to do to survive, thrive, and graduate from LaGrange. Teachers in the Freshman Academy help students with their folder in the 9th grade, and guidance counselors assist students in grades 10–12.

Communication with parents is an integral part of LaGrange's success. The graduation/literacy coach sends numerous emails and newsletters and even conducts home visits. Evening meetings are scheduled for partners at the school, churches, and neighborhood centers so that they have an opportunity to become acquainted with the coach and teachers.

To date, teachers have been trained in Lexiles, vocabulary building, visual maps, and literacy strategies. All new teachers are brought "up to speed" and are given a planning period to meet with peer mentors, which gives them support as they adjust to the various aspects of the initiative. Teachers have also have received training in constructed-response items — test items that require students to provide a specific answer — to better prepare students for state testing and Next Generation Assessments related to the Common Core State Standards.

LaGrange also hired an interventionist who can be consulted by individual teachers when a student has a particular issue. For example, one student was working at a full-time job starting at 3:00 P.M. to help support his family. This start time was causing him to miss some school, and consequently, he was in danger of not graduating. The interventionist met with the student and his employer to develop solutions to the problem so he could graduate on time. While teachers were committed to doing everything they could to help at-risk students, the hiring of an interventionist served a need for those students who were most in danger of not graduating. In addition, a credit recovery program has also been put in place, featuring "I contracts," which are signed by the teacher, student, and parent.

Reflection

LaGrange proves that "literacy by happenstance" can be an effective approach to building a literacy program. As one teacher noted, "We seem to have tried an activity or strategy to see if it would work for us, and that was a good approach." It *was* indeed a good approach, as state test scores are up in both reading and math.

J.E.B. Stuart High School: A Team Approach to Literacy

J.E.B. Stuart High School in Falls Church, Virginia, is another excellent example of a school that has put literacy first through a deliberate, thoughtful, team-oriented literacy initiative. At Stuart High, literacy is the underpinning of the school and all its goals. When Stuart started a literacy initiative, it was a struggling school, but with literacy as its framework, the school has turned itself around. The administration and staff, after looking at student achievement levels, realized that reading and literacy deficits were holding their students back. Their students were thus not prepared for the demands of college and career.

The principal first formed a Literacy Council, comprising teachers across all content areas, plus a counselor and a literacy coach. The team met every two weeks to create and revise plans and to review progress. Because the Council made all decisions, the team approach distributed responsibility for leadership across *all* content areas; policymaking did not reside with just the principal and the literacy coach.

Stuart became the first high school in its district to hire a literacy coach and use diagnostic literacy testing (the Gates-MacGinitie reading assessment). Data acquired by this testing were crucial to the direction and approach adopted by the Council. In the beginning of the initiative, phonemic awareness was the biggest issue for students, so the Council concentrated on issues related to raising the skill levels of all their students in this area. As phonemic awareness improved, fluency and comprehension became the focus.

The students who struggled most were placed in yearlong intensive reading courses. For some, that meant a double block of time *in addition to* language arts (as opposed to being *in place of* language arts). These courses counted as credit toward graduation and were taught by the strongest teachers. Unlike many schools that place their weakest teachers with their weakest learners, Stuart placed the strongest teachers with the students who need the most intervention.

Since the goal was literacy for *all* students, the Council chose strategies that would be used schoolwide over the first year. Twenty strategies were chosen initially, which were then narrowed down to twelve, and then to six. In the end, the Council decided to focus on vocabulary, graphic organizers, and think-alouds to help its students raise their literacy levels most effectively. These strategies were used in all content areas and levels, even in advanced courses, so that all students were learning the same strategies. This unified approach also allowed for the strategies to be reinforced in content area classes while students were learning the strategies in intervention courses. Eventually, the school developed reading and writing rubrics for use by all staff so that teachers had consistent expectations across all content areas.

Following are the beliefs and practices that Stuart High developed (Carnegie Corporation of New York's Council on Advancing Adolescent Literacy, 2010):

Culture

- *All* graduates are college and career ready.
- *All* students can learn.
- Students need time to learn.
- *All* efforts are data-driven.
- The goal is continuous, incremental improvement.
- Teachers work in content teams.
- Literacy instruction benefits *all* students.

Information

- Annual diagnostic reading assessments.
- Common formative assessments.
- Common summative assessments.
- Data are provided on a timely basis.
- Teachers and the entire staff have real-time data on student performance.
- Programs are monitored closely.
- Programs are continually evaluated and re-evaluated.

Resources

- The budget reflects literacy priorities.
- A literacy coach is on staff to provide support.
- The literacy coach devotes 100 percent of time to literacy (no administrative tasks).
- Reading specialists teach reading classes.
- Intervention classes range from 15 to 18 students.

Leadership

- The principal's focus is student learning.
- The principal is the literacy leader.
- The principal works in partnership with the literacy coach.
- Initiatives are based on assessed student needs, not on adult wants.
- The master schedule is constructed based upon the needs of students.

Professional Staff

- Strong teachers are consistently assigned to teach students with the greatest needs.
- Professional development is ongoing, connected, and job-embedded.
- All teachers are required to participate in regularly scheduled professional development.
- Teachers are required to demonstrate proficiency in teaching literacy strategies.
- Peer coaching provides support.
- Peer observation facilitates collaboration.

Differentiated Literacy Instruction

- Multi-tiered interventions are based upon the assessed needs of students.
- Differentiated instruction includes phonemic awareness, vocabulary, comprehension, and fluency, all based on assessed needs.
- Students have additional time to improve literacy skills in addition to English language arts, not in place of English language arts.
- Teachers are trained specialists.
- Literacy courses count toward graduation credits.
- Intervention classes use texts from core academic courses.

Content Area Literacy Instruction

- Literacy is embedded in classroom instruction and is considered a normal part of instruction.
- All core classes include reading and writing instruction.

- Content teachers must demonstrate proficiency in core reading strategies.
- Literacy instruction is provided to advanced students.
- Strategies taught in intervention classes are reinforced in content classes.
- Writing rubrics are developed and used as instructional tools by all teachers.

It is interesting to note that, while this document was created long before schools needed to transition to the Common Core State Standards and the PARCC or SMARTER Balanced assessments, this list reflects what is truly necessary for students to become college and career ready.

Pasadena Independent School District: An Organizational Approach

The Pasadena Independent School District in Pasadena, Texas, is a suburban district offering programs for PreK–12. Its outstanding teachers, innovative campus administrators, and dedicated support staff focus on data-driven decision making and sustained improvement over time. A strong commitment to equipping staff with the tools needed to improve their teaching is embedded throughout the development of the curriculum. As a result, for seven consecutive years, a combination of effective interventions and focused staff development has helped Pasadena earn the distinction of being a Texas Recognized School District. In addition, Pasadena was named the 2008 National Model School District by the International Center based on its impressive progress in student achievement.

With the help of Title I funding, Pasadena uses *READ 180* (now *READ 180 Next Generation*) throughout the district. Originally, *READ 180* was used in all secondary schools but has since been moved to some elementary schools as well. It has been particularly effective for Level 3 ELL students who have at least a 450 Lexile. Learning disabled students have also made gains with the help of this program, as have those students whose decoding skills were adequate but who needed further help with vocabulary and comprehension.

A well-established list of intervention programs is maintained, and the district is adept at tracking data to help each student move forward. To help support these intervention programs, sustainable professional development is provided by the Texas Region 4 Education Service Center as well as by district experts and specialists.

Teacher Training

After teachers are hired, Pasadena works hard to bring all of them up to the same level. The district also hires a large number of alternative certification teachers. During a summer school internship, teachers lead and begin to receive training that will help them learn how to interpret data. Along with all other first-year teachers, incoming teachers receive training throughout the first year in the Rigor/Relevance Framework and participate in an immersion program covering basic literacy strategies.

The district has also hired International Center senior consultants to provide a large portion of its professional development. To date, teachers using the train-the-trainer model have raised the level of rigor and relevance in their classrooms and have learned the importance of discrete vocabulary instruction. They have worked on questioning, graphic organizers, and quick writes, as well as document, technological, and quantitative literacy. After receiving training in quick writes, the Pasadena Memorial High School math department saw a 10 percent increase in its state test scores. When students spent simply one to three minutes a day on writing at the appropriate level of rigor, the school was able to see a significant improvement in scores.

Pasadena also uses leveled databases such as EBSCOhost or SIRS to differentiate materials for students. Moreover, book clubs and book contests celebrate reading.

What sets Pasadena apart from many other districts is its commitment to long-term professional development. To get an idea of its focus, a snapshot of five years of training follows:

- **Year 1:** Laying the foundation for rigor and relevance. Time was spent assessing what literacy practices existed and what was needed. The district found that reading and writing practices and scores were good in English language arts but content area comprehension was lower than desired. This knowledge helped drive training in subsequent years.

- **Year 2:** Training teacher leaders in vocabulary instruction, instructional strategies, and rigor/relevance.

- **Year 3:** Training in quick writes and graphic organizers.

- **Year 4:** Building rigor with text strategies and decoding.

- **Year 5:** Differentiating, scaffolding, and critical thinking. International Center Senior Consultant Lin Kuzmich, who has worked extensively with Pasadena, comments, "You can't differentiate without a big enough toolbox, and by Year 5 their toolbox is big enough."

Reflection

In the 2009–10 school year, Pasadena teachers in the elementary schools were reading *Differentiated Literacy Strategies for Student Growth and Achievement in Grades K–6* (Gregory and Kuzmich, 2004) and secondary school teachers were reading *Differentiated Literacy Strategies for Student Growth and Achievement in Grades 7–12* (Gregory and Kuzmich, 2005). Across its curriculum, Pasadena is seeing the difference that a literacy focus can make. In social studies and science, Pasadena has seen its Texas Assessment of Knowledge and Skills (TAKS) scores rise, and since 2003, the number of schools using technical assistance or corrective action dropped from 29 to 3. Pasadena serves as an excellent example of what a district can do with foresight, a strong focus on literacy, great leadership, and sustained professional development. Pasadena provides yet another illustration of how schools with a strong emphasis on literacy are much better prepared to move toward successful implementation of the Common Core State Standards.

Young Adult Literature as a Best Practice

So far, we have seen a number of different approaches to literacy programs. In those schools, and indeed throughout this book, the emphasis has been on embedded literacy, the kind of reading and writing skills required in the workplace. In the past, our schools have done a poor job of preparing our students in this kind of literacy, so now we must scramble to catch up. Our new race to improve literacy is being built largely on our awareness that embedded literacy has to be improved.

Yet in the midst of all the planning and implementing, and amid our struggles to raise student achievement, we sometimes forget to ask ourselves an important question: "Do students *like* to read?" We do know that using intriguing pre-learning strategies can pique student interest in a particular reading. Teaching students effective during-learning strategies can help them comprehend texts better than ever before, while useful post-learning strategies help them first process what they have learned and then retain that knowledge. These steps, though, may not help students *enjoy* reading and want to read for pleasure. This is why young adult literature can be a valuable component of any literacy initiative — it can persuade students that reading can be fun as well as functional.

Including YA (young adult) literature in the curriculum may mean challenging an existing resistance against such material, which is often — and often unfairly — considered less worthy than "real" literature. As Pam B. Cole states in *Young Adult Literature in the*

21ˢᵗ Century (2009), "Whether it is the fault of state or local standards, or those of *No Child Left Behind*, educators seem to pay more attention to whether high school students can identify authors and titles of the classics and give a short answer regarding the theme of each than we do to whether or not students can actually read." If we use YA literature to promote student enjoyment of reading, we will help them build what we might call their literacy resilience, just at a time when many students become less interested in reading. As students shift from learning to read to reading to learn, texts become increasingly difficult and oftentimes less interesting to students.

While teachers should not, of course, simply abandon Shakespeare and *The Scarlet Letter*, not all students are capable of tackling such difficult texts. As Louise Rosenblatt stated in her groundbreaking text, *Literature as Exploration*, originally published in 1938, "People who read for themselves will come to the classics at the point when particular works have particular significance for them. To force such works on the young prematurely defeats the long-term goal of educating people to a personal love of literature sufficiently deep to cause them to seek it out for themselves at the appropriate time."

Let us take a look, for instance, at a hypothetical high school where the junior year American literature curriculum includes reading *The Scarlet Letter*, which is written at a 1420L. There are 400 students in the junior class, and 75 percent of them have proficient or advanced Lexile scores. Proficient readers score between 1050L and 1300L, so even they may have trouble comprehending the novel, let alone the 100 who did not score as proficient and will thus struggle with the text.

The hypothetical teachers would probably insist that they must teach *The Scarlet Letter* to everyone. Why? The answer is: they always have. Students need to have common literary experiences, experiences that will help them in college. But will reading *The Scarlet Letter* be a valuable learning experience for everyone? A student reading at a 600L surely will not have the same literary experience as a student reading at a 1450L. This student is also not becoming better prepared for college by pretending his or her way through the reading.

But what if these teachers also used *Speak* by Laurie Halse Anderson? *Speak* is the story of Melinda, who is shunned by her classmates for calling the police and breaking up a party. What she does not — and cannot — tell anyone is that a popular senior raped her. Her inability to tell her story, and her ultimate shunning, closely mirrors Hester Prynne's situation. At a 680L, *Speak* is a much more accessible novel for most students, and teachers can cover the same curriculum using *Speak* as they do using *The Scarlet Letter*.

This is just one example of how the use of young adult literature can enhance a school's literacy initiative. With the CCSS emphasizing skills rather than content, differentiating our instruction becomes even more important.

So it remains for us to find a way to instill the love of reading into our students. Students should have the opportunity to learn that reading isn't always about locating information and that it is not just a skill they need to have for their futures as workers.

There are several approaches to this dilemma that can bring students the experience of reading for the joy of it and, at the same time, incorporate the rigor of CCSS: literature circles, book clubs, and RAFT.

Literature Circles

The educational imperative for students to become lifelong readers has yet to be realized. Too often, students are given assignment after assignment of required reading that has little connection to their own lives, making reading an unappealing chore that is thrust upon them rather than an activity in which they participate and can enjoy. While required reading is certainly a necessary part of any curriculum, participating in literature circles (or "lit circles," as they are commonly known) can foster an interest in reading in ways that a traditional literature curriculum cannot.

In literature circles, small groups of students gather together to discuss a piece of literature in-depth. (Schlick Noe and Johnson, 1999) The discussion is guided by students' responses to what they have read. You may hear about events and characters in the book, the author's craft, or personal experiences related to the story.

This definition sums up what, for many students, is the appeal of lit circles. Student response is of the utmost importance, and student choice is often a large part of establishing lit circles in a classroom. Because students are able to choose the material and direct the discussion, there is a feeling of ownership that is not present with teacher-selected material, or with guided reading and discussion. Students may discover a genre, author, or series that is of interest and choose to read further outside the classroom setting.

Even when CCSS and Next Generation Assessments are increasingly important, lit circles can still be a valuable part of a curriculum. Literature standards can be covered just as thoroughly within lit circles as they can with a whole-class selection, even if only once during a semester. Lit circles are also a very effective way to support a school's literacy initiative because they provide one of the few places where students can receive direct instruction that can help to encourage lifelong reading.

Lit circles can even be used in other content areas such as science. Roles such as *discussion director*, *summarizer*, *vocabulary enricher*, and *webmaster* can be assigned to students as they read their textbooks. Thus, rather than being a solitary activity, the reading of the textbook becomes an engaging and interactive endeavor.

Even if a school does not implement a schoolwide initiative, several teachers — or even one teacher — can use lit circles. If department money is not available, the library media specialist can be a valuable resource for obtaining multiple copies of books.

Kaukauna High School: Literacy through Book Clubs

Book clubs are an effective tool for infusing reading for pleasure into a school's culture. Kaukauna High School in Kaukauna, Wisconsin, has implemented an enjoyable and successful book club system. It is a program that works across all content areas and provides a way of approaching Common Core State Standards with a more traditional approach to literature and a major emphasis on promoting love of reading.

When Kaukauna started its literacy initiative in 2004, it quickly became apparent that students were not interested in discussing books in a traditional manner during the lunch hour or after school. Lunch hours were difficult because students were not interested in attending if their friends had to attend one of the other three lunch hours. After school, students were too busy with activities or work. So to "lure them in," Kaukauna staff started offering extra credit for reading the book of the month.

The procedure for Kaukauna's Book of the Month project is:

1. The literacy coordinator selects a high-interest Young Adult title for the month and purchases 25 copies.
2. Students can check out a copy for one week.
3. The literacy coordinator creates a RAFT (Role Audience Format Topic) assignment for students to complete.
4. After reading the book, students write the RAFT paper and turn it in to the literacy coordinator for assessment.

5. From a sheet on the coordinator's door listing teachers and the amount of extra credit they give, students choose which teachers they will receive extra credit from.

6. The literacy coordinator assesses the RAFT paper, makes a copy, and gives the paper to the appropriate teacher, who can then award the extra credit.

With experience, Kaukauna has found ways to make the program more economical. Some titles have been purchased with money donated by local charities. Stickers in the front covers of the books acknowledge each donation. Other high schools in the area run similar programs, and the schools have traded titles to avoid making additional purchases. Five years into the program, Kaukauna is now able to "recycle" titles and use them again, and multiple copies of these books are ideal for lit circles in classrooms across the school. They have also been fortunate enough to have parents run a Scholastic Book Fair, which uses profits to purchase Book of the Month titles.

The payoff has been great. Students see that adults across all subject areas value reading for pleasure enough to offer extra credit in their own classes. Oftentimes, students will spontaneously "book talk" the new title in a class if other students notice they are reading it, which, in turn, leads to more discussions about books enjoyed by both students and teachers. Several staff members make it a point to read the books as often as they can so that they can hold book conversations with students.

Discussion Points about Starting a Book Club

- How would a book club benefit our school?
- How could a book club encourage better relationships between students and teachers?
- How could a book club help students develop thinking skills?
- How might a book club promote cross-disciplinary work among teachers?

While some parents have suggested that the Book of the Month program would be an ideal place to "work through the classics," the school's staff feels strongly that the titles should be more accessible. Great care is taken to find titles that appeal to teens at a Lexile level that makes them readable to most students and that could spark interest in further reading.

Dynamic young adult titles can be chosen that have a curricular tie-in as well. For example, *Briar Rose* by Jane Yolen tells the story of a young woman researching her grandmother's Holocaust experience. This title was "book talked" in social studies, and teachers in the department gave "double extra credit" that month. As Kaukauna High School transitions toward the Common Core State Standards, teachers outside of ELA and math are searching for ways to add more reading and writing experiences to their curriculum. These titles, depending on their subject matter, can be worked into a number of courses when not being used as the Book of the Month. For example, the novel *Flash Burnout*, by L.K. Madigan, is being used in photography class after having been a Book of the Month. The characters' interest in photography creates a natural connection to the curriculum of the course.

Each of the titles in the section that follows was used at Kaukauna. While not every title has a curricular tie-in, these were chosen for a specific curricular purpose. The first example gives the direction; the directions are the same for each title and are posted with each assignment. The rubric stays the same for each month as well.

RAFT

RAFT stands for **Role-Audience-Format-Topic**. It provides a creative way to check for reading and it allows students to demonstrate their knowledge and opinion regarding a book, which is enhanced when students can select between two assignment choices, as is demonstrated in the following examples. While RAFTs can be assigned in any topic area (as shown in Chapter 5), they work particularly well as a replacement for a traditional book report. And while different strategies could be used each month, consistently creating the assignment in the form of a RAFT is important so students know what to expect and do not have to learn a new strategy each month, in addition to reading a new book.

Briar Rose

by Jane Yolen

Description: Growing up, Rebecca's grandmother would tell her a frightening version of Sleeping Beauty. After her grandmother dies, Rebecca realizes that the story holds the clues to her grandmother's past. Traveling to Poland, Rebecca pieces together the story of Sleeping Beauty and her grandmother's Holocaust experience.

RAFT Topic: _____

Directions for Earning Book Club Extra Credit

- To earn extra credit, you must complete a RAFT paper.
- The RAFT must be at least two double-spaced typed pages or two neatly hand-written pages.
- A RAFT paper is a way to demonstrate that you have read and written in a more creative format.
- When you have completed your RAFT paper, turn it in to me.
- After checking my list, decide which teacher/class might provide your extra credit. Write your choice on the top of your paper and/or the rubric sheet. If your paper meets the criteria, I'll let your teacher know you have earned the extra credit.

RAFT Assignment Choice #1

Role: Rebecca

Audience: the general public

Format: newspaper article

Topic: the mystery of her grandmother's belongings

RAFT Assignment Choice #2

Role: you

Audience: me

Format: compare/contrast report

Topic: the correlations between the traditional story of Sleeping Beauty and the story of Rebecca's grandmother

RAFT Student Rubric

Name:		Teacher:		
Book Title:				

Remember to complete your RAFT in two typed pages, including as many details as possible to demonstrate your knowledge of the book. Remember that you are writing as a character. Refer back to the directions on your RAFT topic paper.

	Excellent	Good	Fair	Poor	Missing
Accuracy	5	4	3	2	1
Perspective	5	4	3	2	1
Focus	5	4	3	2	1
Mechanics	5	4	3	2	1
Comments:					

Total Points: _____

Additional RAFT Activities

Other examples for a Book of the Month program follow.

Use *La Linea* in social studies, perhaps when studying immigration laws.

La Linea

by Ann Jaramillo

Description: Fifteen-year old Miguel leaves Mexico to migrate to California across the border to begin a new life. His carefully laid plans suddenly change when his younger sister follows him. Together they endure hardships and danger on their journey of desperation and desire, loyalty and betrayal.

RAFT Assignment Choice #1

Role: Miguel

Audience: Elena

Format: a letter

Topic: your experiences and what led to your ultimate choices

RAFT Assignment Choice #2

Role: Elena

Audience: Miguel

Format: a letter

Topic: your experiences and what led to your ultimate choices

Double Helix could be the book of the month when biology teachers are covering genetics.

Double Helix

by Nancy Werlin

Description: Eli Samuels struggles with the knowledge that he has a 50-50 chance of getting Huntington's disease as he watches his mother disintegrate from having the wrong gene. When Eli takes a job at Wyatt Transgenics, he makes a startling discovery that connects his family to the genetic engineering experiments of the famous geneticist Quincy Wyatt.

RAFT Assignment Choice #1

Role: Eli

Audience: his mother

Format: letter

Topic: his feelings about the decisions she made

RAFT Assignment Choice #2

Role: Eli

Audience: Dr. Wyatt

Format: letter

Topic: the pros and cons of Dr. Wyatt's experiments

The next title offers a great tie-in to economics, health, and business classes.

Chew on This

by Eric Schlosser and Charles Wilson

Description: In *Chew on This*, a *New York Times* bestseller, Schlosser and Wilson unwrap the fast-food industry to bring you a behind-the-scenes look at a business that both feeds and feeds off of the young. Find out what really goes on at your favorite restaurants—and what lurks between those sesame seed buns.

RAFT Assignment Choice #1

Role: a McDonald's executive

Audience: the American public

Format: a press release

Topic: a defense of your practices

RAFT Assignment Choice #2

Role: a concerned citizen

Audience: McDonald's

Format: a letter

Topic: why you won't be eating their fast food anymore

The next title's focus on abuse ties into health classes, family and consumer education classes, and teen parenting classes.

Fault Line

by Janet Tashjian

Description: Seventeen-year-old Becky Martin never thought she'd be one of *those* girls. After all, she doesn't fit the profile. She has great parents and friends, and even has an opportunity to be an amateur comic. Then she meets comic Kip Costello who's cute and hilarious. But he begins to demand more and more of her time and attention. This is a novel about teen dating violence that cuts through the clichés.

RAFT Assignment Choice #1

Role: Kip

Audience: his support group

Format: speech

Topic: why he thinks he acted the way he did toward Becky and what he learned from their relationship

RAFT Assignment Choice #2

Role: Becky

Audience: her support group

Format: speech

Topic: why she thinks she allowed Kip to treat her the way he did and what he means to her now

The last example is about student relationships and bullying; the theme of bullying is a good choice for reflection and discussion.

Shattering Glass

by Gail Giles

Description: Fat, clumsy Simon Glass is a nerd, a loser who occupies the lower rung on the social ladder, until popular Rob Haynes wants to turn Simon from total freak to would-be prom king. But as Simon rises to the top, he shows a devious side that Rob did not anticipate.

RAFT Assignment Choice #1

Role: Young

Audience: Rob

Format: letter

Topic: why he took the punishment that he did

RAFT Assignment Choice #2

Role: Simon

Audience: Rob, Young, Coop, and Bob

Format: speech

Topic: why he overrode the computer's decision for Class Favorite

While a book club is generally a schoolwide program, it also can be managed in a classroom. Teachers could develop RAFT assignments for books that they have already read and maintain in a classroom library. Students could check out these books and complete RAFT papers for extra credit in selected classes.

The Value of Young Adult Literature

Young adult literature can serve as a gateway for teens to discover a love of reading. Finding books that interest teens, that speak to them, and that help them to see themselves as readers is immensely rewarding for students and teachers alike. Consider making young adult literature a part of your own literacy initiative. Lit circles can be a means for students to start developing their own responses to reading that can carry over into any subject area. Book clubs can also be structured so that students are rewarded for finding and reading books that they truly enjoy, and RAFT can help students integrate writing and reading.

Summary

There is no single best approach to a school literacy program, as is made clear by the experiences of the schools cited in this chapter. Each school built a solid and successful literacy program while approaching the initiative from different directions and with slightly different emphases.

Brockton may have developed their program in the most comprehensive manner, starting by assessing where the school was when the process started, and then setting very high expectations and a goal of ongoing, continuous improvement. The program focuses on reading, writing, listening, and reasoning strategies, and engages teachers from all content areas in the teaching of literacy. An early emphasis on the teaching of open-response writing provided a catalyst that proved Brockton's literacy plan was effective and inspired more efforts. This particular initiative grew to become a comprehensive program that produced outstanding results. Brockton's approach, in the end, supports a range of learning opportunities for students, giving them the opportunity to excel as they prepare themselves for college, technical training, or employment, depending upon where their interests lie.

LaGrange High School has taken perhaps the most unsystematic approach to literacy of all the schools examined in this chapter. After an unexpected decline in student achievement, the school took steps to correct its model with a renewed emphasis on literacy. The English department initiated the effort, but it really took off when a literacy coach came on board and began working directly with teachers in the classroom. Student Lexile levels were measured and teachers were trained in how to use them. Consequently, differentiating instruction for students became an effective practice. An interventionist became available to assist with individual students. It happened by happenstance, but the program works.

J.E.B. Stuart High School employs a team approach that has become the foundation for the whole school. It began with a Literacy Council, comprising teachers from all content areas. A literacy coach refocused the literacy emphasis to help bring all students up to proficient levels, and the school added intensive reading classes that helped the weakest learners. The Literacy Council selected a toolbox of strategies that are used in all classes by all students and later added reading and writing rubrics. It's a comprehensive team approach that supports all content areas and all students.

The Pasadena Independent School District takes a more organizational approach to literacy that is data-driven and dedicated to sustained improvement over time. The district sees to it that the staff has the tools they need to succeed. Intervention is provided as needed, and staff development programs ensure that all teachers have the skills and knowledge they need to implement the literacy initiative in their classes. Long-term professional development, in fact, is the hallmark of the Pasadena program.

Kaukauna High School supports literacy through a book club program that promotes a love of reading. The program is precisely structured and engages students by providing young adult books, chosen by the staff, that students will actually enjoy reading.

All of these schools have adopted different approaches to accomplishing the same goal: student literacy. The programs engage students in reading and challenge them to do better. All have set high expectations for their students, and all provide the support needed by staff and students to succeed.

Questions to Consider

- If teachers succeed in giving students a love of learning and the skills needed to read, increased learning is sure to follow. What do you think about this statement? Do you agree?

- Which of the ideas developed by the schools in this chapter can you best envision incorporating into your school's initiative?

- How do the teachers in your school feel about using young adult literature in the classroom? How could your school incorporate more reading for pleasure in your building?

- Compare and contrast Brockton's story with Kaukana's approach to embedded literacy. What are the similarities and differences? Which one strikes you as being closer to a method that your own district might use?

References

Carnegie Corporation of New York's Council on Advancing Adolescent Literacy. *A Time to Act: An Agenda for Advancing Adolescent Literacy for College and Career Success*. New York, NY: Carnegie Corporation of New York, 2010.

Cole, P.B. *Young Adult Literature in the 21st Century*. New York, NY: McGraw Hill, 2009.

Gregory, G. and Kuzmich L. *Differentiated Literacy Strategies for Student Growth and Achievement in Grades K–6*. Thousand Oaks, CA: Corwin Press, 2004.

Gregory, G. and Kuzmich, L. *Differentiated Literacy Strategies for Student Growth and Achievement in Grades 7–12*. Thousand Oaks, CA: Corwin Press, 2005.

Kagan, S. *Cooperative Learning: Resources for Teachers*. San Clemente, CA: Resources for Teachers, 1994.

Rosenblatt, Louise M. *Literature as Exploration*, 5th Ed. New York, NY: Modern Language Association of America, 1995.

Schlick Noe, K.L. and Johnson, N.L. *Getting Started with Literature Circles*. Norwood, MA: Christopher-Gordon Publishers, 1999.

 Chapter 7

Actions for Implementation

In this book, we've looked at many different aspects of literacy. We've considered the state of reading in America, the reading habits of adults, and the characteristics of literacy required in the workplace. We've examined the organizational leadership and teamwork required for a literacy initiative. We've also looked at classroom strategies and programs that can make literacy effective in all subject areas. In Chapter 6, we presented examples of schools that have implemented successful literacy programs. To achieve their high level of literacy instruction, staff in each school addressed these five steps:

- **Step 1:** Identify the literacy issues, needs, and resources within the building.
- **Step 2:** Develop a consensus on the need for change that incorporates training, curriculum, and instructional modifications.
- **Step 3:** Build the capacity to address literacy issues using building staff.
- **Step 4:** Design and implement action steps to support change over time.
- **Step 5:** Monitor, evaluate, and modify plans as success is achieved.

The exact process each school employed in taking these steps differed, and it will differ for your school as well. But regardless of a school's specific characteristics, the process always begins by identifying the school's needs and strengths in literacy and determining how to respond to the challenge of training and supporting teachers so they can help students to process written material more effectively.

Every school raised awareness of the need for literacy training and secured the acceptance of innovative ideas for the classroom. Over time, extensive professional training was provided that was teacher-led, content-specific, and supported by the administration through observations and resources. In each case, the administration reviewed school procedures, rubrics, and protocols to ensure that student and teacher behaviors and expectations enriched the literacy initiative. When engaged in your own literacy planning, consider these essential factors.

- Administrative leadership is involved, supportive, and aggressive.
- Collaboration is built on open communication.
- Data is the starting point for all changes in culture, expectations, and performance.
- Goals and outcomes are clear and communicated frequently.
- All staff members accept responsibility for addressing literacy needs in a school-wide process.
- Resources are identified for the initiative and a long-range commitment is made.
- Successes are celebrated, and new goals are determined.
- A team approach utilizes the expertise of administrators, a literacy coach, and teacher leaders.

When a school successfully engages in literacy planning, it addresses all of these essential aspects of the initiative. They will be achieved through the steps described throughout this chapter.

Step 1: Identify Literacy Issues, Needs, and Resources

Of course, the first task is to assess your students and their literacy levels. You must determine exactly what they know and don't know and what is holding them back. Having done all of this, the task becomes one of developing and implementing a literacy plan to improve instruction.

To begin this step, you and your colleagues should consider your school's unique circumstances by asking critical questions that will identify literacy issues and reviewing the answers as a team.

What Is Our School Doing Now?

Every school has a literacy program in place. It may not be producing all of the desired results, but it is certainly doing many things right. Conduct an in-depth analysis to find out what the program's best practices are. These best practices can form the foundation of the literacy initiative going forward.

The analysis should burrow all the way down to what individual teachers are teaching and how they are teaching. Which strategies are working? Which programs are creating interest among students? When students are truly engaged with learning, what is happening and why?

Now here's a harder question: What is our school doing that is not working? What strategies are being used that are discouraging students or focusing on the wrong goals? The following table lists critical factors that will enter into your planning and provide a format for gathering information.

Gathering Information to Begin a Schoolwide Literacy Program

Check "Yes" or "No" and Respond to Each Factor			
Factor	Yes	No	Explain
Data/evidence exists regarding student literacy skills, levels, and needs.			
Data on student reading skills are accessible to teachers.			
The faculty have a culture of high expectations; rigorous and relevant instruction; and strong, respected relationships.			
The faculty share the belief that achievement levels should be higher.			
The administration encourages a dialogue about expectations, instructional rigor, and student test results.			
The district has taken the time to map the curriculum and align it to the Common Core State Standards.			
Information from recent graduates exists on how well they were prepared for postsecondary education.			
Time and resources exist to support professional development.			

Unique School Histories Influence Literacy Plans

Responding to the Yes, No, Explain sequence in the table facilitates an examination of individual differences found in schools. The school's history will determine what the "best" approach to literacy development should be for that school. Whatever information is gathered via the table will be tempered by what has taken place in the recent history of the school. To define a solid, workable approach to literacy training that will be accepted and embraced by teachers, the following questions can help guide decisions:

- What initiatives have been attempted in the past five years?
- What challenges faced the teachers within the building in recent years?
- Do teachers believe that students can work at higher, more rigorous levels and succeed? If not, what can be done to help all teachers believe?
- Would most teachers, administrators, and the board of education agree on common school goals for improving education outcomes and student performance?
- Is there a consensus of beliefs across disciplines and grade levels about the need for literacy training?
- Are resources available that can support training over time?

The answers to these questions reflect both the culture and the climate of the school's recent history. They are necessary to consider when beginning a long-term, rigorous literacy initiative.

Successful Literacy Plans

The DSEI encompasses three factors needed to ensure student achievement: organizational leadership, instructional leadership, and teaching. Organizational leadership involves a mentality, structure, focus, and commitment to creating an environment in which learning is optimized. The stage must be set from the very top so that everyone involved understands the expectations and vision for a literacy plan and that there will be support to make the plan happen.

Schools that have developed productive literacy programs have employed different approaches to achieving success. Research continues to verify the value of a variety of steps that most schools can and should address in professional development. Birdville Independent School District in Texas, for example, identified five key principles in its staff development activities:

- Allocate time and resources.
- Include instructional leaders — both teachers and administrators.
- Collaborate in teams.
- Engage everyone in meaningful learning and work.
- Use data to make decisions.

In addition to the principles developed by districts such as Birdville, the following four stages describe the process that high-achieving schools and districts have used in organizing targeted, enriched literacy initiatives. To organize a new literacy program, consider how to address each stage to achieve lasting, higher student performance across all curricular areas (Miller, et al., 2009):

Stage 1. Assess Needs

A. Create a common vision.

B. Assess the school culture.

C. Map and align the curriculum.

D. Assess student performance data.

E. Incorporate school history.

F. Identify challenges and supporting conditions.

Stage 2. Plan for Change and Improvement

A. Share leadership and decision making.

B. Build trust.

C. Apply the Learning Criteria.

D. Involve stakeholders.

Stage 3. Implement Action Steps

A. Focus on literacy strategies.

B. Design professional development.

C. Use the leadership team.

D. Organize instructional support.

E. Meet the needs of *all* students.

Stage 4. Sustain Improved Performance

A. Assess progress toward program goals.

B. Use the Learning Criteria to evaluate and monitor progress.

C. Modify goals, action plans, and expectations.

D. Recognize and celebrate success.

After responding to the questions posed earlier in this chapter that focus on the school's unique history, address the following questions, which involve the concrete decisions needed to complete a written plan for implementation.

Questions to Consider When Constructing a Literacy Initiative

- How should a school address steps that have achieved schoolwide literacy, such as the steps taken by schools like Brockton?
- Who should be involved and consulted?
- What time frame would be appropriate for a literacy initiative?
- What policies, procedures, and school structures will need to be discussed?
- Where do we stand in terms of aligning our curriculum to the CCSS?
- What new or existing resources will be needed for a literacy plan?
- How should staff training be designed and implemented?
- Are there steps taken by schools like Brockton or others that are not, in fact, necessary for every school?

Is the school at a stage of development wherein a full multi-year program can be designed, or should the process proceed one step at a time (allowing "happenstance" to guide the implementation process)?

Step 2: Consensus for Change

The instructional leadership aspect of the DSEI is directly focused on instructional effectiveness and, ultimately, student achievement. The leadership team needs to reinforce the vision set by organizational leadership by means of data-driven decision making as well as focused professional collaboration and growth. It is critical that the leadership committee collaborate to ensure successful implementation.

260

Everyone needs to be on board for a literacy initiative to succeed, so the leadership committee should begin working toward consensus right away. Building consensus enables you to do the following:

- Develop more creative solutions.
- Build enthusiasm.
- Implement the plan with more energy.
- Build respect and understanding.

The number one path toward consensus is through open discussion. Administration, teachers, parents, and all stakeholders must understand the need for change. First, take your findings from Step 1 to the staff. Then, share the good news and the bad news. Build a consensus for change. Present and explain your comprehensive database to demonstrate the need for a literacy initiative to all stakeholders. Discuss what the data show and how the initiative will be designed to solve the weaknesses in current literacy instruction. Explain how literacy impacts learning in every content area.

Don't leave any stakeholders out of the loop. The staff, parents, and community need to understand that the initiative will affect instruction for all students and in all content areas, and also that support and training for teachers will be provided as needed.

You may want to build a contact list of all interested stakeholders and regularly update them on progress, issues, decisions, and other developments as the literacy committee proceeds. Emails, newsletters, Facebook posts, and notes delivered to school mailboxes can be a valuable way of keeping everyone up to date. As a result, there will be no surprises, and more importantly, everyone will be made to feel included in the process.

A major part of building consensus involves reaching out to teachers to get them involved in the initiative. The degree of their passion and commitment to the change will influence its success a great deal. Seek out the leaders, the most experienced and skilled teachers, and draw them into the literacy committee. Even those who can't commit as much time as the committee will require should be consulted and their ideas requested. Many of these teachers can be involved in mentoring or trying out new strategies, thus becoming "experts" who can be a resource for other teachers. This involvement will foster greater commitment to making sure the changes are successful. As acknowledged leaders on the staff, they will engender more support among other members of the staff.

Because bringing literacy instruction into the content areas requires science, math, music, and other content-area teachers to teach literacy skills for what may be the first time in their careers, they will need extra support and encouragement to reassure them that they have the skills needed to implement the change. One way to do this is to set up a training program early on to demonstrate the school's commitment to giving them the resources and support so they can succeed. A calendar of training opportunities that stretches several years ahead, like the one discussed in Chapter 6 that was created by the Pasadena School District, can build more confidence.

The curriculum will have to be addressed and consensus gained for necessary changes to be made. The CCSS demand more rigor and relevance, which means that some aspects of the curriculum will need to be upgraded and changed. Plus, time will need to be provided for direct literacy instruction in classes that were normally conducted without it. Students who are not performing up to level have, in the past, been given less complex materials instead of the support they need to manage texts and reach higher expectations. Textbooks and other curriculum materials are being aligned to the CCSS and may ease some of the transition. In any case, these changes will represent another adjustment for teachers and students. Sharing reasons for the changes and explaining their extent and their benefits will help to ensure broader acceptance.

Reaching the "Tipping Point"

Throughout the process of building consensus, school leadership is critical. The leadership includes the principal, department heads, and the literacy coach. It also includes those who may not hold an official leadership position, but who help connect and influence the ideas and actions of the staff. Often these are experienced teachers who lead by example and are respected by those around them. Malcolm Gladwell, in his acclaimed book *The Tipping Point*, also points out three groups of people who may not be part of any of the groups already mentioned. He calls them the "connectors," "mavens," and "salesmen." (Gladwell, 2000)

Connectors are people who have a knack for linking larger groups of people together. They seem to know and communicate with everyone. Mavens are "information specialists." They are the people that others come to in order to get the facts and background on some new idea, like a literacy initiative. Salespeople are the "persuaders." These are people that seem to win agreement easily. When they talk up an idea, others jump on board.

If the literacy committee can win the approval of the connectors, mavens, and salesmen, a consensus will likely follow, and then participation and commitment will ensue. So how do you win over these key people? Gladwell offers a couple of ideas. The "stickiness factor" is a term he uses to describe the degree to which an idea is memorable or not. Understandably, the presentation of an idea affects how readily it is received and how memorable it becomes. So articulate your message carefully to make it clear and straightforward. When an idea is sticky, it catches on. People remember it and talk about it and act upon it.

When all these pieces come together, a "tipping point" is reached. This moment occurs when enough people have become interested in an idea and bought into it that it suddenly begins to spread like an epidemic. When this happens, you know that consensus has been reached.

So an important route to building a consensus is to engage people by opening the doors to ideas and participation. Reach out to people who connect to and lead others by their actions and personal charisma. Search out people who will be the cheerleaders for the initiative.

Step 3: Build Capacity to Address Literacy Issues

Professional Development

Plan for professional development, and plan for it to correspond to stages in the implementation of your initiative. It should be presented just in time for teachers to try it in class right away, not in six months' time, or last week. Professional development will be central to the success of the initiative because teachers are being asked to expand and broaden their skills and to try things that they may not have been asked to do since college (or ever!), such as teaching literacy. The extent of this challenge for teachers can easily be overlooked.

For example, the literacy needs in math are different from the literacy needs in a language arts course. Math textbooks are structured differently from language arts or even science texts, and the way students extract information from math books differs from how they access it in a literature text. Math teachers, because most have little or no experience in teaching literacy, will not have the requisite skills to implement the new literacy requirements. Moreover, much of the conversation about literacy will not seem to have an obvious or direct application to math, so math teachers may return to their classrooms with little idea of how to proceed. Adding to the confusion, the school's literacy experts may not have much experience applying literacy strategies to math. The same applies to other content areas as well, although perhaps not to such a degree.

Thus, a professional development program aimed at content-area literacy support is a necessity, if the DSEI is going to move beyond organizational leadership and instructional leadership toward what actually happens in the classroom. If organizational leadership does its job of establishing an overarching vision and mission, and if instructional leadership makes the necessary tools, data, and support available and accessible to teachers, then the vanguard of instructional effectiveness — teaching — will be well supported in addressing the daunting challenges of the classroom.

Similar needs for professional development exist to support teachers of ELL and special needs students. As mentioned earlier, CCSS requires a rigorous approach to instruction for all students. Simplifying instruction for ELL or special learners is not the solution. Rather, they need to be brought up to higher achievement levels. To assist teachers with strategies and support to accomplish this objective, professional development must be provided.

Literacy Coach

Put a literacy coach or coordinator in place to support teachers. The role of a literacy coach should be broad and extend to every classroom. The responsibilities and benefits of employing a literacy coach include the following. A literacy coach:

- **Represents the literacy initiative.** In many ways, the literacy coach is the daily representative of the literacy initiative as it goes forward in the school. All members of the literacy committee are present in the school and are "talking up" the program, but the literacy coach is the one who interacts with all of the teachers, the principal, and the other members of the literacy committee on a regular basis. The coach is also the person who spearheads many of the strategies and assessments that have been put in place for the program. So the literacy coach carries information back and forth throughout the staff, making sure everyone is aware of all issues and problems, and translates responses into individual classroom solutions.

- **Sustains collaborative discussions with all teachers.** A literacy coach must be available to all teachers, both individually and in groups. Individual sessions are critical, but group meetings can yield surprising results as the literacy coach, experienced teachers from various content areas, and new teachers discuss and share ideas. In this way, everyone becomes involved in the "coaching" process.

- **Monitors and assesses student achievement.** Everyone is involved in overseeing student progress, but the literacy coach has ongoing access to the big picture. The literacy coach sees the assessments and knows how those scores compare from class to class and subject area to subject area. As needed, the coach can step in with interventions to assist individual students and to help teachers incorporate intervention techniques into their classrooms.

- **Provides ongoing professional development.** The literacy coach observes classroom performance and can form judgments about how well particular strategies are working in various classrooms and for particular teachers. This insight enables the coach to refine strategies and provide personalized coaching for each teacher based on classroom observations. Because the literacy coach has daily contact with teachers and gets to know their strengths and weaknesses, the coach can help teachers gain new knowledge and learning so that they can integrate new strategies and practices into their teaching on an ongoing basis.

Mentor Teachers and Peer Support

Develop mentor teachers or "experts" who are available to assist and advise other teachers. Encourage staff to take advantage of these in-house resources. Mentor teachers can support the initiative in a variety of ways:

- Assist other classroom teachers in developing and improving instructional strategies.
- Introduce and model new strategies.
- Provide support and encouragement as less-experienced teachers apply new strategies and adjust to change.

In addition, there should be some mechanism put in place to promote peer-to-peer visits and support — perhaps lunches or other relaxed situations in which teachers may share experiences and ideas. Teachers who are working in relative isolation in a classroom may not even know what they don't know; it is important to have a conduit for information. Strategies or resources may exist that can solve a problem or make a form of instruction easier or more effective, but only if teachers know they exist. Simple conversations with peers can often reveal these secrets of the trade.

Provide a means for sharing best practices, including strategies, texts, and classroom presence. Use action labs to enable teachers to use strategies while expert teachers observe and offer suggestions and ideas.

Resources

Two types of resources are vital to support teachers and literacy instruction: a well-chosen student library and a professional library. The student library should indicate Lexile levels for every book. The professional library should include materials such as websites, DVDs, professional books, and curriculum materials that will support teachers in bringing the ideas of the initiative into the classroom.

In addition, consider a technology-based intervention solution such as *Read 180 Next Generation* for students who are not as likely to succeed with embedded literacy solutions.

Step 4: Design and Implement Action Steps

By this point in developing the initiative, much discussion will have taken place, and major decisions will have been made. The task now is to boil it all down into specific action steps that will be implemented by staff and at the classroom level.

As these steps are defined, remember that the initiative will be developed over time, so the steps being addressed are not limited to what must be done today or this semester; these steps should take into account how the program will develop over a period of at least three years.

Keep It Simple, Direct, and Clear

Most literacy plans that fail to produce desired results fail because they are too complicated and involve too many steps. Plan to do just what you and the staff can reasonably accomplish. This is why vertical alignment is so important: all levels of the organization must "be on the same page" so that everyone understands the expectations and the plan. If you try to do more than your school and teachers can comfortably manage, some things won't get done, people will feel overworked, tasks that have been rushed to completion will not function effectively, and a feeling of discouragement will replace the optimism such an initiative needs in order to thrive.

Keys to a Successful Plan

- **Measurability.** How will you assess whether the plan is working? What assessment tools will you use?
- **Coherence.** Your plan should have a clearly stated objective, and each piece of the plan must connect directly to that stated purpose.
- **Concreteness.** General statements of action are difficult to measure. Each step of the plan should describe a specific action, not something that teachers should think about or consider. What, exactly, should they *do*?
- **Transparency.** This is a matter of language. Don't couch the plan in language that could be confusing or difficult to comprehend. Direct statements describing direct actions are critical.

The action plan should include the following information:

- **Goals.** Your action plan will include many goals. These goals may involve collecting data, analyzing data, doing research, hiring a literacy coach, choosing classroom strategies, teaching teachers, and so on.
- **Tasks.** Each goal will be broken up into a series of discrete tasks that must be clearly stated. Each goal should precisely define the actions to be taken.
- **Persons responsible.** The action plan should identify which person or committee will be responsible for completing each task.
- **Resources.** The various tasks will require a variety of resources, such as a budget, staff time, instructional materials, training, information or data, and so on.
- **Timeframe.** Every task should have a beginning date and an end date. The timeframe for completion should be clearly stated.

Goals typically are accomplished by completing a series of tasks that might be divided among several individuals or committees. A plan can be illustrated by the following diagram:

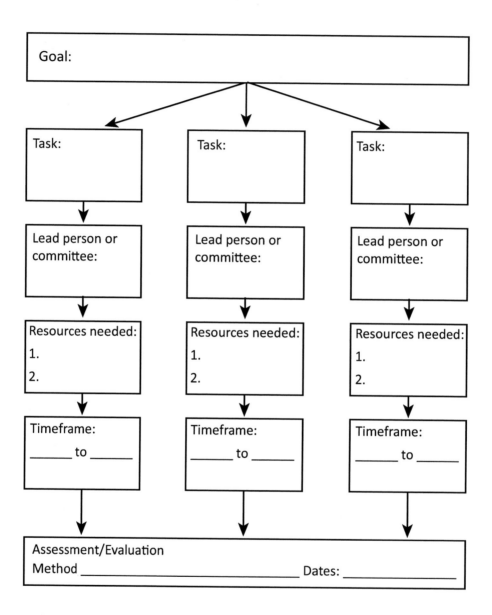

Goal:

Task:

Task:

Task:

Lead person or committee:

Lead person or committee:

Lead person or committee:

Resources needed:
1.
2.

Resources needed:
1.
2.

Resources needed:
1.
2.

Timeframe:
_____ to _____

Timeframe:
_____ to _____

Timeframe:
_____ to _____

Assessment/Evaluation
Method _____ Dates: _____

Assessment/Evaluation

When all the tasks are completed, the goal should be achieved. However, depending on the goal, the success of the efforts may not be obvious. Accordingly, the team must develop some method for assessing success. The success of hiring a literacy coach might be relatively easy to assess. Did one get hired? Does the person know her field? Does she work well with the staff? Is she a good trainer? Other goals might be more difficult to assess, especially if many variables are involved. It might take time to evaluate a new teaching strategy that has been introduced, and it might have to be assessed in a variety of ways. Do the teachers understand it? Do they use it? Why or why not? Do students understand what is being taught using this strategy? Does the strategy work as it is, or does it need refinement? Is there a better strategy for teaching literacy?

For many of these more complex goals, an ongoing cycle of evaluations and refinements may be required.

Step 5: Monitor, Evaluate, and Modify to Improve Success

A literacy initiative cannot be considered complete merely because it is in place and operating. It must be monitored and evaluated on a regular basis to ensure not only that it continues to work, but also to determine how it can be improved. One of the risks in implementing this step is that staff may regard it as another onerous task to be completed merely for the sake of getting it done and over with. But monitoring and evaluating are crucial, and everyone involved needs to have a clear understanding of the purpose of gathering and evaluating data to modify the program. If some people fail to understand the *why, how,* and *what-for* of this step, the quality of the data and the evaluation can be compromised. Thus a clear statement of purpose should be written early in the process of implementing the initiative. The statement should include answers to these questions:

- What is our purpose in collecting and evaluating these data?
- What data are we going to evaluate?
- How are we going to evaluate the data?
- What are we going to do with our evaluation when we have it?

There are three stages to a monitoring program: collecting information, analyzing and evaluating the information, and taking action to enhance student learning based on the information.

Collecting Information

Many different kinds of information can be collected, including both hard data and soft data. The term *hard data* refers to information that can be measured, such as test scores. *Soft data* refers, on the other hand, to information that cannot be strictly measured but that is meaningful nonetheless. Examples include observations of classroom behavior and student attitudes.

Information collection begins with data from standardized tests and daily classroom work. Information can be garnered, for instance, from portfolios, projects, surveys, interviews, informal formative assessments, and questionnaires, among other sources.

Observations are another important source of information. Teachers should be watching to see how students respond and behave with respect to various instructional approaches. They should note which strategies or materials engage them and which do not. They should also observe student attitudes and comments. Information collection can, furthermore, be extended to what families say about their children's progress or experiences. Department heads and other observers should themselves be collecting similar hard and soft data to contribute to the pool of information.

Do not neglect the experiences and attitudes of teachers. Employ interviews, surveys, and questionnaires to find out which strategies teachers think work effectively and which do not. Ask teachers which strategies apply best to certain content areas and which ones are most difficult to plan, implement, and assess. Questionnaires might also inquire about whether teachers feel sufficiently prepared to use each strategy.

All of these sources of information can shed additional light on how well the program is working and give clues to how it can be improved.

In the end, it may be impractical to accumulate information from all of these sources. An excess amount of data can be overwhelming, and if the data cannot be evaluated, they are useless. In order to manage and digest data effectively, a systematic method should be established to collect data and the kinds of data to be collected should be precisely determined. Along with hard data, soft data should be part of what is collected because they can yield important perspectives on the success of the program.

Analyzing and Evaluating Information

Meaningful analysis of information is only part of the process of improving literacy instruction rather than an end in itself. Set clear objectives for evaluating data.

- What is our standard, or measure, for success?
- How do we judge whether student literacy is improving?
- How do we make the connection between what is being learned and the instruction we are giving?

Before data can be analyzed or evaluated, a certain amount of organization and data consolidation must be completed in order to make it usable. Hard data, when quantifiable, can be organized into tables so that clear judgments can be made about student achievement. An important element of this process is to consider whether the data display format should include comparisons of sub-groupings to show whether different groups are achieving more or less success. For example, are success rates different for girls and boys or according to race? Is literacy achievement improving faster for good readers than for poor readers? Data can be organized to reveal these kinds of disparities.

Soft, or qualitative, data will also need to be organized into descriptions or summaries. These kinds of data are, of course, more difficult to evaluate and more time-consuming, both to collect and organize, but they can help build a complete picture of how well the initiative is progressing and delineate whatever shortcomings the initiative may have. Soft data can also help to tell a story in a way that hard data cannot. A substantiated anecdote, for instance, so long as it is representative, can illustrate a point much more vividly and memorably than a statistically significant collection of hard data. Numbers can quantify and measure trends, but soft data can convey, quite powerfully, what it is like for a person to be impacted by those trends. Representative individual stories, when coupled with relevant hard data, can help others better understand the big picture and may even make the hard data more accessible.

Whether the data in question are hard or soft, the literacy committee, department heads, and teachers should all analyze and evaluate these data, looking at them with four questions in mind:

- What do the data say about literacy instruction on the schoolwide level?
- What do the data say about literacy instruction in the different departments?
- What do the data say about literacy at each grade level?
- What do the data say about literacy instruction in individual classrooms?

With data in hand, evaluators should take these actions:

- **Look for patterns or themes.** Are literacy results the same in all content areas? Are certain groups of students showing higher or lower achievement levels? Are students who participate in certain programs, such as book clubs, achieving better results? Are most but not all teachers having success with particular strategies?
- **Compare data from different sources.** Do results from standard assessments, class exams, portfolios, and other assessments yield the same results? Why or why not? Do test results reinforce or contradict teachers' responses to certain strategies?
- **Compare results with what was expected.** Did the literacy committee have high expectations for a set of strategies that ultimately yielded less than spectacular results?

As always, ask questions of the data. Whether results are good or bad, why did they happen? How well were teachers supported in learning and applying these new strategies? Which students participated in these programs? What outside factors may have influenced the results?

It may not be best to put off evaluation until the end of the semester or the end of the year, because at that point, the amount of data collected may be too great to grasp. More frequent or ongoing rounds of evaluation may be more fruitful. Regardless of timing, do put in place and follow a schedule for collecting and evaluating data.

Modifying the Initiative over Time

After collecting and evaluating data, put in place an action plan that reflects the evaluation. In most cases, the plans will target elements of the literacy program, such as strategies or teacher training, but nothing should be taken off the board. Anything that is not working should be modified or eliminated altogether and replaced with something else that may work better. You may find, for example, that your district needs a strong intervention such as *Read 180 Next Generation* for those students who are still struggling or significantly lacking in literacy skills.

272

When making changes, it is important to share the data and evaluations with the affected parties so that reasons for the changes are understood. The action plan should also include a methodology both for implementing the changes and for monitoring them to see how well they work.

This diagram describes a process of developing, evaluating, and modifying many elements of a literacy initiative.

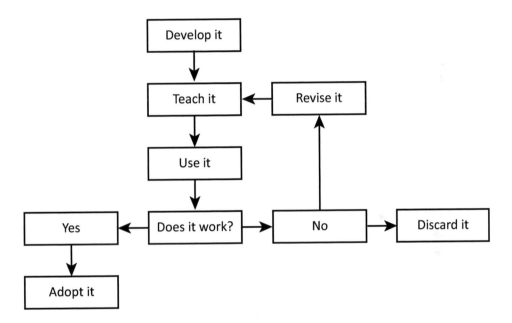

Obstacles and Risks

One problem with a monitoring and evaluation program is that it is easy to shove it onto a back burner. When an initiative is first proposed, the need for monitoring and evaluation is obvious, since the literacy team needs to know where literacy instruction stands. After the program is up and running, it is easy to become lax and thereby avoid the work required to acquire the information needed to drive additional changes and refinements.

It is also true that it takes time and effort to collect and evaluate data and to develop and implement new approaches. Teachers and administrators are already short on time, and tolerance for the extra effort required to start up a new program may wane over time. There is no easy answer to this problem, except to acknowledge that this step is vital. There is no point in initiating a new literacy program unless you make the effort needed to assess its impact over time and to find the instructional approaches that work best.

One way to attack this problem involves creating an efficient, regular plan for assessment and evaluation so that the process becomes ongoing and automatic. Just as plans for teacher training are put in place as an ongoing component of the initiative, a prescribed time and method for collecting and evaluating data should also form part of the literacy program's planning from day one. With the adoption of the Common Core State Standards and PARCC or Smarter Balanced Assessments, the cost of ignoring any of these steps is too great.

Takeaways on Embedded Literacy

This book has covered a great deal of ground, leading from the critical need for embedded literacy given the new CCSS expectations through this chapter on implementing a successful literacy initiative. The need is great and immediate, and the process may seem overwhelming at times. It may be useful to keep these key points in mind as you proceed.

Literacy for College and Career

Current textbook readability levels and the ability of current students to confront and interpret complex texts are not keeping pace with the realities of the workplace and college expectations. Community colleges and universities are engaging in too much remedial work just to bring students up to competency, and international workers are often better prepared to deal with workplace literacy than U.S. workers are. This situation is unacceptable, and public schools are where the change must happen.

Literacy in the Literature

A strong body of research supports the incorporation of literacy skills and strategies across the curriculum. The move toward assessment-driven learning and the prerequisites for Next Generation Assessments mean that students need to read and write competently in all content areas. Across the curriculum, lesson plans and assessments must provide increased rigor and relevance.

Literacy and Leadership

Organizational Leadership must create the culture and vision that support an embedded literacy initiative and then work to align the school's structures and systems to that vision. Instructional Leadership must work to align the curriculum to the new standards, noting especially where former ELA standards now cross content areas. They can and should use data to determine where students are, where they need to be, and how they will know when students get there. Professional development will be critical for teachers whose backgrounds do not include much in the way of literacy training. As daunting as a literacy initiative might appear from the outset, many schools have succeeded in implementing such initiatives and have seen reading, writing, speaking, listening, and language skills improve dramatically.

Literacy and Instruction

All teachers need to add an aptitude for literacy instruction to their strong content knowledge. They must increase the rigor and relevance of their lesson plans and use learning progressions to fashion logical lessons and to differentiate instruction. They must work to develop strong relationships with students that enable students to explore their own learning metacognitively and to recognize their own strengths and needs. Teachers within a given school should start using similar rubrics to assess writing and should explore the sorts of literature — including rigorous, relevant YA novels in the middle and high school — that might encourage students to read with enjoyment and pleasure.

A great deal of sharing is needed to make a literacy initiative work effectively. Teachers should share best practices across disciplines and across grades. A literacy coach can help to make that happen.

Summary

This final chapter examines some of the steps and the rationale involved in developing an action plan to implement a literacy initiative. While this plan must necessarily be tailored to the specific needs and situation in your particular school, every school should consider certain elements.

The first step is to assess students and determine where the literacy program in your school currently stands. Do you have data on student literacy levels and needs? Do faculty members have high expectations for student achievement? What resources does your school or district have to support moving forward with a literacy initiative? It's also important to consider your school's unique history with implementing literacy initiatives. Literacy issues have been around for a long time, and most schools have grappled with them before, but has your school's experience been positive, or not so positive? The answers to these questions will make a big difference in how you approach the matter this time around.

Certainly, school leaders can simply develop a literacy initiative, provide professional development, and implement the plan, but a plan without committed teachers is unlikely to succeed. This is why all levels of the DSEI — organizational leadership, instructional leadership and teaching — are given equal consideration. Teachers will be most effective if the organization has created a clear vision and the instructional leaders have supported teachers. Only then will teachers feel safe enough and confident enough to implement strategies and differentiate instruction for students. Everyone should agree with both the need for change and the methods for making it happen. In building consensus, every school should strive to reach the "tipping point" for schoolwide collaboration.

In building your school's capacity to address literacy issues, several key steps must be taken. First, a well-designed, layered approach to professional development must be established. This must prepare teachers to use the strategies of the initiative on a daily basis in the classroom. The training needs to be ongoing so that teacher skills steadily improve. A literacy coach or coordinator is imperative, along with mentor teachers and a program for peer support.

Once the groundwork has been laid for an initiative, draw up the action plan. Remember to keep it simple, direct, and clear so that everyone knows and understands what will be done when, by whom, and for what purpose.

Finally, the initiative must be continuously monitored, evaluated, and modified. In some ways, this may be the most difficult step of all, because over time, the passion that drove the early efforts will almost certainly dissipate, and yet the initiative can never be regarded as complete. There will always be better ways of doing things, better assessments, and better instructional strategies. Students can always achieve more, and part of our responsibility is to enable them to reach their potential. Only through a systematic approach to monitoring and evaluating instructional practices can their potential, and the promise of our hard work, be achieved.

Questions to Consider

- Based on the information you have right now, what are the major literacy issues facing your school? What is your school currently doing to address them?

- Is there a consensus of opinion about the state of literacy instruction in your school?

- How effective has your school been in the past in communicating concerns, goals, and other issues to staff and other stakeholders? What might you do to improve this?

References

Gladwell, Malcolm. *The Tipping Point: How Little Things Can Make a Big Difference.* Boston, MA: Little Brown, 2000.

Miller, M., Bell, E., and Holland, D. "Slow Turn Ahead." *Journal of Staff Development* 30: 46–50, 2009.